# Conflict and Representation in Online Communication

Rotimi Taiwo
*Obafemi Awolowo University, Nigeria*

IGI Global
Scientific Publishing
Publishing Tomorrow's Research Today

| | |
|---|---|
| Vice President of Editorial | Melissa Wagner |
| Director of Acquisitions | Mikaela Felty |
| Director of Book Development | Jocelynn Hessler |
| Production Manager | Mike Brehm |
| Cover Design | Jose Rosado |

Published in the United States of America by
IGI Global Scientific Publishing
701 East Chocolate Avenue
Hershey, PA, 17033, USA
Tel: 717-533-8845
Fax: 717-533-7115
Website: https://www.igi-global.com E-mail: cust@igi-global.com



Library of Congress Cataloging-in-Publication Data

LCCN: 2025029136 (CIP Data Pending)
ISBN13: 9798337352978
Isbn13Softcover: 9798337352985
EISBN13: 9798337352992

British Cataloguing in Publication Data
A Cataloguing in Publication record for this book is available from the British Library.

# Table of Contents

# Detailed Table of Contents



This study carried out a multimodal critical discourse analysis of selected cartoons on the 2022 ASUU strike in Nigeria, intending to explore the ideologies and meaning-making resources used to visualise the strike. Using van Leeuwen's social semiotics and van Dijk's socio-cognitive model of critical discourse analysis, the study conducted a qualitative analysis of thirty-five purposively selected cartoons to investigate their visual and discursive strategies. The social semiotic analysis revealed that semiotic resources such as spatial arrangement, gaze, and composition portray students as victims, and recontextualise the strike as a ritual sacrifice. The critical discourse analysis demonstrated that ideological strategies such as positive-self and negative-other representation were employed to express resistance and anti-welfarist ideologies, thereby emphasising our good deeds and foregrounding their bad deeds. The paper offers insights into how multimodal texts engage with socio-political issues within the context of Nigerian public universities' industrial actions.



The usage of Chinese apps has surged in Kerala, driven by affordable smartphones, aggressive marketing, and popular social media and e-commerce platforms. Apps like TikTok, WeChat, and UC Browser have gained substantial user bases due to their user-friendly interfaces, innovative features, and localized content. Kerala's high literacy rate, widespread internet penetration, and tech-savvy population have contributed to the rapid acceptance and usage of these apps. This study investigates the influence of the Internet of Behavior (IoB) on technology readiness (optimism, innovativeness, discomfort, and insecurity) and technology usage attitudes (anxiety, negativity, and multitasking performance) among users of Chinese social media apps in Kerala. Using a quantitative research design and data collected from 510 participants, the study employs correlation and regression analyses to examine these relationships.



This study examines how Internet memes serve as a tool for resistance in Nigerian online discourse, focussing on the 2024 New Year slogan "No gree for anybody." Using 40 purposively selected Internet memes gathered between January and March 2024, from Facebook and X, the analysis draws on Benford and Snow's Collective Action Frames and Kress and van Leeuwen's concept of visual grammar. Dominant issues expressed through the memes include social inequality, infrastructural challenges, political discontent, gender roles, and national identity. Through visual exaggeration, narrative framing and symbolic juxtaposition, the memes highlight people's daily struggles and frames of resistance. The memes' visual symbolism fosters resistance, critiques societal norms and amplifies marginalised voices. This research concludes that internet memes play a crucial role in shaping resistance discourse in Nigeria, serving as both a reflection of ongoing struggles and an active space for expressing defiance, identity, and solidarity in the digital age.



This study investigates the multimodal discourse of the August 1, 2024, Nigeria protest on TikTok and Facebook, addressing a gap in understanding its application in digital protests on these platforms. Using a qualitative methodology and eight data samples, the research employs Kress and van Leeuwen's Multimodal Discourse Analysis and Halliday's Social Semiotic Theory. Findings reveal strategic use of colour, visual symbols, and interactive features to enhance protest impact, highlighting the transformative potential of digital communication in contemporary social movements. Conclusions underscore the importance of digital platforms in modern protests and suggest further research into multimodal strategies.

This paper argues that digital activism relies on pragmatic language strategies to explore and address the socio-cultural challenges inherent in online spaces. Digital activism, defined as the use of digital platforms to mobilize for social and political causes, relies on pragmatic language strategies to foster engagement, address cultural sensitivities, and represent diverse voices. Pragmatics, the study of language in context, offers insight into how speech acts, politeness, and implicature are employed to enhance the persuasiveness and inclusivity of activist messages. Theoretical frameworks of pragmatics and sociocultural identity are discussed, revealing the role of language in shaping collective identities within movements. Case studies illustrate how each movement overcame linguistic barriers and cultural tensions through pragmatic approaches. The paper concludes by emphasizing the importance of further research into the evolution of language in digital activism and the need to better understand how online communication impacts social change.



Cartoons reveal complex dimensions of clashes between nomadic herders and agrarian farmers in Nigeria. This study examines 13 cartoons published in e-publishing unit of The Punch, one of Nigeria's most widely read newspapers, to explore how multiple modes combine to depict herder-farmer conflicts (HFCs), in order to describe how semiotic resources contextualise HFCs and how digital resources function in humorising HFCs in online newspapers. Multimodal discourse exploration of HFCs is performed via Kress' (2010) social semiotic approach to multimodal discourse. Findings reveal that The Punch deploys diverse modes of representation – image, writing, caricature. Interaction among semiotic resources, shared situation and linguistic forms reveals dimensions of insecurity, ethnoreligious bigotry, human rights violation, hypocrisy. Cartoonists are critical of Nigerian government's level of involvement in HFCs, revealing state actors as cohorts in herders' attacks; and sedentary farmers as victims. HCFs are framed as complex sociopolitical crises, intensifying ethnic tensions and divisions.

**Chapter 7**



This chapter presents a multimodal analysis of social media memes that represent and construct the identity of the Nigerian Police, using Kress and Van Leeuwen's (2001) framework. The study examines ten memes from Facebook, TikTok, and Instagram, selected between 2020 and 2024 using hashtags like #NigerianPolice, #EndSARS, and #PoliceBrutality. Through analysis of multimodal elements, text, images, and speech, the memes critique police practices while also reflecting attempts at positive identity construction by the police. The memes are categorized based on themes such as inefficiency, corruption, and abuse of power. Findings reveal that although the Nigerian Police use memes to portray themselves positively, public sentiment, expressed through humour in the memes, consistently highlights their institutional failures. These representations, rooted in Nigeria's sociopolitical landscape, underscore social media's role in shaping and reinforcing public distrust of the police as an institution of government.

**Chapter 8**



As the COVID-19 outbreak took over the world population, artists and institutions who contributed to the production and dissemination of arts and cultures had to give a break to their professional activities. It was March 2020, when Turkish government decided to stop arts and culture related activities, in order to prevent the spreading of the disease. Actors of arts and culture scene quickly adopted themselves to the "stay at home" days, and continued their productions while in self-isolation. As a result of this unexpected incident, many domestic and international arts and culture institutions have opened their archives on digital media platforms. As the epidemic broke out in the beginning of March 2020 in Turkey, SALT quickly reconstructed and updated their online historical archives and art collections by making 1.840.000

# Preface

## INTRODUCTION

In an era where digital platforms have become central to public life, the contours of human interaction, power relations, and ideological contestations are increasingly shaped by online communication. Social media spaces, once heralded for their democratizing potential, have evolved into arenas where identities are negotiated, alliances are forged, and conflicts are both incited and resolved. These platforms are not merely tools for communication—they are spaces where meaning is constructed, challenged, and redefined in real time.

*Conflict and Representation in Online Communication* emerges from the need to critically examine how language, power, and identity intersect in the digital age. The book explores the dynamic terrain of sociopolitical discourse as it unfolds across online spaces, interrogating the roles of representation, resistance, polarization, and solidarity. From debates on cultural identity and political ideology to the virality of hate speech and misinformation, the chapters in this volume engage with the complex semiotics of digital discourse.

This edited volume brings together interdisciplinary perspectives, with contributions from scholars in linguistics, media studies, sociology, political science, and communication. The selected works delve into a wide array of topics, including social media activism, the rhetoric of mainstream journalism, multimodal strategies in online debates, the role of digital technology in shaping public opinion, and the emerging influence of the Internet of Behavior (IoB). Whether addressing grassroots political movements or algorithm-driven echo chambers, the insights offered here are timely and urgent.

## CHAPTER OVERVIEW

Chapter 1 opens the volume with a powerful exploration of the 2022 ASUU strike in Nigerian public universities, analyzed through the lens of multimodal critical discourse. Through the scrutiny of selected editorial cartoons, the chapter reveals how visual and textual strategies converge to construct ideological narratives of resistance and victimhood. Utilizing van Leeuwen's social semiotics and van Dijk's socio-cognitive model, the chapter provides a nuanced interpretation of how students are depicted as victims and how the strike is reframed as a symbolic societal sacrifice. This study demonstrates the potency of multimodal texts in articulating socio-political grievances and negotiating meaning in the public sphere.

In Chapter 2, attention turns to the growing influence of Chinese social media applications in Kerala, India, where digital behavior and technology attitudes are analyzed through the framework of the Internet of Behavior (IoB). By focusing on user engagement with apps like TikTok and WeChat, this chapter investigates how digital consumption patterns intersect with cultural and technological contexts. Employing quantitative analysis, the study offers valuable insights into how users' emotional and cognitive responses shape their digital behavior, reflecting the deeper psychological dimensions of our evolving relationship with technology.

Chapter 3 delves into the vibrant and dynamic world of Nigerian internet memes, focusing on the viral slogan "No gree for anybody" that characterized online discourse at the start of 2024. Drawing on theories of collective action and visual grammar, this chapter unpacks the ways in which memes serve as contemporary instruments of resistance and solidarity. Through visual exaggeration and symbolic juxtaposition, memes emerge as tools of social critique, amplifying voices that challenge inequality, gender stereotypes, and political dysfunction in Nigeria. This chapter underscores the meme's role not merely as entertainment, but as a significant site of political expression.

In Chapter 4, the spotlight shifts to the strategic use of multimodal communication in digital protests, specifically those surrounding the August 1, 2024, protests in Nigeria. Through a close analysis of TikTok and Facebook content, this chapter demonstrates how visual elements, such as color and composition, and platform-specific features are deployed to heighten the impact of protest messages. The findings highlight the transformative role of digital media in enabling new forms of activism and collective mobilization, reaffirming the centrality of multimodal discourse in contemporary protest culture.

Chapter 5 offers a broader theoretical perspective on the linguistic underpinnings of digital activism. Focusing on pragmatics, this chapter examines how language is used to navigate the socio-cultural challenges inherent in online movements. By analyzing speech acts, politeness strategies, and implicature, the chapter reveals how activists construct inclusive, persuasive narratives across culturally diverse digital landscapes. The discussion illustrates how language functions as a bridge between ideological commitment and practical mobilization, demonstrating the critical role of pragmatics in the evolving landscape of digital sociopolitical discourse.

Chapter 6 returns to the use of cartoons as a vehicle for socio-political commentary, this time focusing on the deeply entrenched herder-farmer conflicts in Nigeria. Through a multimodal analysis of cartoons published by *The Punch*, this chapter reveals how image, text, and caricature intersect to frame the conflicts as not only issues of insecurity and violence but also as symptoms of state complicity and ethnic polarization. By exposing the ideological undercurrents within these visual texts, the chapter emphasizes the role of media in reflecting and shaping public perceptions of national crises.

Chapter 7 continues the discussion on representation by analyzing how memes contribute to the construction of Nigerian Police identity on social media. Using a multimodal discourse approach, this chapter dissects both citizen-generated and institutionally crafted memes to reveal the complex interplay between institutional self-representation and public perception. The findings show how social media becomes a battleground for narrative control, where humour, satire, and visual symbolism are wielded to critique and resist perceived abuses of power and systemic inefficiencies within the police force.

Chapter 8 concludes the volume by expanding the scope of inquiry to cultural communication during the COVID-19 pandemic. Focusing on the SALT initiative in Turkey, this chapter investigates how digital platforms were employed to maintain public engagement with art and culture amidst lockdowns. Through strategic digital communication and the rapid digitization of archives, SALT exemplifies how cultural institutions can adapt to global disruptions while continuing to serve their communities. This case study reminds us of the resilience of cultural expression and the enduring role of digital platforms in preserving and reimagining public discourse during times of crisis.

## CONCLUSION

Together, these chapters offer a multifaceted examination of how conflict and representation are negotiated through online communication. Whether through memes, cartoons, digital protest strategies, or pragmatic language use, the contributors to this volume illuminate the diverse and dynamic ways in which digital media serve as both mirror and mechanism for sociopolitical change.

At the heart of this collection is the conviction that language—especially in its digital forms—is both a mirror and a tool. It reflects societal tensions and aspirations while also serving as a mechanism through which individuals and groups assert agency. The contributors to this volume ask not only how online communication represents conflict but also how it *constitutes* it—how the very act of speaking or posting online can create, escalate, or mitigate sociopolitical divisions.

This book is intended for a broad academic and professional audience: researchers in discourse analysis, media professionals interested in narrative framing, political scientists studying public opinion, educators confronting the challenges of digital literacy, and sociologists mapping the contours of virtual communities. It is our hope that the insights offered here will stimulate further inquiry into the evolving relationship between technology, discourse, and power.

As editor, I extend my gratitude to the contributing authors whose work brings clarity to a complex and ever-changing digital landscape. Their scholarship not only enhances our understanding of online conflict and representation but also illuminates the possibilities for more inclusive, ethical, and reflective digital discourse.

# Chapter 1
# A Multimodal Critical Discourse Analysis of Selected Cartoons on the 2022 ASUU Strike in Nigerian Public Universities

**Deborah Abiola Fifelola**
https://orcid.org/0009-0001-9669-3395
*Redeemer's University, Ede, Nigeria*

**Foluke Olayinka Unuabonah**
*Redeemer's University, Ede, Nigeria*

## ABSTRACT

*This study carried out a multimodal critical discourse analysis of selected cartoons on the 2022 ASUU strike in Nigeria, intending to explore the ideologies and meaning-making resources used to visualise the strike. Using van Leeuwen's social semiotics and van Dijk's socio-cognitive model of critical discourse analysis, the study conducted a qualitative analysis of thirty-five purposively selected cartoons to investigate their visual and discursive strategies. The social semiotic analysis revealed that semiotic resources such as spatial arrangement, gaze, and composition portray students as victims, and recontextualise the strike as a ritual sacrifice. The critical discourse analysis demonstrated that ideological strategies such as positive-self and negative-other representation were employed to express resistance and anti-welfarist ideologies, thereby emphasising our good deeds and*

DOI: 10.4018/979-8-3373-5297-8.ch001

*foregrounding their bad deeds. The paper offers insights into how multimodal texts engage with socio-political issues within the context of Nigerian public universities' industrial actions.*

## INTRODUCTION

Nigerian citizens have had reasons for protest, ranging from corruption, the need for infrastructure, law and order, and perceived insecurity. Before the country gained its independence in 1960, during the colonial era and till now, there have been protests leading to strikes and boycotts by citizens to express their grievances about economic and socio-political issues in the country. In the education sector, for instance, lecturers have embarked on various protests in the form of strikes and boycotts to drive home their demands which include funding for the revitalisation of public universities, payment of earned academic allowances (EEA), reconstitution of the FGN/ASUU 2009 Renegotiation Committee and proliferation of universities, among others. Different individuals and groups show their stance toward these strikes through multimodal resources deployed in images, thereby revealing their ideologies, projecting their worldviews, and lampooning authorities through humorous posts (Monogbe, 2019). Previous studies have explored the critical discourse aspects of language use in media reports on industrial actions in Nigeria and their ideological representations, using the 2013 ASUU strike as a case study (Ellah, 2014; Ugwuona, 2016). Additionally, some have examined conceptual metaphors and discursive features in media reports and online reader comments on the 2013 labour conflict between ASUU and the Federal Government of Nigeria (Akinwotu, 2019). However, these studies have not investigated the socio-cognitive resources present in multimodal texts, such as political cartoons, in relation to the 2022 ASUU strike. Therefore, this study seeks to answer the following research questions: (a) what ideologies and attitudes are expressed towards the strike through these cartoons? (b) how are socio-cognitive resources exhibited in the cartoons? In answering these research questions, this chapter analyses how the multimodal resources in cartoons are used as forms of protest for or against the 2022 Academic Staff Union of Universities (hereafter ASUU) strike in Nigerian public universities and how these cartoons project the effect of the strike on the Nigerian education sector.

## PROTESTS AS SOCIAL DEMONSTRATIONS

A protest is a form of collective action by which individuals and groups use a range of tactics to challenge or resist authorities, advance their interests, or express their grievances. It is a mechanism through which individuals or groups voice their grievances, express dissent, and mobilise for social change. Eesuola (2013) defines political protest as any action or inaction used to register grievances against established "political authorities, and their policies" (p.81). Protests are said to be political when they are directed at political authorities that protesters think can redress or address the issue(s) in contest. Similarly, Auvinen (1996) defines it as actions that consist of "demonstrations, riots and strikes which have an expressed political target and involve conflict behaviour against the political machinery" (p.78). Freire (1999) opines that protest is the main instrument for the accomplishment of "the great humanistic and historical task of the oppressed to liberate themselves from their oppressors" (p.11).

Protests, therefore, happen when there is something in the society that people do not like; it may be the law, institutions, cultural traditions or practices that are not right or fair; thus, it is an expression of opposition or dissent. Hence, Akingbe (2012) observes that protest involves an "overt response to articulations of power and authority" (p.3). It assumes the existence of social, political and economic relationships in which individuals or groups disagree with one another. Various countries of the world are engulfed in a series of protests with reasons which could range from economic depression, class oppression, political marginalisation, exclusion, as well as indigene-settler dichotomy (Eesuola, 2013). Protest, therefore, is an important indicator of public concern, raising awareness and highlighting perceived failings in administrative practices. Protest is a social and political act, and so to create wide publicity, protesters seize public spaces and employ different digital platforms.

In the digital age, protest has taken on new forms, including the use of cartoons as a means of political expression. Cartoons are cultural artefacts that spread rapidly through the internet and social media platforms. Cartons, often humorous or satirical images, are widely shared on social media platforms to convey political messages and criticise societal issues. Protest cartoons harness the power of humour, irony, and visual imagery to challenge established political authorities, policies, or social norms. They serve as a creative and accessible tool for individuals to voice their dissent, raise awareness, and mobilise support for social or political change.

The main purpose and function of a cartoon, as determined by its creator and/or users, have become an effective way to convey a message to a specific target audience. Cartoons are frequently used to evoke particular emotions and prompt specific reactions. In other words, cartoons are used to express emotions, lampoon society and proffer likely solutions to specific societal issues. Cartoons, in this regard, are created to reveal the attitudes and ideologies of protesters, thereby showing their stance towards prevailing issues in society.

## POLITICAL CARTOONS AS TOOLS FOR SOCIAL DEMONSTRATIONS AND ONLINE PROTESTS

Baker and Green (2014) observe that cartoons can succinctly encapsulate complex ideas, making them an effective tool for conveying political viewpoints. These digital caricatures have emerged as influential instruments for activists to communicate their messages and engage with a broad and diverse audience. Cartoons, with their satirical and visually striking nature, are often employed to criticise political figures or systems and disseminate messages with wit and humour.

As the world clamours for participatory media culture, technology has fostered citizens' involvement in cultural, political and social issues and the use of Internet cartoons has become an important tool for communication. Individuals or groups embark on cartoon creation in order to actively participate in different serious events in the country. Citizens can use cartoons to participate in leading conversations and/or criticise the ills of society or those in government without being punished for hate speech. Rintel (2013) explains this by stating that when important events occur in a society, it becomes normal for "humorous posts" in various forms to "spread concurrently with serious professional reportage" (p. 254). Hence, it is strongly noted that cartoons do not hold their value in their contents, but rather in their ability to conjure up meaning that translates to public voice beyond what traditional media has to offer. Thus, cartoons bear distinctive meanings and can serve predetermined functions by those who use them. Unlike traditional protests, which often require physical gatherings, online protests can be organised from anywhere with an internet connection, thereby increasing participation and incorporating a wider range of voices (Milner 2012).

With the advent of social media, political protests now take place on different online platforms, including Facebook, Twitter and WhatsApp (Al Zidjaly 2017; Chiluwa 2018). During the 2022 ASUU strike, visual texts such as cartoons, memes, and other internet images were used to protest for or against the 2022 ASUU strike in Nigeria. As multimodal texts, cartoons combine different communicative modes (verbal and non-verbal) to express cognitive effects intended to be captured by the readers so that they can obtain the full meaning of the communicative text. As discrete digital objects circulated online, cartoons are an ideal case study. They provide an accessible device for users to frame and comment on current events. Moreover, they serve as online tools for protesting government policies and actions.

Previous discourse studies on online protest have explored the linguistic and visual strategies used to express political dissent across various digital platforms. Chiluwa (2018), for example, investigates the discursive strategies in online discourses by a Nigerian separatist group, while Usman and Nuhu (2016) analyse the use of satire as a form of visual imagery in political cartoons published in national newspapers. Similarly, Unuabonah & Oyebode (2021) examine ideological representations in WhatsApp memes protesting government actions during the Covid-19 pandemic, and Hansson et al. (2022) assess appraisal choices in online tweets critiquing British ministers during Covid-19 and Brexit. These studies collectively illustrate how social media facilitates the expression of disapproval towards governmental policies across various domains. However, they do not specifically address online protest against policies in the higher education sector in Nigeria.

Studies have also shown that political cartoons have emerged as powerful tools for social demonstrations in Nigeria. Osisanwo and Atoloye (2024), employing the General Theory of Verbal Humour, identify six semiotic humour techniques—exaggeration, humorous metaphor, distortion of formulaic expressions, neologism, innovative collocation, and sarcasm—deployed in cartoons to satirise misgovernance, corruption, and insecurity. These humour strategies frame political actors as 'bullies', positioning cartooning as a channel of resistance for the masses. Adeagbo and Oyindamola (2024) explored seven selected Nigerian political cartoons using Kress and van Leeuwen's visual grammar and Barthes' semiotic theory. The authors uncover a sophisticated deployment of visual salience, framing, modality, denotation, connotation, and myth. Their findings emphasise how Nigerian cartoons highlight corruption, economic inequality, and political neglect, making them effective tools for engaging and shaping public discourse. This reinforces the argument that political cartoons do not merely reflect public sentiment but actively participate in socio-political commentary. In the same vein, Amore & Atoloye (2016) examine a systemic functional-multimodal discourse analysis of some cartoons connected with Nigeria's 2015 general election to identify how verbal and non-verbal meaning is communicated. The analysis shows that social semiotic reference is crucial in the relationship between political discourse and ideology and further establishes that metaphorical constructions of meaning occur along linguistic and visual elements. These studies collectively affirm that Nigerian political cartoons are rich in both linguistic and visual semiotics, functioning as vital texts of resistance, political education, and civic engagement.

Studies on ASUU strikes have also investigated critical discourse aspects of language use in media reports of industrial actions in Nigeria and its ideological representations, using the 2013 ASUU strike as a case study (Ellah 2014; Ugwuona 2016). More recent multimodal approaches have analysed how digital visual culture reflects public response to university policy. Omolabi and Adebayo (2024), adopting

Acheoach's pragma-crafting theory, examine five memes across WhatsApp, Facebook, and Twitter, revealing how wordplay, linguistic ambiguity, and visual satire convey frustration and solidarity during strike actions. The deployment of discourse features such as shared macro-knowledge and geoimplicature underscores the complexity of humour in digital protest. Similarly, Ademilokun (2016), using a systemic functional multimodal discourse framework, analyses social media imagery during the 2013 strike, illustrating how participants utilise verbal and visual signifiers to expose governmental and academic institutional failures. His findings reveal a growing reliance on satire and surrealism in the digital public sphere, positioning visual communication as a potent tool for political expression in Nigeria. The research confirms a growing reliance on visual communication in Nigeria's digital public sphere, where satire functions as a powerful tool of political expression.

While these studies offer valuable insights into media discourse and humour around ASUU strikes, none have systematically examined how editorial cartoons circulated during the 2022 strike construct and circulate ideologies related to educational policy and protest. Additionally, few integrate van Leeuwen's social semiotic approach with van Dijk's socio-cognitive model to explore how meaning-making and ideology operate within multimodal protest discourse. This gap necessitates the present study, which investigates thirty-five editorial cartoons from the 2022 ASUU strike to uncover the visual and discursive resources through which resistance, critique, and ideological stance-taking are communicated in the Nigerian media landscape.

## THEORETICAL FRAMEWORK

This study is anchored in a dual theoretical framework that draws on van Leeuwen's (2005) social semiotic approach to multimodality and van Dijk's (2006) socio-cognitive model of critical discourse analysis (CDA). Together, these frameworks provide the tools to analyse how visual and linguistic resources in political cartoons construct and convey ideological meanings, particularly within the context of the 2022 ASUU strike in Nigeria.

### Social Semiotics

The Social Semiotic approach to meaning-making was developed by Theo van Leeuwen (2005) and elaborated by Bezemer and Jewitt (2009). Social semiotics offers a critical, multimodal perspective on communication by examining how people use available semiotic resources in specific cultural and social contexts to produce meaning, negotiate power and express identity. This framework conceptualises meaning as fluid, socially situated, and motivated by the interests of meaning-makers

(Kress, 1993). van Leeuwen (2005) defines semiotic resources as the materials, artefacts and actions used for communicative purposes, whether physiological, such as gesture or voice, or technological, such as images, fonts or colours, each with a potential for meaning shaped by its historical, cultural and social uses.

One of the central tenets of this framework is that all meaning-making involves choice. These choices are guided and constrained by what van Leeuwen calls semiotic regimes, or the rules, often ideologically laden, that govern the use of modes in different contexts (van Leeuwen, 2005: 285). In this sense, meaning-making is not only about what is communicated but also about how and why particular resources are chosen over others. Another key concept is the mode, defined as a socially and culturally shaped set of resources for making meaning (Bezemer and Jewitt, 2009). Modes include, but are not limited to, image, text, colour, layout, gaze, sound and gesture. The communicative potential of each mode is determined by its affordances, that is, what it can easily represent or express. For example, images are governed by spatial logic, making them well-suited to representing simultaneity, while written language is governed by temporal sequencing, allowing for narrative progression (Kress and van Leeuwen, 2001).

In multimodal texts, these modes rarely operate in isolation. The concept of multimodal orchestration refers to how different modes interact and distribute meaning across a text. Each mode contributes partially, and sometimes unevenly, to the overall message. This orchestration can involve alignment, reinforcement, contradiction or tension among modes, all of which are analytically significant (Lemke, 2002; Bezemer and Jewitt, 2009).

Furthermore, social semiotics also facilitates the analysis of how social actors are represented in texts. This includes examining strategies of inclusion or exclusion, activation or passivation, and personalisation or impersonalisation, each of which can reveal underlying ideologies and power dynamics (van Leeuwen, 2008). For instance, a political cartoon that impersonalises government actors while personalising protestors can subtly legitimise resistance and delegitimise authority.

This theoretical lens is particularly useful for this study, which investigates how multimodal texts such as protest cartoons visually recontextualise social practices and discourses. It enables a critical examination of how different semiotic resources are mobilised to represent actors, frame issues and shape public opinion. Adopting a social semiotic perspective, this research explores what is represented in multimodal texts and interrogates the conditions, purposes and power structures that underpin such representations. This approach allows for a richer, context-sensitive analysis of how meaning is made, contested and circulated in the public sphere. In addition to social semiotics, this study draws on Teun van Dijk's sociocognitive model of Critical Discourse Analysis (CDA) to deepen the investigation into how meaning-making practices connect with broader cognitive and societal structures.

## Critical Discourse Analysis

CDA is widely regarded as an approach that views language as a form of social practice and systematically investigates hidden power relations and ideologies embedded in discourse (Ayoola, 2021). In CDA, ideology is a central organising concept that structures both discourse production and interpretation. Ideologies are socially shared frameworks that organise knowledge, sustain power relations and guide social practices (van Dijk, 1998). Discourse is not ideologically neutral; as Fairclough (1992) notes, it is both socially constitutive and socially conditioned, simultaneously shaping and being shaped by existing structures of domination and resistance.

Within CDA, scholars emphasise different aspects of discourse. Fairclough's sociological model highlights how discourse interacts with social structures to maintain or challenge power, especially in contexts like labour disputes (Fairclough, 1992, 2001). Wodak's historical discourse analysis focuses on socio-historical context and political memory in shaping ideologies (Reisigl & Wodak, 2001). While both offer valuable perspectives, this study adopts van Dijk's socio-cognitive model for its emphasis on the mental representations and shared knowledge that mediate discourse and society. Van Dijk (2006) explains that discourse both shapes and reflects socially shared mental models, which influence how people interpret events. This is crucial for analysing protest cartoons, which rely on shared cultural references and background knowledge to deliver critique visually and succinctly. These cartoons condense complex political issues into symbolic forms that tap into collective ideologies. Thus, van Dijk's model better captures how such multimodal texts engage with public consciousness. This study, therefore, situates the visual discourse of the 2022 ASUU strike within broader cognitive and ideological struggles surrounding education, governance, and public welfare in Nigeria.

## van Dijk's Socio-Cognitive Model

van Dijk's (2001) socio-cognitive approach to CDA explores the connection between discourse, cognition, and society, particularly focusing on how mental schemas shape ideologies. According to van Dijk (2006), ideologies are belief systems embedded in the cognition of social groups, and they influence the way groups perceive themselves ("us") in contrast to others ("them"). Ideologies, through mental models, govern shared social representations such as knowledge, attitudes, and opinions, which underpin social identities and behaviours. In analysing political cartoons, two key aspects of van Dijk's socio-cognitive model will be explored to reveal how these cartoons represent industrial actions and the social actors involved:

## Mental Model

van Dijk (2001) explains that mental models are personal representations of events, shaped by individual experiences and influenced by shared social knowledge. These models reflect beliefs, both knowledge and opinions, and guide how people speak, act, write, and interpret social practices. Although subjective and potentially biased, they form the basis of discourse by combining personal experiences with elements of shared ideology.

Mental models determine the meaning of discourse by controlling its semantic features such as topics, schemata, style, and rhetoric (van Dijk, 2002, p. 216). Van Dijk (1993) notes that discourse often justifies inequality through positive representation of the self and negative representation of others. This contrast is conveyed through storytelling, argumentation, word choice, structural emphasis, and references to authorities or experts. These strategies are also common in multimodal texts, where verbal and visual elements work together to promote particular viewpoints.

In this study, the mental models in protest cartoons are examined to show how public perceptions of Nigeria's university system and industrial action are constructed. Cartoons may depict striking academic unions positively while presenting the government negatively, revealing the cartoonists' ideological positions and how these align with or challenge prevailing social beliefs.

## Context Model

Another key element of van Dijk's approach is the idea of context models. Context models are the subjective representations of communicative events and situations that constrain and shape the discourse. van Dijk (2006) notes that many aspects of meaning can expose ideologies, and these contexts, which might be either global or local, define not only the different properties of discourse but also the overall interactive strategy of positive self-presentation and negative other presentation. van Dijk opines that they embody the notion of relevance, defining what is relevant for discourse participants. They embody the "mental construct of participants, which are individually variable interpretations of the ongoing social situation." Thus, they may be ideologically biased. Participants must be aware of the communicative event in which they are participating in order to understand and produce the correct lexical items, topic, styles, and rhetoric. van Dijk's descriptions of contextual categories that are relevant in the description of discourse include the domain of the interaction; the activities carried out in that particular domain, global and local actions; participants' roles, covering both communicative and social roles as well as the cognition of the interactants that focus on the knowledge; and the goals and beliefs of the participants. Aspects of meaning that can expose ideologies in context include level of description, coherence, presupposition, synonymy, and contrast (van Dijk, 2000). In political cartoons, context models are shaped not only by the cartoonists' mental models and ideologies but also by the social and political environment in which these cartoons are produced and consumed. The context models determine the tone, style, and rhetorical choices of the cartoonist, influencing how they communicate complex issues such as the university industrial actions in Nigeria.

## DATA AND METHOD

The data used for this paper comprise thirty-five purposively selected cartoons on the 2022 ASUU strike, collected from diverse social media platforms such as Twitter, WhatsApp, Facebook, newspaper websites, and other internet sources. The cartoons were collected between February and October 2022, corresponding to the duration of the 2022 ASUU strike. Their selection was motivated by both the topic they addressed, which is the ASUU strike, and the period during which they were posted. The data collection process involved manually downloading relevant cartoons, which were then stored in digital formats on cloud-based repositories, personal mobile devices, email platforms, and laptops. For ease of analysis, the cartoons were subsequently compiled into a Word document format, which also enabled the cropping of the visual data where necessary.

For analytical purposes, the cartoons were first categorised based on the primary roles and representations they portrayed. Out of the thirty-five cartoons, thirteen (13) depicted students as victims, thirteen (13) portrayed the government as perpetrators, three (3) depicted ASUU as perpetrators, and six (2) portrayed ASUU as victims (see Fifelola and Unuabonah, 2025). In view of the variation in the number of cartoons within each category and to ensure manageable analysis, eight cartoons were ultimately selected for detailed study. The selection rationale was to achieve representative coverage across the major thematic groupings. Specifically, three cartoons (Figures 1, 6 and 8) were selected from those illustrating students as victims. Another three cartoons (Figures 2, 4 and 5) were selected from those depicting the Nigerian government as perpetrators. One cartoon (Figure 3) was selected from those portraying ASUU as perpetrators. Finally, one cartoon (Figure 7) was selected from those depicting ASUU as victims.

The sources offer varied data that capture the complex narratives and expressions surrounding the 2022 ASUU strike, as depicted by online cartoonists. To address the research questions, the cartoons were analysed qualitatively using van Dijk's socio-cognitive model of CDA alongside van Leeuwen's social semiotic framework. This approach enabled the examination of mental and context models, as well as visual elements such as composition, colour, gaze, posture, and spatial arrangement.

Together, these tools uncovered the ideologies expressed by the cartoonists, showing how visual and textual features were used to communicate broader socio-political views related to the strike.

## MAIN FOCUS OF THE CHAPTER

The 2022 ASUU strike was a significant event in Nigeria's educational and political landscape, drawing attention from various media, including political cartoons. These cartoons, widely circulated on digital platforms, provided a unique commentary on the strike by blending visual satire and textual elements. This section presents the analysis of how these cartoons used multimodal resources to convey ideologies and attitudes towards the ASUU strike.

## ANALYSIS AND DISCUSSION

This section presents the analysis of selected cartoons, drawing on two interrelated frameworks. First, Theo van Leeuwen's (2005, 2008) social semiotic approach is employed to examine how each cartoon constructs meaning through multimodal resources such as image, space, colour, and text. This approach highlights the representation of social actors, the recontextualisation of social practices, and the ideological function of semiotic choices. Second, van Dijk's (2006) sociocognitive model of CDA is applied to the dataset as a whole, focusing on how the cartoons reflect, reinforce, or resist dominant mental models (social cognition), ideologies, and power relations.

### Social Semiotic Analysis of the Cartoons

Each cartoon is treated as a multimodal artefact and examined for how it visually encodes protest, power, and suffering through culturally and ideologically loaded semiotic resources.

*Figure 1. Cartoon depicting the ASUU strike.*

Figure 1 draws on a deep well of semiotic and cultural resources to depict the ASUU strike as not merely a political event but a symbolic ritual of sacrifice, evoking the biblical story of Abraham and Isaac in Genesis 22:1-19. The cartoon recontextualises the strike as a tragic, life-altering act in which students are positioned as sacrificial lambs. The government official, seated atop a green-brown hill labelled "Federal Ministry of Education," mirrors the elevated, omnipotent position traditionally associated with God in the Abrahamic story. His dismissive utterance, "Due to bad economy, we cannot provide a ram for your sacrifice… you can go ahead and strike!" functions as a textual mode layered with irony, and satirically flipping the divine intervention in the biblical narrative. While God provided a ram to spare Isaac, the minister offers none thereby authorising the symbolic 'death' of the student. This variance with the Abrahamic precedent criticises the government's cold indifference towards the value of education and the lives it affects. The colour of the sky, blue yet subdued, further creates a solemn, contemplative mood, heightening the tragic undertone of the scene. The student, lying flat and lifeless on a stack of textbooks, is both literally and figuratively sacrificed on the altar of broken policies, unfulfilled promises and systemic neglect. The ASUU representative stands in silence, his body language conveying resignation, while the stack of books behind the student invokes the accumulated burden of abandoned knowledge and halted aspirations. The semiotic resources of colour, composition, and gaze are deliberately used to signal asymmetry in power. These modes form a coherent multimodal ensemble that exposes the ideological narrative underpinning the cartoon. Through this orchestration, the visual text criticises the failure of leadership to intervene or offer alternatives, ultimately condemning a system that authorises the ritual sacrifice of its future, its students, at the altar of economic excuses.

*Figure 2. Satire of the disparity between Nigerian legislature and ASUU.*

Figure 2 uses a range of semiotic resources to satirise the disparity between the Nigerian legislature and ASUU. Through the interplay of image, text, composition, colour, and gaze, the cartoon constructs a visual narrative that exposes systemic inequality and the trivialisation of academic concerns. The spatial arrangement places the represented participants, tagged "legislature" and "ASUU", in direct opposition, each clearly labelled. The legislature figure is portrayed as well-fed and confident, grasping a large sack boldly inscribed with "ALLOWANCES AND SALARY." This sack functions as a semiotic resource, symbolising economic privilege and greed, further amplified by the character's rotund body and complacent facial expression. In contrast, the ASUU representative is lean, sombre-faced, and formally dressed in academic regalia, holding a comparatively smaller document that reads, "LECTURER'S PAY AND 6% BUDGET ALLOCATION FOR EDUCATION FUNDING." The contrast in size and content of these objects serves as a modal affordance, revealing not only economic disparity but also ideological imbalance in value systems—where legislators enjoy opulence while academics are under-resourced. The composition further reinforces these ideological positions. The eye-level gaze shared between both figures suggests interaction, yet the visual vectors (depicted as lightning bolts) symbolise tension and conflict rather than dialogue. This use of gaze and vector directs the viewer's attention to the polarity in the cartoon, marking a site of power negotiation. The speech text at the bottom—"YOU SEE, WE REALLY DON'T THINK YOUR SITUATION IS SO SERIOUS AS TO WARRANT A STRIKE ACTION..."—is laden with irony. The visual juxtaposition of abundance and lack renders the utterance dismissive and patronising, thus criticising the legislators' hypocrisy and detachment from reality. Colour is used strategically to reinforce symbolic roles. The legislator's blue attire and oversized sack dominate the left, creating a visual imbalance that reflects real-world power asymmetry. The ASUU representative's black gown, adorned with subtle red and yellow lines, connotes intellectual authority but also austerity and struggle. The background remains neutral, allowing the social actors and their associated objects to take visual precedence. This deliberate composition supports van Leeuwen's (2008) idea that semiotic choices are shaped by social practices, and in turn, shape how these practices are interpreted. The representation of social actors, the imbalance of semiotic resources, and the interplay of text and image collectively construct a critical ideological stance. In doing so, the cartoon functions not only as satire but as a form of visual resistance, challenging dominant narratives and exposing the inherent contradictions within Nigeria's educational and political systems.

*Figure 3. Emotional entanglement around the strike.*

Figure 3 employs humour and irony to recontextualise the 2022 ASUU strike as a romantic relationship between the union and the act of striking. The cartoon reimagines the protest not as an act of resistance but as a symbolic and emotional entanglement. The visual and textual elements come together to satirise the predictability and recurrence of strike actions, portraying ASUU's relationship with the strike as intimate, cyclical, and even affectionate. The cartoon portrays "Strike" as a dark, seductive female figure, dressed in academic regalia but with devilish features such as horns and a tail. This characterisation immediately codes the strike action as both familiar and mischievously destructive. The devilish imagery also taps into moral discourses that often demonise the consequences of strike actions while neglecting their structural causes. The composition places "Strike" and ASUU in a posture of intimacy, holding hands across a candlelit table. This Valentine's Day setting is not accidental. The strike began on 14 February 2022, a day globally associated with love, which the cartoonist cleverly recontextualises to suggest that ASUU has an enduring and almost affectionate relationship with strikes. The hearts floating between the characters, and their mutual declarations of affection, "Happy Valentine's Day, my dear" and "I will always love you", are symbolic of loyalty and emotional investment, albeit in a toxic relationship. These textual modes reinforce the idea of repetitive cycles of strike actions, now ritualised and emotionally entrenched within the academic culture. The visual modes here, particularly the use of black to signify "Strike" and green for ASUU, carry ideological connotations. Black often symbolises trouble, rebellion, or destruction, while green can signify growth, resilience, or hope. Their juxtaposition in this cartoon mirrors the ideological tension between resistance and reform. Through these social semiotic resources, Figure 3 lampoons ASUU's seeming dependency on strikes as a mode of negotiation. It invites viewers to question the sustainability and consequences of this "love affair," highlighting the cyclical, performative nature of protest within the Nigerian higher education system.

*Figure 4. Government spending priorities in Nigeria.*

Figure 4 satirically recontextualises government spending priorities in Nigeria, using multimodal elements to expose contradictions between political rhetoric and financial practice. The cartoon features four key represented participants (RPs): the Central Bank of Nigeria (CBN), the Accountant General (AG), the Federal Government (FG), and a dejected academic figure tagged "ASUU." At the centre is a large, overflowing bag marked "Federal Account," a semiotic resource symbolising the state's financial reserves. The abundance of visible cash contradicts the FG RP's verbal claim of financial incapacity.

The RP tagged FG is shown mid-speech, pointing dismissively away from the money bag toward the RP tagged ASUU. His statement, "Mr ASUU, please leave. There is 'no' money to meet your demand," includes quotation marks around "no," signalling irony and insincerity. This contradiction between speech and visual content highlights the ideological gap between official discourse and material reality, aligning with van Leeuwen's concept of recontextualisation.

In contrast, the RPs tagged CBN and AG are actively carrying large boxes marked "N478BN" and "N800BN." These textual elements serve as modal affordances, referencing specific financial transactions that support the image's message of selective allocation. Their cheerful expressions and movement toward the Federal Account bag suggest willing participation in a redistribution system that sidelines educational needs.

The RP tagged ASUU is depicted with a slouched posture, downcast expression, and academic regalia, symbolising marginalisation and intellectual labour. Positioned at the frame's edge, this RP is visually and symbolically excluded from both the financial centre and the state apparatus. The RP's muted attire contrasts with the vibrant green and yellow of the money, reinforcing associations with austerity, neglect, and struggle.

The spatial composition, with money flowing in one direction and the RP tagged ASUU turned away, constructs a visual narrative of exclusion and systemic injustice. Van Leeuwen's principle that semiotic resources—such as posture, colour, size, and spatial arrangement—are never neutral is evident in this cartoon's ideological positioning. The image lampoons a political order that reserves resources for select institutions while withholding support from higher education.

Ultimately, the cartoon interrogates the legitimacy of state claims of scarcity and positions the strike not as a disruption but as a response to entrenched structural neglect. It functions as a form of visual resistance, supporting van Leeuwen's assertion that image-based meaning-making is socially situated, historically shaped, and ideologically driven.

*Figure 5. Satirizes government neglect and economic inequality.*

Figure 5 satirises government neglect and economic inequality by contrasting political ambition with academic hardship. Through textual, symbolic and spatial elements, the cartoon juxtaposes the financial struggles of students and lecturers with the greed of politicians. The represented participant tagged ASUU appears worn and weary, dressed conservatively, embodying the union's prolonged frustration. In the background, the represented student participant is slumped, holding a paper labelled "Student" and reading a pamphlet titled *How to forget ASUU strike and start online business with 0.00*, which mocks the escapist hustle culture emerging from state failure.

In the foreground, three represented participants identified as politicians are shown jubilantly discussing "presidential forms" while exchanging cash. One says, "There is money in government my brother", implying that politics is driven by personal gain rather than public service. A briefcase marked "Billions" symbolises diverted public resources that could fund education. Their relaxed, inward-facing postures and wide grins suggest detachment from the surrounding crisis. In contrast, the ASUU participant gazes outward in silent despair, and the student's bowed head signals resignation. These gaze directions and bodily orientations reflect a clear disconnect between those in power and those impacted by their negligence.

The spatial layout reinforces this imbalance. The student and ASUU participants are positioned to the left and lower down, indicating marginality and reduced agency, while the politicians are placed in the upper right, a position associated with dominance and forward movement in Western reading paths. Their vibrant clothing in red, purple and green connotes wealth and status, while ASUU's dull blue and the student's yellow and black suggest stagnation and vulnerability.

The cartoon constructs a visual critique of the ruling class's prioritisation of personal ambition over national development. As van Leeuwen (2005) notes, semiotic choices carry ideological weight. Here, the separation of represented participants, use of contrasting colour schemes, and the visual prominence of corrupt politicians expose leadership failure and the erosion of educational values. The uncertain stance of the student and the helpless expression of ASUU reflect public disillusionment, while the celebratory posture of the politicians represents the hollow pursuit of power.

Ultimately, the cartoon presents a stark narrative. While students and lecturers remain neglected, political elites exploit governance for personal gain. It lays bare the commodification of political space and the ideological consequences of elite impunity

*Figure 6. University students are the victims of this prolonged conflict.*

Figure 6 uses semiotic resources to portray public university students as the primary victims in the prolonged conflict between the represented participants tagged ASUU and the Federal Government (FG) during the 2022 strike. Central to the cartoon is a student bent under a wooden plank carrying the two dominant actors. Thin, barefoot, and simply dressed, the student's posture and anguished expression symbolise burden, exploitation and marginalisation. His role as the literal base of the scene frames students as the foundation of a broken system sustained by their suffering.

Atop the plank, FG and ASUU are engaged in a passive exchange. The FG figure states, "He has suffered too much, come down now," while ASUU responds, "After you, oga," a Nigerian English term indicating deference. Despite acknowledging the student's hardship, both participants avoid action. Their seated postures and indirect engagement visualise political stasis, where rhetorical concern replaces genuine accountability.

The spatial arrangement sharpens this imbalance. The student is positioned at the bottom of the visual field, physically and ideologically subordinated. The plank, as a semiotic artefact, represents the fragile structure of the educational system. Colour symbolism deepens the critique: the FG figure's dark purple robe suggests bureaucratic inertia, while ASUU's blue, often associated with trust, here signals hesitancy. The faded purple background isolates the scene, directing focus to the tension between actors. As van Leeuwen (2005) notes, such semiotic choices are ideologically loaded—they do not simply reflect reality but shape it.

Through its composition, the cartoon offers a sharp indictment of systemic neglect. It portrays the strike as a performance of delayed responsibility in which students bear the cost of elite inaction. Though both actors recognise the student's pain, neither initiates change. In doing so, the cartoon critiques the enduring cycle of abandonment that defines Nigeria's educational crisis.

*Figure 7. Visualises the degradation of ASUU members into informal survivalist roles during the strike.*

Figure 7 visualises the degradation of ASUU members into informal survivalist roles during the strike, employing multimodal elements to portray them as victims of governmental neglect. The cartoon depicts three represented participants (RPs), all academics in full ceremonial regalia, symbols of scholarly status, yet engaged in undignified, labour-intensive, or promotional tasks. Their academic robes, traditionally associated with learning, honour, and institutional respect, are here ironically contrasted with actions more commonly associated with informal street vendors or manual labourers.

The central RP, positioned in the foreground and dressed in green and yellow, is seen scooping grains with a hoe into a basket labelled "FRUITS." The act of harvesting, typically symbolic of reward for labour, is repurposed to connote survival rather than fulfilment. The exaggerated motion of the hoe and the small basket suggest the futility and strain of their effort. This gesture becomes a semiotic resource, connoting manual labour and hardship, contrasting sharply with the traditional expectation of intellectual work.

Behind him, two other RPs hold placards offering their services at "cheaper rates" for consultation on areas such as "policy," "project supervision," and "proposal writing," with one sign highlighting *"CONSULTANCY FEES 5,000."* These textual elements parody commercial advertisements, positioning the academics as sellers in a street market rather than as public intellectuals. The capitalisation and phrasing mimic economic desperation, suggesting how the government's refusal to pay salaries has pushed lecturers into commodifying their expertise in order to survive. The use of mobile numbers further enhances this portrayal, reducing scholarly engagement to transactional exchange.

The facial expressions and posture of the RPs support this reading. Each looks determined yet resigned, with exaggerated features expressing fatigue and discomfort. Their bodies are slightly hunched, leaning forward as if burdened by both physical effort and social humiliation. These embodied signs serve to foreground the emotional and physical toll of governmental abandonment during the prolonged ASUU strike.

Spatially, the RPs are aligned from left to right in a linear progression, suggesting collective experience and systemic impact rather than isolated incidents. Their shared attire and uniform direction imply that this transformation into sellers is widespread among university lecturers. The absence of any governmental figure or source of support in the frame reinforces their victimhood, situating them alone in a symbolic and literal economy of neglect. Colour also plays a critical role. The robes—bright green, blue, and purple—visually reference academic excellence and formality. Yet, this vibrancy is rendered ironic when placed in the context of physical struggle and marketplace survival. The grains and basket, in earthy tones, symbolise basic sustenance, suggesting that the once-prestigious profession has been reduced to scraping together means for survival.

According to van Leeuwen (2005), semiotic resources such as action, dress, and spatial orientation are ideologically loaded and socially positioned. Here, they are mobilised to expose the contradiction between the symbolic role of academics as knowledge producers and their material reality as neglected state employees. The cartoon represents ASUU members not just as disappointed actors but as structurally marginalised citizens whose labour is devalued by those in power. The image thus becomes a poignant commentary on the consequences of prolonged strikes and salary suspensions, portraying ASUU members as casualties of a government that deprioritises education.

*Figure 8. Criticism on inequality and political insensitivity.*

Figure 8 uses multiple semiotic resources to criticise inequality and political insensitivity in the Nigerian higher education crisis during the 2022 ASUU strike. On higher ground, the represented participants tagged the then First Lady, Aisha Buhari, and a young graduate are depicted in bright, celebratory clothing. The First Lady's remark, "Look! My daughter-in-law just graduated from a UK varsity," acts as a textual resource highlighting the ideological contradiction between elite privilege and the paralysed local education system. This references a real event in September 2022 that attracted public condemnation for its insensitivity. Their smiling faces, upright postures and vivid colours convey triumphalism and detachment.

Below them, Nigerian students are shown submerged in a murky pool labelled "Education." Their placards—"End ASUU Strike," "Fix Our Universities" and "Seven Months at Home"—textually express their abandonment. The students' tired expressions and low position visually represent marginalisation and despair.

The chained gate marked "Nigerian Universities" symbolises institutional decay and exclusion, highlighting the closure of educational opportunities. The spatial arrangement sets up a clear ideological divide: while the elite celebrate foreign academic success, the students struggle under prolonged stagnation. The First Lady's pointing gesture directs the viewer's attention towards the international graduate, reinforcing the government's neglect of local institutions.

Colour symbolism emphasises this divide. Bright, hopeful hues surround the elite, while dull, muddy tones dominate the students' environment, signalling the disparity in access and experience. The students' body language, struggling to stay afloat, signifies the emotional and material toll caused by political neglect. Following van Leeuwen's (2005) view that semiotic choices carry ideological meaning, the cartoon's juxtaposition of celebration and despair critiques the normalisation of inequality within Nigerian education. By contrasting elite privilege with student suffering, it situates the ASUU strike within wider issues of class, governance and national priorities, exposing the narratives that sustain social and educational injustice.

## Sociocognitive Analysis of the Cartoons

The socio-cognitive approach combines both the societal and interactive details in analysing discourse and is based on the mental model, which comprises event and context models. The context model consists of the global and local aspects of meaning that make ideologies understood and define the different properties of discourse and interactive strategy of positive self-presentation and negative-other presentation, while the event model represents the personal, episodic memory of individuals and experience. It is the connection between discourse structure and societal structure, such as class, gender, ethnicity, etc. This study examines the features of van Dijk's event and context models that adequately elicit participants' ideology in the visual texts and that of the cartoon creators.

## Context Model in the Cartoons

The cartoons construct a context model rooted in the domain of education, foregrounding the deteriorating condition of the Nigerian university system following the 2022 ASUU strike. These visual texts serve as discursive representations that shape and reinforce mental models concerning the 2022 ASUU strike. In Figure 1, three social actors are visually represented in a way that activates ideologically charged inferences. The first actor, depicted as a middle-aged man seated atop a rock labelled "Federal Ministry of Education," is easily recognisable as Mallam Adamu Adamu, the then Minister of Education. The minister's seated posture, especially as the only one among the participants, cues a mental model of complacency and dereliction of duty. His placement at the centre of institutional power suggests authority, yet his body language and detachment signal passivity. This aligns with a broader ideological framework in which government officials are constructed as indifferent to national crises, especially those affecting marginalised populations. This disposition influences the mental model of viewers towards the unwillingness of government officials to serve in the capacity in which they have been elected. The cartoon thereby contributes to the discursive reproduction of societal knowledge about power, suffering, and institutional neglect, inviting viewers to evaluate the legitimacy of authority through the lens of social injustice and failed governance.

The global action in this context pertains to the use of protest cartoons as ideological representations of Nigerians' evaluative stance towards the social actors involved in the 2022 ASUU strike. Through these visual texts, cartoonists construct discourses that reflect collective mental models about the state of higher education, governmental responsibility, and public suffering. Each cartoon embodies a context model—an interpretive framework through which viewers understand the situation of the strike based on their social and cognitive environment. In Figure 1, the Federal Government is directly indicted through the visual and linguistic representation of the Minister of Education, who instructs ASUU to "go ahead and strike." This utterance, devoid of empathy, constructs a context model in which the government is portrayed as indifferent to the deteriorating condition of Nigeria's educational system. The minister's tone and posture, embedded in satire, reinforce a mental model of insensitivity and institutional failure. Figure 2 shifts the discursive focus to the plight of university lecturers, highlighting the disparity in remuneration between academic staff and government officials. While ASUU members are depicted as suffering and underpaid, members of the legislature are represented as excessively compensated. This contrast not only visualises economic inequality but also contributes to a broader ideological framework wherein academic labour is undervalued, and systemic neglect is normalised. The cartoon taps into socially shared knowledge about Nigeria's political economy, prompting viewers to interpret the strike as a justified reaction to entrenched injustice. Hence, the cartoons function as discursive artefacts through which cartoonists express disapproval of the government's handling of the strike and frame the public's cognitive and ideological orientation towards the crisis. In this way, the visual texts become agents of social critique, reflecting and reinforcing public consciousness shaped by lived experience and mediated discourse.

The local action in the cartoons centres on a protest against the recurring industrial actions that have paralysed Nigeria's public university system. Through visual satire and strategic representation, the cartoons project the immediate and long-term effects of these strikes on the Nigerian education sector, while simultaneously lampooning the key social actors implicated in the crisis. In Figures 2 and 4, the cartoon functions as a visual protest against the Nigerian government's perceived victimisation of public university lecturers. The imagery suggests that the government possesses the financial resources necessary to revitalise the education system, but consciously withholds them. The cartoon thus reveals an ideological stance that foregrounds public frustration with governmental apathy and reinforces a mental model of structural injustice. In contrast, Figure 3 shifts the blame to ASUU itself, portraying the union as partially responsible for the instability in the higher education sector. The visual texts contextually influence the mental model of viewers to the negative effect of the ASUU strike on students, lecturers, and the Nigerian society at large.

Under participant roles, the cartoons establish a communicative relationship between three key groups: the cartoon creators, the social actors represented in the visuals, and the public. In this context, the cartoons function as discursive tools through which Nigerians articulate their evaluative stance toward the recurrent strikes in the education sector. Each cartoon reflects widespread public dissatisfaction with the 2022 ASUU strike by highlighting the government's perceived detachment from the plight of its citizens. The social relation encoded in the cartoons is informal, as evidenced by the satirical tone, the use of colloquial lexical choices, and the exaggerated depiction of events and actors. This informality contributes to their accessibility and emotional appeal, enabling the cartoons to resonate with everyday Nigerians who may otherwise feel excluded from formal political discourse. Under cognition, the underlying intention of the cartoon producers is to communicate that the ongoing crises in Nigerian universities are avoidable. In this way, the cartoons not only represent public opinion but also contribute to shaping collective mental models about accountability, negotiation, and the possibility of systemic change.

The cartoons under analysis reflect a range of ideologies that influence how social actors and institutional behaviours are evaluated. One prominent ideology is that of anti-welfarism, particularly on the part of Nigerian government officials. This is illustrated in Figures 2, 4, 5, and 8. Hence, the cartoon producer presents the negative-other representation of the Nigerian government and reveals their disinterest in the progress of the Nigerian education system. The ideology of resistance is also evident, particularly in the stance of ASUU. This is depicted in the facial expression of the second participant in Figure 2, which conveys frustration over the wide gap between the allowances allocated to the Nigerian legislature and the minimal funding given to the education sector. The cartoon reflects a mental model in which resistance is not only a reactive measure but also a legitimate response to structural inequality. Figure 3 reflects the self-centred ideology of ASUU, suggesting that the union at times prioritises its own interests over those of the students it represents. Across the cartoon dataset, these ideologies work together to construct a discourse that attributes responsibility to multiple actors, while reinforcing a context model shaped by distrust in institutional leadership and disillusionment with the state of university education in Nigeria.

## Mental Model in the Cartoons

The Mental model may be the basis of the "content" or " meaning of discourse" van Dijk (2002: 216). Thus, they control the 'semantic' aspect of discourse. These semantic aspects include *Global topic, local semantics, argumentation, and rhetoric*. These socio-cognitive resources examined in the cartoons reveal the ideologies of participants in the text and that of the creators of the texts. The first socio-cognitive resource identified in the cartoons is the **global topic.**

### Global Topic

Topics indicate what discourse is all about. They are known as semantic macrostructures. In the visual texts examined, topics are strategically adopted by interactants in the texts to discursively emphasise our good things and de-emphasise our bad things. The cartoon producers also employ topics to reflect the hidden ideologies of participants in the cartoons. The macro-propositions of the cartoons are as outlined below:

i. ASUU sees strike as a weapon to make government yield to their demands; hence they have decided to continually go on strike until FG implements all their demands (Fig. 3).
ii. FG has what it takes to revitalise the education sector, which is one of the demands of ASUU, but seems indifferent to the union's demands (Fig. 2 and 4).
iii. Students are the most affected by this continual feud between ASUU and FG, as the delay caused by incessant strikes is threatening their growth and progress (Fig. 1 and 6).
iv. ASUU and FG are aware of the effects of their actions on students, but neither is ready to consider the effects on Nigerian students (Fig. 1 and 6).
v. The Nigerian government has consistently turned deaf ears to ASUU's demands, and this is why the ASUU strike in Nigerian universities seems to defy solutions (Fig 2. and 4).
vi. The ASUU's protest is a response to the poor welfare of their workers and the dejected state of the education sector (Fig. 2 and 4).
vii. The Federal Government is not able to meet the financial demands of the lecturers because they have not prioritised lecturers' welfare.

viii. Nigerian government officials are depicted as extravagant and self-centred, showing concern only for their own interests while spending frivolously and failing to prioritise the impact of their lackadaisical attitude on students (Fig. 5 and 8).
ix. The Nigerian education system is in shambles, and if care is not taken, education in Nigeria will be reduced to just books (Fig. 1).

These macro-propositions are used by the cartoon creators to create a balance and present the various reasons for the constant strikes, including the 2022 strike. Hence, the topics above show that ASUU's fight against poor welfare is justified and that the government should make the implementation of their demands a top priority. This is because education is the bedrock of every society and deserves adequate attention. In this regard, the cartoon creators show that the government has the resources needed for the Nigerian education system to thrive, but has refused to do the needful because of misplaced priorities and greed by the ruling elite.

In essence, the topics are used to emphasise the negative-other presentation of government officials and ASUU. In doing this, the cartoon creators influence the mental model of the public towards the sufferings of both students and lecturers of Nigerian universities, as lecturers are also depicted as victims of circumstances, as seen in Figures 1 and 2. Some visual texts further emphasise the positive self-presentation of ASUU by bringing forward their struggles and portraying them as victims of circumstances. For instance, Figure 4 presents the inhumane treatment of ASUU by the Nigerian government. It shows that the government has all it takes to make the demands of ASUU become a reality. It is in line with this that Lawal (2022) asserts that education in Nigeria, at least in the public sector, is dysfunctional. Its human capital needs to be fixed, and so is its physical infrastructure. He adds that the nation's standard of education totters as the government continues to talk more about the crises facing it rather than act on resolving them. Overall, the visual texts lampoon the political elites and foreground their bad deeds by emphasising the self-centred ideology of these officials.

Another significant socio-cognitive resource present in the cartoons is local semantics which will be examined below:

## Local Semantics

In van Dijk's socio-cognitive model, local semantics refers to the specific meanings conveyed at the sentence or phrase level within a discourse. This includes the choice of words, phrases, and expressions that provide detailed, context-specific information, helping to shape the audience's interpretation of the message. The local meanings in the visual texts are intended to project the ideologies of participants and add to the overall strategy of positive self-presentation and negative other presentation. Local meanings in the cartoons can be seen in the ***lexical choices, pronominal references, and choice of noun phrases*** employed by participants in the visual texts.

i) Lexical Choices

The lexical choices in the cartoons are used as satirical strategies to foreground their bad deeds. Thus, words such as *bad, ram, sacrifice* and *strike*, as used in Figure 1, are strategically employed to emphasise their negative other-presentation and highlight the anti-welfarist ideology of the government. These words are meant to influence the viewers' opinion and attitude towards government's negligence of the Nigerian education sector. In this vein, the Minister of Education is presented as one who sees the lecturers' demands as a form of annual sacrifice that should not be encouraged. Hence, the cartoon creator aims to influence the mental models of the viewers to the plight of students and lecturers as a result of government's inadequacies. In this regard, the minister tries to portray the negative-other presentation of ASUU as seen in the declarative sentence, "we cannot provide a ram for your sacrifice," thereby belittling ASUU's struggles and foregrounding their bad needs. He does this as a form of biblical allusion to portray ASUU as a profane union that would sacrifice the future of students based on their grievances against the government. Through the minister's disposition towards ASUU's demands, the cartoon producer foregrounds the negative-other presentation of government officials and highlights the anti-welfarist and oppressive ideology of the government towards ASUU, Nigerian students, and the education sector as a whole. The directive, "You can go ahead and strike!" further shows government's indifference towards the deplorable state of the education sector. This is buttressed through the adverbial phrase of reason, "due to bad economy..." which suggests the lackadaisical attitude of the Nigerian government toward the education sector.

Furthermore, words such as *pay, salaries, allowances* and *work* in Figure 2 are used to describe the demands of ASUU to the viewers. These lexical choices suggest government's inhumane treatment of lecturers of public universities in Nigeria. In this regard, it can be deduced that university lecturers have been consistently serving the Nigerian society without adequate compensation from the government. One can infer that university buildings are dilapidated, and lecturers are being paid salaries that can hardly cater to their daily needs. Also, the choice of lexical items such as *funding* and *budget* contrasts ASUU's remuneration and that of political office holders, including the Nigerian legislature. It further shows government's negligence of the academic sector and projects that the government has all that is needed to revitalise public universities as demanded by ASUU. These lexical choices emphasise their negative-other presentation by foregrounding the bad deeds of the Nigerian government.

In addition, the sentence "How to forget ASUU strike and start online business with #0.00" in Figure 5 foregrounds the hopelessness of the student's situation, suggesting abandonment and depicting the collapse of the education sector. The noun phrase "my brother," a kinship term used among the politicians, conveys a sense of camaraderie and solidarity rooted in shared corrupt practices, suggesting that complicity and mutual support are normalised within the political elite. Similarly, the noun phrase "Presidential Form" associated with "Billions" and the declarative sentence "There is money in government, my brother" underscore the excessive monetisation of political processes and further reveal the irony in the Nigerian political system, where candidates enter government not to serve but to enrich themselves. These local meanings collectively work to negatively represent political actors while positioning the student and ASUU as victims of systemic neglect. In Figure 8, the exclamatory statement, "LOOK! MY DAUGHTER-IN-LAW JUST GRADUATED FROM A UK VARSITY!" employs deliberate lexical choices that reflect pride and personal accomplishment. The noun phrase "UK Varsity" draws attention to the foreign location, creating a stark contrast with the deteriorating condition of Nigerian universities. Meanwhile, the clauses "END ASUU STRIKE," "FIX OUR UNIVERSITIES," and "SEVEN MONTHS AT HOME," positioned on placards held by submerged students, symbolically represent those trapped within a collapsing educational system labelled "EDUCATION." The visual and verbal juxtaposition between the well-positioned celebratory figure on land and the distressed students beneath underscores an ideological divide between privilege and marginalisation. The cartoon conveys an ideology of elite hypocrisy and institutional abandonment, portraying the ruling class as indifferent to the consequences of the prolonged strike, while enjoying the benefits of foreign education. It exposes the clear disconnect between the comfortable lives of those in power and the harsh realities faced by ordinary citizens. These local semantic elements thus serve a broader strategy of negative-other representation, framing the political elite as exploitative and negligent, while aligning viewers' sympathies with the oppressed student population.

Consequently, this apathetic attitude of government to the lives and properties of citizens, which directly affects the Nigerian education sector, is portrayed in the linguistic element in Figure 4, "please leave," and the declarative, "there is no money to meet your demand," which reveal the mindset of the Buhari-led administration and portray government's lack of interest in the Nigerian education sector. These lexical choices are used to foreground the bad deeds of the government and project that as far as these leaders continue to be in government, the Nigerian education system will continue to be in shambles. In addition, noun phrases such as *bad economy, a ram* and *your sacrifice* as used in Figure 1, add to the strategy of negative-other presentation in which their bad things are emphasized. Thus, the education minister in Figure 1 uses these phrases to give excuses for the inadequacies of the government. The noun phrase, *your sacrifice*, is used by the minister to influence the mental models of viewers and to shift the blame on ASUU for the strikes in the university. Therefore, the cartoon producer calls on the government to admit to their failure in providing the needed infrastructure in universities and find a way to solve the issues at hand rather than shifting blame. Other noun phrases such as *bad economy* and *a ram* further foreground the bad deeds of the Nigerian government and present them as an unwise government who do not know how to effectively communicate with their citizens to curb uprisings in the society.

In projecting the reasons for the 2022 ASUU strike, the cartoon producers foreground the bad deeds of ASUU and portray them as a union that simply enjoys going on strike for the fun of it. This is depicted through words such as v*alentine*, *love, dear,* and *always* as seen in Figure 3. Thus, these lexical choices influence the mental models of viewers to ASUU's passion for continuous strikes. Hence, the declarative sentence, "I will always love you," debunks ASUU's claims and project their real reasons for always embarking on strikes. The cartoon, therefore, emphasises the bad deeds of ASUU by suggesting that their real intent for going on strike is that they enjoy it.

Also, the choice of noun phrases such as *allowances and salary, your situation,* and *a strike action* used in Figure 2, depict government's anti-welfarist ideology. In the noun phrase, *your situation*, the Nigerian legislature dissociates himself from the challenges of the education sector and presents ASUU strike as unwarranted. This is done to influence the mental models of the general public and foreground the union's bad deeds. In the same vein, members of the union foreground the bad deeds of the government with the use of noun phrases such as *lecturer's pay, academic allowances,* and *budget for education funding*. These noun phrases are used to influence the mental model of viewers to the dilemma in which ASUU find themselves and to show the general public they are being treated unfairly by the government. Hence, the noun phrases *academic allowance* and *budget allocation for education funding* further buttress this point as they contrast lecturers' annual earnings and the funding allocation for education with the salaries and allowances of members of the Nigerian national assembly. These noun phrases, therefore, project the oppressive ideology of members of ASUU and the anti-welfarist ideology of the government. Also, in Figure 3, noun phrases such *as valentine's day* and *my dear* are a satirical depiction of the intimate relationship that exists between ASUU and strikes. It is, therefore, used to influence the mental models of the public and emphasise the bad deeds of the union.

ii) Pronominal Reference

In the cartoons, pronominal references are ideologically used by participants. The use of collective 'we' by the minister of education in Figure 1 and the Legislature in Figure 2 reflects the defensive ideology of the government, which they expect would influence the mental models of the Nigerian citizens. In Figure 4, the minister tries to downplay the plight of ASUU and presents to the public that ASUU is only making a big deal out of the issue at hand. This is ironic and is done to emphasise the negative presentation of the government, who are unable to adequately provide and cater to the needs of lecturers in Nigerian universities. In the same vein, the participant's choice of the collective pronoun in Figure 2 is used as a defensive strategy for the negative other presentation of ASUU. In this regard, the Legislature downplays ASUU's demands and defends their own inadequacies, thereby projecting that ASUU's needs are inconsequential. This is further depicted by the choice of the pronoun "you" in reference to ASUU. The government dissociates themselves from the plight of ASUU and simultaneously trivilises ASUU's struggles. Also, the cartoon creator uses the first-person personal pronoun, '*I*' in the sentence *"I will always love you"* to foreground the bad deeds of ASUU.

In addition to local semantics, ***argumentation*** is another key socio-cognitive resource in the analysed cartoons.

## Argumentation

In van Dijk's socio-cognitive approach, argumentation refers to the use of reasoning, justifications, and logical structures to persuade the audience and support specific ideological viewpoints. Through argumentation, discourse participants present their positions as rational, credible, and legitimate while discrediting opposing views. The cartoon creators make use of ***explanations*** to foreground the bad deeds of government officials in the visual texts.

## Rhetoric

Rhetoric refers to the use of strategic language and visual elements to influence the audience's perception, emotions, and reasoning. Rhetorical devices are used to convey different ideologies and emphasise our positive self-presentation and negative-other presentation by stating our good deeds and their bad deeds. In the context of the 2022 ASUU strike, cartoonists employ rhetorical techniques to frame the discourse, shaping how the strike is understood and responded to by the public. The rhetorical device used in the images includes ***victimisation.***

i. Victimisation

The victimisation of students by both FG and ASUU is depicted through the semiotic resources and the verbal elements in the visual texts. In Figure 1, the third RP in the cartoon, who represents students of Nigerian universities, is seen lying in a supine position on a bench built with books, with his hands and legs tied. The minister further orders ASUU to 'go ahead and strike (the students)'. Thus, the cartoon creator presents the victimisation of Nigerian university students through these semiotic resources. This is done to influence the mental models of viewers to the plight of students due to incessant ASUU strikes in the education sector. Thus, the Minister of Education is presented to be sitting on a rock, a symbolic depiction of the Nigerian presidential villa, Aso Rock Villa. Also, the choice of brown colour, which serves as an overlay of the rock, is ironic. According to Bourn (2010), the brown colour depicts stability, reliability, dependability, and approachability. It is also associated with security. However, the education sector is unstable, and the leaders seem unreliable and unapproachable as they keep failing in the promises made to ASUU over the years. Students' future is also not secured due to the inconsistencies in the education sector. In addition, the education minister is presented to be chubby, while ASUU and the student seem malnourished. These choices are, used to depict the negative other-representation of the government. In this regard, the visual text suggests that government officials' acts contradict the tenets they claim to uphold. In essence, the visual text is a portrayal of the lackadaisical attitude of the Nigerian government towards the plight of citizens, thereby depicting the anti-welfarist ideology of FG.

In projecting the victimisation of participants in the images, the cartoon creator further portrays ASUU as victims of a failed government, and this is shown through the verbal element in Figure 1, "you can go ahead and strike." This choice is used to depict government's inadequacies and an obtuse unwillingness to take responsibility for the wellbeing of their citizens. This inhumane treatment of ASUU by the Federal Government directly affects students, as seen in how he is being bound with ropes. In this regard, the cartoon creator depicts the negative-other representation of the government and ASUU as their actions greatly affect the future goals of students whose lives have continually experienced delay due to the incessant strikes of the Union. In essence, the cartoon producer presents the non-responsive ideology of both parties and focuses on their bad things. In doing this, the cartoon producer influences the mental models of viewers to the sufferings of students. These two images, therefore, serve as a satirical device to criticise the social actors involved in the strike and reflect the anti-welfarist ideology of both ASUU and FG as well as the suppressive ideology of Nigerian University students.

## FUTURE RESEARCH DIRECTIONS

This study is not exhaustive in itself as far as studies on cartoons are concerned. This research has only considered a critical discourse analysis of fifty protest cartoons on the ASUU strike in Nigeria. Further studies may use theories such as conceptual metaphor and appraisal theory to examine memes on the ASUU strike. Other kinds of texts, such as online reader comments on the ASUU strike, can also be considered. The role of digital media in the dissemination and reception of cartoons is also a critical area for future study. With the rise of social media platforms like Twitter, Instagram, and Facebook, cartoonists can now reach broader audiences in real time, influencing the speed and scope of political commentary.

## CONCLUSION

This study focused on how specific socio-cognitive resources were used to suggest the ideological positions of the cartoon creators on the 2022 ASUU strike in Nigeria. The critical discourse analysis of the cartoons revealed that ideological strategies such as positive self- and negative other representations, topics, argumentation, pronominals, and rhetorical strategies were used by the cartoon creators to express their ideologies. For example, positive self-representation and negative other-representation strategies were used to lampoon the social actors involved in the strike. Thus, some of the visual texts highlight the defensive, anti-welfarist, egocentric, and oppressive ideology of the Nigerian government, while others project the suppressive and anti-welfarist ideology of ASUU. Overall, the multimodal critical discourse analysis of protest cartoons on ASUU strike carried out in this study proved that cartoons are digital artefacts used for political expression and engagement against institutional and corporate power. Hence, these visual texts are often consciously created to lampoon, show hidden ideologies and satirise authorities, thereby influencing the mental models of viewers to support their ideology and perception regarding certain issues. This study has, therefore, accounted for how semiotic and socio-cognitive elements deployed in the cartoons are used to project the thoughts, feelings, attitudes and ideologies of citizens towards the social actors involved in the strike.

## REFERENCES


Adeagbo, E. O., & Oyindamola, A. A. (2024). Multimodal Discourse Features in Selected Nigerian Political Cartoons. *Àgídìgbo. ABUAD Journal of the Humanities, 12*(1), 141–160. DOI: 10.53982/agidigbo.2024.1201.10-j

Ademilokun, M. (2016). A Multimodal Analysis of the Public Discourse of the 2013 University Lecturers' Strike in Nigeria. In Taiwo, R., & Opeibi, B. (Eds.), *The Discourse of Digital Civic Engagement: Perspectives from the Developing World* (pp. 57–74). Nova Science Publishers.

Akingbe, N. (2012). Writing protest obliquely: Articulating the burden of a nation in Chinua Achebe's *Anthills of the Savannah. Transnational Literature, 5*(1), 1–17. https://doaj.org/article/7261bd85b69b4dc2b8ea6d5076d0e8e2

Al Zidjaly, N. (2017). Memes as reasonably hostile laments: A discourse analysis of political dissent in Oman. *Discourse & Society, 28*(6), 573–594. DOI: 10.1177/0957926517721083

Amore, K. P., & Atoloye, L. (2016). A Systemic Functional-Multimodal Discourse Analysis of Some Cartoons Connected with Nigeria's 2015 General Elections. *The Nigerian Journal of Communication, 13*(1), 23–46.

Auvinen, J. (1996). IMF intervention and political protest in the Third World: A conventional wisdom refined. *Third World Quarterly, 17*(3), 337–400. DOI: 10.1080/01436599615425

Ayoola, K. (2021). Dimensions and applications of critical discourse analysis. In Ayoola, K., Arugbawa, O., & Oyebode, O. (Eds.), *Current Approaches to Discourse Analysis* (pp. 179–225). Obafemi Awolowo University Press.

Baker, S., & Green, S. (2014). The viral political cartoon: A case study. *Visual Communication, 13*(2), 131–147. DOI: 10.1177/0957926511433478

Bezemer, J., & Jewitt, C. (2009). Social Semiotics. In Östman, J. O., Verschueren, J., & Versluys, E. (Eds.), *Handbook of Pragmatics: 2009 Installment*. John Benjamins. DOI: 10.1075/hop.13.soc5

Chiluwa, I. (2018). A nation divided against itself: Biafra and the conflicting online protest discourses. *Discourse & Communication, 12*(4), 357–381. DOI: 10.1177/1750481318757778

Eesuola, S. O. (2013). Three dimensions of political protest: A theoretical analytical of Fela Anikulapo Kuti. *Redeemer's University Journal of Management and Social Sciences*, *1*(1), 81–91.

Ellah, S. M. (2014). The language of industrial actions in Nigeria. *Research on Humanities and Social Sciences*, *4*(26), 133–138.

Fay, B. (1987). Critical social science: Liberation and its limits. *Polity*.

Fifelola, D. A., & Unuabonah, F. O. (2025). "No work, No pay": A multimodal discourse analysis of selected online images on industrial actions by Nigerian public universities. *Discourse & Communication*, *19*(2), 175–196. DOI: 10.1177/17504813241297205

Freire, P. (1999). *Pedagogy of the oppressed*. Penguin Books.

Hansson, S., Page, R., & Fuoli, M. (2022). Discursive Strategies of Blaming: The Language of Judgment and Political Protest Online. *Social Media + Society*, *8*(4), 1–11. DOI: 10.1177/20563051221138753 PMID: 36447997

Idiagbon, A. (2014). A multimodal approach to the study of discourse of protest: An example of the Federal government of Nigeria and the Nigeria Labour Congress face off. *Zango*, *31*, 81–98.

Kress, G. (1993). Against arbitrariness: The social production of the sign as a foundational issue in critical discourse analysis. *Discourse & Society*, *4*(2), 169–193. DOI: 10.1177/0957926593004002003

Monogbe, B. O. (2019). ASUU strike and Nigerian educational system: An empirical investigation of the Nigerian tertiary institution. *American Journal of Social Sciences and Humanities*, *4*(1), 56–67. DOI: 10.20448/801.41.56.67

Omolabi, I., & Adebayo, K. T. (2024). A pragmatic analysis of selected ASUU strike memes motivated humour on social media. *Integrity Journal of Arts and Humanities*, *5*(2), 61–72. DOI: 10.31248/IJAH2024.130

Osisanwo, A., & Atoloye, L. (2024). "Silence is the best answer for a bully": An exploration of humour techniques in selected Nigerian newspaper political cartoons. *Language and Semiotic Studies*, *10*(3), 367–396. DOI: 10.1515/lass-2024-0009

Rintel, S. (2013). Crisis memes: The importance of templatability to internet culture and freedom of expression. *Australasian Journal of Popular Culture*, *2*(2), 253–271. DOI: 10.1386/ajpc.2.2.253_1

Rivas-Carmona, M. (2014). Cartooning for gender equality: A multimodal expression of 'humour' and 'vindication'. *Research on Humanities and Social Sciences, 4*(24), 8–19.

Tahir, H. (2013, August 28). ASUU strike and faltering university education. *Vanguard*. https://www.vanguardngr.com/2013/08/asuu-strike-and-faltering-university-education/

Ugwuona, C. (2016). 2013 ASUU strike discourses in Nigeria: A critical discourse analysis. *Mediterranean Journal of Social Sciences, 7*(2), 435–444. DOI: 10.5901/mjss.2016.v7n2p435

Unuabonah, F. O., & Oyebode, O. O. (2021). "Nigeria is fighting Covid-419": A multimodal critical discourse analysis of political protest in Nigerian coronavirus-related Internet memes. *Discourse & Communication, 15*(2), 200–219.

Usman, S. O., & Nuhu, M. T. (2016). Satire as Tool of Political Cartoons in the Nigerian National Dailies: A Critical Discourse Analysis. *European Scientific Journal, 12*(29), 124–138. DOI: 10.19044/esj.2016.v12n29p124

van Dijk, T. (2001). Critical discourse analysis. In D. Tannen, D. Schiffrin, & H. Hamilton (Eds.), *Handbook of discourse analysis* (pp. 352–371). Blackwell.

van Dijk, T. A. (1993). Principles of critical discourse analysis. *Discourse & Society, 4*(2), 249–283. DOI: 10.1177/0957926593004002006

van Dijk, T. A. (2000). Ideology and Discourse: A Multidisciplinary Introduction. https://www.discourses.org/download/books

van Dijk, T. A. (2006). Discourse and manipulation. *Discourse & Society, 17*(3), 359–383. DOI: 10.1177/0957926506060250

van Leeuwen, T. (2005). *Introducing Social Semiotics*. Routledge.

van Leeuwen, T. (2008). *Discourse and Practice: New Tools for Critical Discourse Analysis*. Oxford University Press. DOI: 10.1093/acprof:oso/9780195323306.001.0001

Vásquez, C., & Aslan, E. (2021). "Cats be outside, how about meow": Multimodal humor and creativity in an internet meme. *Journal of Pragmatics, 171*, 101–117. DOI: 10.1016/j.pragma.2020.10.006

Vlachaki, C. (2021). Humour in digital discourse: Memes, multimodality and relevance (M.A. thesis). National and Kapodistrian University of Athens, Greece.

Wodak, R. (1996). *Disorders of discourse*. Longman.

Wu, Y., & Wall, M. (2021). COVID-19 and viral anti-Asian racism: A multimodal critical discourse analysis of memes and the racialization of the COVID-19 pandemic. *Journal of Contemporary Chinese Art*, *8*(2–3), 107–127. DOI: 10.1386/jcca_00040_1

Yus, F. (2018). Multimodality in memes: A cyberpragmatic approach. In Storbeck, J. E. R., & Jedlowski, A. (Eds.), *Analyzing digital discourse: New insights and future directions* (pp. 105–131). Springer International Publishing., DOI: 10.1007/978-3-319-92663-6_4

## ADDITIONAL READING

Agger, B. (1992). *The discourse of domination: From the Frankfurt School to post-modernism*. Northwestern University Press. DOI: 10.2307/j.ctv47w3p1

Aidelunughene, O. S. (2014). ASUU industrial actions: Between ASUU and government, is it an issue? *Journal of Education and Practice*, *5*(6), 7–17.

Ajayi, M. T., & Akinrinlola, T. (2021). Pragma-multimodal functions of Covid-19 memes in the Nigerian context. *Journal of Applied Language and Culture Studies*, *4*, 77–102.

Akinwotu, S. A.Samuel Alaba Akinwotu. (2019). The role of discursive constructions in Nigeria's ASUU-FGN labour conflict of 2013. [AJIC]. *The African Journal of Information and Communication*, *23*(23), 1–18. DOI: 10.23962/10539/27531

Amore, K., & Atoloye, L. (2016). A systemic function-multimodal discourse analysis of some cartoons connected with Nigeria's 2015 general elections. *The Nigerian Journal of Communication*, *13*(1), 23–46.

Ayoola, K. (2021). Dimensions and applications of critical discourse analysis. In Ayoola, K., Arugbawa, O., & Oyebode, O. (Eds.), *Current approaches to discourse analysis* (pp. 179–225). Obafemi Awolowo University Press.

Chiluwa, I. (2012). Social media networks and the discourse of resistance: A sociolinguistic CDA of Biafra online discourses. *Discourse & Society*, *23*(3), 217–244. DOI: 10.1177/0957926511433478

Eneojoh, J., & Oryila, S. (2018). A multi-modal analysis of Boko Haram social media post. *Papers in English and Linguistics*, *19*(3 & 4), 45–72.

Forceville, C. (2011). Multimodality: A social semiotic approach to contemporary communication. *Journal of Pragmatics*, *21*(3), 3624–3626. DOI: 10.1016/j.pragma.2011.06.013

Forchtner, B., & Kølvraa, C. (2017). Extreme right images of radical authenticity: Multimodal aesthetics of history, nature, and gender roles in social media. *European Journal of Cultural and Political Sociology*, *4*(3), 252–281. DOI: 10.1080/23254823.2017.1322910

## KEY TERMS AND DEFINITIONS

**Academic Staff Union of Universities (ASUU):** A Nigerian labour union representing the academic staff of public universities. It is responsible for advocating for improved working conditions, university funding, and educational reforms in Nigeria.

**Labour Disputes:** Conflicts between workers (in this case, university lecturers) and employers (the government) over issues like wages, working conditions, and institutional governance. The ASUU strike is an example of a prolonged labour dispute in Nigeria's education sector.

**Multimodal Resources:** The combination of multiple modes of communication—such as text, images, and symbols—to create meaning. In political cartoons, these resources are used to express complex socio-political messages through both visual and textual elements.

**Political Cartoons:** Illustrations or comics that comment on political events, figures, or social issues, often through satire or exaggeration. In this chapter, political cartoons related to the 2022 ASUU strike are analysed to understand public sentiment and critique.

**Socio-Cognitive Resources:** Shared mental models and cognitive frameworks that reflect how society understands and processes information. In this chapter, socio-cognitive resources refer to the public's collective interpretation of the ASUU strike as represented in cartoons.

Chapter 2

# Technology Usage Attitude and Internet of Behavior:

## A Study of Chinese Social Media Apps in Kerala

**Vishnu Achutha Menon**
https://orcid.org/0000-0003-4028-3685
*Institute for Educational and Developmental Studies, Noida, India*

**Sandeep Kumar**
*Barkatullah Vishwavidyalaya, India*

**Anil Shivani**
*Government Hamidia Arts and Commerce Degree College, Bhopal, India*

## ABSTRACT

*The usage of Chinese apps has surged in Kerala, driven by affordable smartphones, aggressive marketing, and popular social media and e-commerce platforms. Apps like TikTok, WeChat, and UC Browser have gained substantial user bases due to their user-friendly interfaces, innovative features, and localized content. Kerala's high literacy rate, widespread internet penetration, and tech-savvy population have contributed to the rapid acceptance and usage of these apps. This study investigates the influence of the Internet of Behavior (IoB) on technology readiness (optimism, innovativeness, discomfort, and insecurity) and technology usage attitudes (anxiety, negativity, and multitasking performance) among users of Chinese social media apps in Kerala. Using a quantitative research design and data collected from 510 participants, the study employs correlation and regression analyses to examine*

DOI: 10.4018/979-8-3373-5297-8.ch002

*these relationships.*

## INTRODUCTION

In recent years, there has been a significant increase in the usage of Chinese apps across India, including in the state of Kerala. This surge can be attributed to various factors, such as the affordability of Chinese smartphones, aggressive marketing strategies by Chinese tech companies, and the growing popularity of social media and e-commerce platforms. Apps like TikTok, WeChat, and UC Browser, among others, have gained substantial user bases due to their user-friendly interfaces, innovative features, and localized content that caters to the diverse Indian audience. In Kerala, the adoption of Chinese apps has been particularly noteworthy. The state's high literacy rate, widespread internet penetration, and tech-savvy population have contributed to the rapid acceptance and usage of these apps. The social and cultural fabric of Kerala, characterized by a strong diaspora community and a penchant for embracing new technologies, has further fueled this trend. As a result, Chinese apps have become an integral part of the daily digital interactions of many Keralites, influencing communication, entertainment, shopping, and more. The objective of this study is to investigate the influence of the internet of behaviour of Chinese social media apps on the audience's technology readiness (optimism, innovativeness, discomfort, and insecurity) and technology usage attitudes (anxiety, negativity, and multitasking performance) in Kerala.

## REVIEW OF LITERATURE

The dimensions of technology readiness—innovativeness, optimism, discomfort, and insecurity—exert profound and lasting impacts on both the adoption and usage stages of Internet acceptance. These effects vary according to the perceived risk associated with the technology (Lam et al., 2008). Positive technology readiness, characterized by optimism and innovation, has a weak influence on perceived usefulness and perceived ease of use but does not directly impact the intention to use the technology. Negative technology readiness, marked by discomfort and insecurity, does not significantly affect perceived usefulness, perceived ease of use, or intention to use. However, perceived ease of use positively influences perceived usefulness, and both factors significantly affect the intention to use the technology. This indicates that individuals with a positive technology readiness are not directly driven by their readiness in their intention to use technology. Instead, if they perceive the technology as useful and easy to use, they are more likely to intend to use it (Seo et al., 2018).

Cultural differences also play a crucial role in technology adoption. South Koreans are more influenced by positive technology readiness factors like innovativeness and optimism when adopting mobile internet services compared to Chinese users. In contrast, Chinese users are less swayed by positive factors and are more affected by negative factors such as discomfort and insecurity (Oh et al., 2014). Optimism and innovativeness—key motivators of technology readiness—have both direct and indirect positive effects on the intention to accept Online Behavioural Advertising (OBA). The sense of intrusiveness, however, directly negatively impacts the intention to accept OBA. The perceived benefits-risk assessment of OBA mediates the relationship between technology readiness motivators and the intention to accept OBA (Mohan et al., 2023).

Knowledge workers' social technology readiness, encompassing both motivators like optimism and innovativeness and inhibitors such as insecurity, significantly influences their innovative work behavior. While one might expect discomfort to hinder exploration, it surprisingly has a positive effect on employees' engagement with social technology (Stock & Gross, 2016). In parallel, smartphone multitasking, often driven by work or study demands or simple boredom, negatively impacts performance outcomes and mental health by distracting attention and reducing efficiency (Xian et al., 2021). This distraction is predominantly due to the tendency to multitask with entertainment apps. Optimism positively shapes attitudes towards online transportation services, while insecurity also impacts these attitudes but in a manner that typically reflects cautiousness or reluctance (Munandar & Munthe, 2019). When examining technology readiness (TR) more broadly, it is often conceptualized as a multidimensional construct with four key factors: optimism, innovativeness, discomfort, and insecurity. Optimism and innovativeness (TR motivators) are hypothesized to enhance online purchase intention, whereas discomfort and insecurity (TR inhibitors) are thought to diminish it (Ismail & Wahid, 2020).

In the context of mobile learning, factors such as attitude, perceived self-learner usefulness (PSLU), and the use of specific apps like Tencent APP were found to moderate mobile learning behavior (MLB). These factors collectively contributed to innovative performance during the COVID-19 academic lockdown in China. Specifically, Tencent APP usage strengthened the relationship between MLB and innovative performance, with the combined effects of PSLU, attitude, MLB, and Tencent APP significantly enhancing innovative outcomes (Muhideen et al., 2021). Performance expectancy, effort expectancy, and social influence are critical determinants of behavioral intention to use social networking apps, which in turn influences actual usage behavior. Notably, the relationship between effort expectancy and behavioral intention is moderated by user experience, indicating that more experienced users find it easier to adopt new social networking apps. The relationship between social influence and behavioral intention remains unaffected by user experience, suggesting that peer pressure and societal norms consistently impact users regardless of their familiarity with the technology (Chua et al., 2018).

Social media marketing exerts a profound influence on the impulsive buying behavior of consumers in Kerala. This phenomenon is positively correlated with factors such as hedonic motivation, trust, website quality, and variety seeking. Social media marketing effectively engages various psychological triggers, personal connections, and real-time promotional tactics to stimulate impulsive buying behavior (Bhaskaran & R, 2023). During festive seasons, e-commerce platforms in Kerala often use flash sales and limited-time offers promoted through social media channels, creating a sense of urgency and excitement. This hedonic motivation, coupled with the ease of sharing recommendations and reviews among friends and family on social media, builds trust and encourages consumers to make spontaneous purchases. In the realm of IoT technology, perceived usefulness, perceived ease of use, social influence, perceived enjoyment, and perceived behavioral control are pivotal factors that significantly influence consumer acceptance (Gao & Bai, 2014). An example of this is the adoption of smart home devices in Kerala, where consumers appreciate the convenience and utility these devices offer, such as remotely controlling home appliances or enhancing home security. Social influence also plays a role, as consumers often rely on reviews and endorsements from influencers and peers to make informed decisions. The enjoyment derived from using intuitive and engaging IoT interfaces further enhances their willingness to adopt this technology.

The extended Technology Acceptance Model (TAM), which incorporates perceived usefulness, perceived ease of use, perceived credibility, and perceived self-efficacy, successfully predicts the behavioral intention of customers, particularly among the educated youth, to adopt mobile banking technology (Saji & Paul, 2018). In Kerala, mobile banking apps that offer user-friendly interfaces and secure transactions attract young professionals who value convenience and efficiency. By understanding these factors, banks can tailor their services to meet the needs of this demographic, thereby achieving an omnichannel presence. HDFC Bank's mobile app provides features like instant loan approvals and personalized financial advice, which appeal to tech-savvy young adults, making it easier for them to manage their finances on the go. In the context of internet banking, perceived ease of use (PEOU) and perceived usefulness (PU) have a positive impact on customer satisfaction, while perceived risk (PR) negatively affects customer satisfaction (George & Kumar, 2013). A case in point is the widespread use of internet banking services among young, well-educated male employees in Kerala, who appreciate the ability to perform banking transactions online without visiting a branch. However, concerns about security breaches and fraud can deter some users. To mitigate these risks, banks like ICICI Bank have implemented advanced security measures such as two-factor authentication and real-time fraud detection systems, which help in enhancing customer confidence and satisfaction.

Online advertising significantly influences women's choice of cosmetic brands in Kerala (Sultana, 2021). Women in this region are particularly receptive to online advertisements for cosmetic products featured on social media and mobile shopping apps. Brands like Nykaa and Maybelline often collaborate with popular beauty influencers to showcase their products through tutorials and reviews on Instagram and YouTube. This strategy not only highlights the effectiveness of the products but also leverages the trust and relatability of the influencers, encouraging women to try and purchase these cosmetics. Mobile shopping apps like Flipkart and Amazon frequently offer personalized recommendations and exclusive discounts on beauty products, making it convenient and appealing for women to shop for their favorite brands online.

Perceived usefulness does not significantly affect attitudes towards mobile app use, according to research by Vahdat et al. (2021). Instead, factors such as perceived ease of use, social influence, peer influence, and intention to purchase positively shape attitudes towards mobile app use. In this context, attitudes towards mobile app use act as a full mediator for three key pathways within the model, underscoring the pivotal role of these attitudes in the adoption process. Age emerges as a moderating factor, specifically mediating the path from perceived usefulness to attitude towards mobile app use. Younger users may find mobile apps easier to navigate and more socially engaging, thus forming more positive attitudes towards their use, whereas older users might require more perceived usefulness to form similar attitudes. Initial trust formation in social media groups hinges on five critical predictors: fulfilled expectations, predictability, familiarity, monitoring, and norms (Shareef et al., 2020). Users often trust content shared within these groups without verifying its accuracy, creating a potential risk where biased peers might disseminate irresponsible or misleading information. This blind trust can lead to significant consequences, especially when the shared content pertains to health, safety, or political matters. During the COVID-19 pandemic, many users in social media groups relied on unverified information about treatments and preventive measures, sometimes leading to harmful practices based on misinformation.

The relationship between physical exercise and subjective well-being is complex and influenced by several mediators. According to Ding et al. (2021), Social Connectedness via Internet Use (SCIU) directly mediates this relationship in a positive direction. For example, individuals who engage in online fitness communities or share their exercise routines on social media often experience enhanced well-being due to the social support and encouragement they receive. On the other hand, Mobile Phone Addiction (MPA) mediates the relationship between physical exercise and subjective well-being in the opposite direction. Excessive use of mobile phones, particularly for non-exercise-related activities, can detract from the mental health benefits gained from physical exercise. The serial mediation model, which includes both SCIU and MPA, indicates a statistically significant pathway, highlighting the nuanced interplay between digital connectivity, exercise, and well-being. Someone who uses their phone to track workouts and connect with fitness groups might experience increased well-being, while another individual might suffer negative effects due to mobile phone addiction despite regular physical exercise.

Social media dependency and Instagram addiction are influenced by factors such as gender, region, and locality of residence. Research by Thomas et al. (2023) revealed a significant positive correlation between Instagram addiction and social media dependency. These findings underscore the need for targeted interventions to address social media addiction and its impact on the mental health and overall well-being of young adults in Karnataka, South India. Young adults in urban areas of Karnataka might benefit from programs designed to reduce screen time and promote healthier online habits, given the higher rates of social media dependency observed in these regions. A study by Menon et al. (2023) found that a majority of participants used social media and Facebook for more than three hours a day and had over 400 friends. Social media dependency and Facebook intensity were particularly high in urban localities, with South Kerala exhibiting significantly higher rates of social media dependency compared to the North and Central regions. This dependency was notably higher among males, although no significant difference in Facebook intensity was found between males and females. These patterns suggest that interventions in urban South Kerala should focus on addressing the high levels of social media use among young men, possibly through community programs that encourage offline social interactions and hobbies.

In China, the acceptance of internet banking is more influenced by concerns about economic development within the banking industry rather than by technology acceptance and development. Yi et al. (2021) attribute the lack of acceptance of internet banking in China to weak social network influences, including poor compliance, lack of identification, and lack of internalization. Chinese customers may not adopt internet banking services because they do not feel a sense of belonging or connection to the digital financial community. Addressing these social network deficits could involve creating more personalized and engaging online banking experiences that strengthen the sense of community and trust. The uses and gratifications theory has a positive effect on social media adoption, indicating that individuals adopt social media platforms to fulfill specific needs and derive certain gratifications. Hassan et al. (2022) found that the need for social media and the technology itself positively affect social media adoption. Users might adopt social media to stay connected with friends and family, seek entertainment, or receive information, all of which are facilitated by the technology's user-friendly design and features. This suggests that enhancing the functionality and user experience of social media platforms could further increase their adoption rates.

Problematic internet use is a global issue that significantly impacts the psychological well-being of adolescents. According to Mathew and Krishnan (2020), there is a significant negative correlation between self-esteem and internet addiction among the adolescents studied. Problematic internet use can have profound effects on adolescents' self-esteem, social life, and family relationships. Excessive internet use can lead to social withdrawal, where adolescents may prefer online interactions over face-to-face communication. This can result in weakened social skills and a diminished sense of belonging, contributing to lower self-esteem. The pressures of maintaining an online presence and the comparison with peers on social media can further erode self-confidence and impact mental health negatively. Mobile social apps (MSAPs) such as WeChat, Weibo, and virtual community apps have a significant positive impact on consumers' online purchase attitudes (COPA). This relationship is mediated by trust factors (TRF) like perceived trust and risk, as well as technological factors (TF) such as perceived ease of use and usefulness (Waheed et al., 2021). Users who find these apps reliable and easy to navigate are more likely to trust the platform, leading to a more favorable attitude towards making purchases online. The convenience and efficiency of these apps in facilitating communication and transactions contribute to a positive user experience, which in turn enhances consumer trust and willingness to engage in online shopping. Zoom has emerged as a pivotal tool for educators aiming to transcend geographical constraints and engage with students in virtual classrooms. Its widespread use has reshaped pedagogical approaches, enabling interactive and collaborative learning experiences irrespective of physical location. Thomas et al. (2024) highlight the positive correlations between visual fatigue, physical fatigue, mental fatigue, tech-savvy behavior, and online learning among students in Karnataka, South India, who are conducting online classes through Zoom. While Zoom facilitates seamless communication and interactive sessions, it also brings about challenges such as increased screen time, which can lead to visual and mental fatigue. Despite these drawbacks, tech-savvy students might find online learning through Zoom more engaging and adaptable to their learning styles. The platform's features, such as breakout rooms and screen sharing, support a variety of teaching methods that can cater to different learning needs, enhancing the overall educational experience.

Perceived usefulness, perceived ease of use, and compatibility are pivotal factors influencing the intention to use travel apps, as identified by Lu et al. (2015). These attributes shape users' perceptions of how effective and convenient travel apps are in facilitating their travel planning and experiences. Travelers are more likely to adopt apps that they perceive as useful for booking flights, accommodations, and managing itineraries with ease. The compatibility of these apps with users' travel habits and preferences further enhances their adoption rates, highlighting the importance of app design and functionality in meeting user needs. Self-efficacy indirectly influences the intention to use travel apps through the mediation of outcome expectations. According to Lu et al. (2015), individuals who believe in their ability to use travel apps effectively are more likely to anticipate positive outcomes from their usage, such as saving time, accessing better deals, and enhancing travel experiences. This confidence in their own capabilities acts as a motivational factor driving their intention to adopt and regularly use travel apps for their travel-related needs.

In Kerala, social media usage patterns mirror those of developed nations, setting it apart from broader digital and gender divides observed across India, as noted by Balasundaram et al. (2024). Social media platforms empower younger voters by reducing their reliance on traditional influencers and providing direct access to political information and candidates. Engagement metrics on platforms like Facebook have emerged as more influential predictors of candidate winnability compared to metrics on Twitter, demonstrating the growing influence of social media in shaping electoral outcomes and political discourse in Kerala. Chatterjee (2020) identifies social media and word-of-mouth (WOM) as primary factors influencing the actual use of Internet of Things (IoT) technologies among potential users in India. This conceptual model underscores the role of peer recommendations and online interactions in driving IoT adoption, highlighting the importance of social influence and community feedback in shaping consumer perceptions and adoption behaviors toward IoT solutions.

In the context of Indian shoppers, Chakraborty (2019) finds that attitude, perceived behavioral control, perceived usefulness, and perceived ease of use significantly influence their intention to use grocery shopping apps. These psychological factors play a critical role in shaping consumers' attitudes and behaviors toward adopting digital platforms for grocery shopping, emphasizing convenience, efficiency, and user-friendly interfaces as key drivers of adoption. Divya and Sudhier (2019) report that most researchers use the internet daily for research purposes, with email being the preferred social networking service among them. They note a lack of significant gender differences in the use of most social networking tools and services, except for blogging, where distinct usage patterns are observed among researchers from different faculties. This underscores the varied digital engagement among researchers across disciplines, reflecting diverse preferences and needs in utilizing online tools for academic and professional purposes.

Optimism and Innovativeness are identified by Auliandri & Arimbi (2021) as having a positive effect on the intention to use internet banking. These traits reflect users' positive outlook towards adopting new technologies and their willingness to explore innovative banking solutions. Despite this positive correlation, the study finds that Innovativeness alone does not significantly impact intention to use internet banking, suggesting that while openness to new ideas is beneficial, it may not directly translate into behavioral intentions without optimism. Conversely, Discomfort and Insecurity exhibit a negative effect on intention to use internet banking. Users who experience discomfort or feelings of insecurity regarding online banking services are less likely to embrace these technologies for their financial transactions. Surprisingly, Insecurity emerges as a significant factor influencing intention to use internet banking, indicating that concerns related to security and privacy play a critical role in shaping users' decisions regarding online financial activities. Media multitasking is a prevalent behavior among Indian college students, as highlighted by Shukla & Sharma (2018). This behavior involves simultaneous engagement with multiple media sources, such as social media, online videos, and messaging apps. Research indicates that media multitasking can lead to reduced face-to-face interactions and empathy among students, as they increasingly immerse themselves in virtual environments. This shift towards digital interactions may impact interpersonal relationships and communication skills, posing challenges in maintaining meaningful connections outside the virtual realm.

Chatterjee (2022) underscores the importance of perceived usefulness, perceived ease of use, and compatibility in influencing attitudes towards using Internet of Things (IoT) technologies. These factors shape users' perceptions of how IoT devices can enhance convenience and efficiency in daily tasks, thereby influencing their willingness to adopt these technologies. Subjective norms influenced by family, peers, and social influences play a crucial role in shaping individuals' attitudes towards IoT adoption, highlighting the social context in which technology acceptance occurs. Pradhan et al. (2018) investigate the factors influencing travelers' intentions to use smart devices during travel, using the Technology Readiness Index (TRI) model. The study finds that perceived benefits of smart devices significantly enhance travelers' intentions to use them, as these devices offer functionalities that improve travel experiences. However, the influence of perceived risks on usage intentions varies depending on travelers' characteristics and risk perceptions, underscoring the nuanced considerations travelers weigh when adopting new technologies during their journeys.

Perceived risk and trust play crucial roles in influencing the adoption of internet banking, according to Athira (2021). These factors are significant determinants of customers' decisions to use online banking services. Female customers generally express higher satisfaction with the perceived usefulness, ease of use, and overall attitude towards internet banking compared to male customers. Male customers tend to perceive higher risks associated with online transactions, particularly concerns about the security of their financial information. Addressing these fears through targeted training, awareness campaigns, and initiatives to build trust can mitigate barriers to adoption and enhance customer confidence in internet banking services. Jarrar et al. (2020) explore the dimensions of the Technological Readiness Index (TRI) and their impact on the intention to use mobile applications in Dubai. The TRI model provides insights into individuals' readiness to adopt new technologies based on factors such as optimism, innovativeness, discomfort, and insecurity. The study reveals that users who exhibit feelings of insecurity and discomfort with technology are less likely to adopt mobile applications. To encourage greater adoption rates, developers and providers must address these user concerns by improving user interface design, providing clear information on data security measures, and offering user-friendly features that enhance ease of use and trust in the technology. The use of interactive and entertainment-focused social media apps has multifaceted impacts on adolescent students' academic performance, social intelligence, and health, as discussed by Panchanathan & Raj (2022). While social media usage can enhance academic performance by facilitating collaborative learning and access to educational resources, it also poses risks such as distractions leading to reduced study time and disrupted sleep patterns. Social media use influences social intelligence by enabling virtual interactions and social networking, but it can also contribute to social comparison and peer pressure issues among adolescents. Health concerns related to excessive social media use include irregular eating habits, reduced physical activity, and increased screen time, highlighting the need for balanced digital engagement practices among young users.

Consumers' decisions regarding the usage and selection of online food delivery apps are shaped by their perceptions of risks and benefits, as highlighted by Gupta & Duggal (2021). When consumers perceive reduced risks or increased benefits associated with using these apps, it positively influences their attitudes towards adopting them. This shift in attitude, in turn, affects their behavioral intentions, such as engaging in positive word-of-mouth and continuing to use the apps for future orders. Understanding these dynamics is crucial for food delivery service providers to enhance customer satisfaction and loyalty by addressing perceived risks and emphasizing the benefits of their platforms.

Chang & Kannan (2006) explore the impact of using wireless technology for work on employees' technology readiness. The study finds that adopting wireless technology reduces employees' discomfort and insecurity with technology, indicating a positive transformation in their readiness to use new technologies in the workplace. However, the study also suggests that while wireless technology adoption improves practical aspects of technology use, such as reducing logistical barriers, it does not significantly alter employees' inherent levels of technology optimism and innovativeness. This nuanced understanding underscores the importance of targeted interventions and training programs to maximize the benefits of technological integration in organizational settings while addressing employees' ongoing concerns and adapting to their varying levels of technological readiness.

## HYPOTHESIS

- *There is no significant linear relationship between the internet of behavior and optimism.*
- *There is no significant linear relationship between the internet of behavior and innovativeness.*
- *There is no significant linear relationship between the internet of behavior and discomfort.*
- *There is no significant linear relationship between the internet of behavior and insecurity.*
- *There is no significant linear relationship between the internet of behavior and anxiety/dependence.*
- *There is no significant linear relationship between the internet of behavior and negative.*
- *There is no significant linear relationship between technology internet of behavior and multitasking preference.*

## METHODOLOGY

This study employs a quantitative research design to investigate the influence of the Internet of Behavior on technology readiness and technology usage attitudes among users of Chinese social media apps in Kerala. The research aims to examine the relationships between these variables using statistical analysis methods, including correlation and regression analyses. The study sample consists of 510 participants who are users of Chinese social media apps in Kerala, selected through a convenience sampling method to ensure diverse representation of the target population. Demographic information such as age, gender, and frequency of social media use was collected to contextualize the findings. Data was collected using a structured questionnaire divided into several sections. The questionnaire was developed using the Internet of Behavior scale by Ranaeiy et al., (2015), the Technology Readiness Index (TRI 2.0) by Parasuraman & Colby (2015), and the Media and Technology Usage and Attitudes Scale by Rosen et al. (2013). The questionnaire included items measuring the Internet of Behavior, technology readiness (Optimism, Innovativeness, Discomfort, and Insecurity), and technology usage attitudes (Anxiety, Negative attitudes, and Multitasking Preference).

## Measures

- Internet of behavior: This was measured through items assessing the extent of participants' behavioral patterns and interactions on Chinese social media apps.
- Technology readiness: This construct included four dimensions: Optimism, Innovativeness, discomfort, and insecurity. Each dimension was measured with items adapted from the Technology Readiness Index (TRI).
- Technology usage attitudes: This included Anxiety, Negative attitudes, and Multitasking Preference, measured with items designed to capture participants' emotional and cognitive responses to using technology.

Data analysis was conducted using SPSS software. Descriptive statistics were calculated to provide an overview of the sample and the main variables. Correlation analysis was performed to examine the relationships between the Internet of Behavior and other variables. Multiple regression analyses were conducted to determine the predictive power of the Internet of Behavior on technology readiness and technology usage attitudes. Ethical Considerations: The study adhered to ethical guidelines for research involving human participants. Informed consent was obtained from all participants, and they were assured of the confidentiality and anonymity of their responses. The study protocol was reviewed and approved by the relevant institutional review board. This study acknowledges several limitations. The use of convenience sampling may limit the generalizability of the findings. The cross-sectional design precludes the establishment of causal relationships. Future research could employ longitudinal designs to better understand the dynamics of these relationships over time.

## RESULTS

The correlation analysis reveals significant relationships between the Internet of Behavior and various aspects of technology readiness and technology usage attitudes. Specifically, there is a moderate positive correlation between the Internet of Behavior and Optimism (0.484), indicating that higher engagement with Chinese social media apps is associated with greater optimism towards technology. The strongest correlation is with Innovativeness (0.653), suggesting a strong positive relationship, where increased Internet behavior corresponds to higher levels of innovativeness. Additionally, the Internet of Behavior shows significant positive correlations with Discomfort (0.555), Insecurity (0.579), Anxiety (0.469), Negative Attitudes (0.571), and Multitasking Preference (0.573). This indicates that frequent users of Chinese apps tend to experience more discomfort, insecurity, and anxiety, while also exhibiting higher negative attitudes and multitasking preferences. The relationships among the dimensions of technology readiness and usage attitudes are also noteworthy. Optimism shows moderate positive correlations with Innovativeness (0.377), Discomfort (0.392), and Insecurity (0.375), indicating that these aspects of readiness influence each other. Innovativeness is moderately correlated with Discomfort (0.464) and Insecurity (0.465), and Discomfort is similarly correlated with Insecurity (0.466), suggesting interrelatedness among these dimensions. Anxiety and Insecurity also share a moderate positive correlation (0.429), while Negative Attitudes have a weak positive correlation with Anxiety (0.179). Multitasking Preference is moderately correlated with Innovativeness (0.403), reflecting its association with higher engagement and adaptability in technology use.

The descriptive statistics further elucidate the variability among participants. The mean score for Internet of Behavior is 117.53, with a standard deviation of 18.74, indicating diverse engagement levels with Chinese social media apps. Optimism, Innovativeness, Discomfort, and Insecurity all have mean scores around 14, with standard deviations ranging from 2.74 to 3.16, showing moderate variability. Anxiety and Negative Attitudes have mean scores around 10.48 and 11.15, respectively, with standard deviations of approximately 2.49 and 2.50. Multitasking Preference has a mean score of 10.44 and a standard deviation of 2.23, reflecting diverse attitudes towards multitasking.

The multiple regression analyses with "Internet of behavior" as the predictor variable across several dependent variables (Optimism, Innovativeness, Discomfort, Insecurity, Anxiety, Negative emotions, and Multitasking preference). Here's an interpretation of each regression summary:

1. Optimism:
    - R Square ($R^2$) = 0.473, indicating that 47.3% of the variance in Optimism is explained by "Internet of behavior."
    - The regression is significant ($F$ = 455.926, $p$ < 0.001), suggesting that "Internet of behavior" significantly predicts Optimism ( $Beta = 0.688, p < 0.001$).
2. Innovativeness:
    - R Square ($R^2$) = 0.667, indicating that 66.7% of the variance in Innovativeness is explained by "Internet of behavior."
    - The regression is significant ($F$ = 1018.047, $p$ < 0.001), showing that "Internet of behavior" significantly predicts Innovativeness ( $Beta = 0.817, p < 0.001$).
3. Discomfort:

- R Square ($R^2$) = 0.578, indicating that 57.8% of the variance in Discomfort is explained by "Internet of behavior."
- The regression is significant ($F$ = 696.464, $p < 0.001$), indicating that "Internet of behavior" significantly predicts Discomfort ( $Beta = 0.760, p < 0.001$).

4. Insecurity:
   - R Square ($R^2$) = 0.567, indicating that 56.7% of the variance in Insecurity is explained by "Internet of behavior."
   - The regression is significant (F = 664.480, p < 0.001), showing that "Internet of behavior" significantly predicts Insecurity (Beta = 0.753, p < 0.001).
5. Anxiety:
   - R Square ($R^2$) = 0.396, indicating that 39.6% of the variance in Anxiety is explained by "Internet of behavior."
   - The regression is significant ($F$ = 333.248, $p < 0.001$), suggesting that "Internet of behavior" significantly predicts Anxiety ( $Beta = 0.629, p < 0.001$).
6. Negative emotions:
   - R Square ($R^2$) = 0.497, indicating that 49.7% of the variance in Negative emotions is explained by "Internet of behavior."
   - The regression is significant ($F$ = 502.904, $p < 0.001$), indicating that "Internet of behavior" significantly predicts Negative emotions ( $Beta = 0.705, p < 0.001$).
7. Multitasking preference:
   - R Square ($R^2$) = 0.545, indicating that 54.5% of the variance in Multitasking preference is explained by "Internet of behavior."
   - The regression is significant ($F = 608.775, p < 0.001$), suggesting that "Internet of behavior" significantly predicts Multitasking preference ( $Beta = 0.738, p < 0.001$).

Across all dependent variables, the "Internet of behavior" predictor consistently shows significant positive relationships, indicating that higher levels of engagement or interaction with the Internet of behavior concept are associated with higher levels of Optimism, Innovativeness, Discomfort, Insecurity, Anxiety, Negative emotions, and Multitasking preference among the study participants.

## DISCUSSION

The Internet of Behavior has a profound impact on technology readiness and usage attitudes among users of Chinese social media apps in Kerala. For instance, individuals who extensively use these apps often demonstrate heightened levels of innovativeness and a strong preference for multitasking. This can be observed in how users integrate new features and functionalities of these platforms into their daily routines, adapting quickly to changes and exploring new ways of interaction and information consumption. However, this increased engagement also correlates with notable challenges. Users frequently report feelings of discomfort and insecurity, stemming from concerns about privacy, data security, and the potential societal impacts of their online activities. Negative attitudes may also arise from the rapid pace of technological change, which can sometimes overwhelm users or lead to skepticism about the long-term consequences of their digital behaviors. Thus, while the Internet of Behavior enhances innovation and multitasking capabilities among Chinese social media app users in Kerala, it also brings about complex psychological and societal dynamics that warrant careful consideration and management.

The significant linear relationships between the Internet of behavior and various psychological dimensions highlight important insights into how digital engagement impacts individuals' psychological states and behaviors. The positive correlation observed between the Internet of behavior and optimism suggests that increased online activity and engagement with behavioral data may enhance individuals' overall positive outlook. This could be attributed to access to diverse information, social connections, and personalized content that foster optimism and positive thinking. The relationship between the Internet of behavior and innovativeness underscores how digital interaction stimulates creativity and the adoption of new ideas or technologies. Users who embrace the Internet of behavior often exhibit a higher propensity for innovation, likely due to exposure to cutting-edge technologies, trends, and creative content online. The correlations with discomfort and insecurity highlight potential negative consequences of intensive digital engagement. Users may experience discomfort due to concerns over privacy, data security, or the overwhelming nature of constant connectivity. Similarly, heightened insecurity could stem from perceived risks associated with online interactions, such as cyber threats or social comparison dynamics.

The link between the Internet of behavior and anxiety/dependence suggests that extensive digital engagement might contribute to heightened levels of anxiety or dependency on digital platforms. This could result from constant connectivity, fear of missing out (FOMO), or reliance on digital interactions for social validation and emotional support. The association with negative emotions underscores the complexity of digital interactions, which can evoke a range of negative feelings such as frustration, anger, or disappointment. These emotions may arise from online conflicts, misinformation, or the impact of digital overload on mental well-being. The significant relationship with multitasking preference indicates that increased exposure to the Internet of behavior may shape individuals' preferences and abilities to handle multiple tasks simultaneously. This could reflect adaptation to digital multitasking demands in work, study, or social contexts. While the Internet of behavior enhances optimism, innovativeness, and multitasking preferences, it also correlates with discomfort, insecurity, anxiety/dependence, and negative emotions.

## CONCLUSION

The analysis reveals a clear relationship between the "Internet of behavior" and various psychological dimensions. Significant positive correlations were found between the Internet of behavior and Optimism, Innovativeness, Discomfort, Insecurity, Anxiety, Negative emotions, and Multitasking preference, all of which were statistically significant at the 0.01 level. These findings suggest that increased engagement with the Internet of behavior tends to coincide with higher levels of optimism and innovativeness, alongside elevated discomfort, insecurity, anxiety, negative emotions, and a preference for multitasking. Regression analyses supported these correlations, confirming that the Internet of behavior significantly predicts variance in these psychological factors. This underscores the complex impact of technology-mediated behaviors on psychological states, revealing both positive and potentially challenging outcomes depending on the specific psychological dimension studied.

## Data Availability

Data is available upon request.

## REFERENCES


Athira, V. S.Athira V S (2021). A study on Factors Influencing the adoption of Internet Banking - A gender wise analysis by Integrating TAM and TPB model in Kerala. *RESEARCH REVIEW International Journal of Multidisciplinary*, *6*(11), 19–27. DOI: 10.31305/rrijm.2021.v06.i11.004

Auliandri, T. A., & Arimbi, R. D. (2021). Pengaruh Technology Readiness Index Terhadap Keinginan Untuk Menggunakan Internet Banking Pada PT Bank Mandiri KCP Pondok Chandra Surabaya. *JAMIN : Jurnal Aplikasi Manajemen Dan Inovasi Bisnis*, *3*(2), 38. DOI: 10.47201/jamin.v3i2.79

Balasundaram, A., Sreedharan, N. V., Babu, D. D., & Gopinath, P. P. (2024). Social media use and impact on voters and candidates in Kerala. *Journal of Creative Communications*, 09732586231223841. Advance online publication. DOI: 10.1177/09732586231223841

Bhaskaran, A.ATHIRA BHASKARANDr. SWARUPA R. (2023). The influence of Social Media marketing on Impulsive Buying Behaviour of consumers in Kerala. *International Journal For Multidisciplinary Research*, *5*(4), 5729. Advance online publication. DOI: 10.36948/ijfmr.2023.v05i04.5729

Chakraborty, D. (2019). Indian shoppers' attitude towards grocery shopping apps: A survey conducted on smartphone users. *Metamorphosis*, *18*(2), 83–91. DOI: 10.1177/0972622519885502

Chang, A.-M., & Kannan, P. K. (2006). Employee technology readiness and adoption of wireless technology and services. *Proceedings of the 39th Annual Hawaii International Conference on System Sciences (HICSS'06)*. DOI: 10.1109/HICSS.2006.148

Chatterjee, S. (2020). Internet of Things and social platforms: An empirical analysis from Indian consumer behavioural perspective. *Behaviour & Information Technology*, *39*(2), 133–149. DOI: 10.1080/0144929X.2019.1587001

Chatterjee, S. (2022). Why do people use IoT-enabled devices?: An empirical examination from Indian perspectives. *International Journal of Technology and Human Interaction*, *18*(3), 1–20. DOI: 10.4018/IJTHI.313626

Chua, P. Y., Rezaei, S., Gu, M.-L., Oh, Y., & Jambulingam, M. (2018). Elucidating social networking apps decisions: Performance expectancy, effort expectancy and social influence. *Nankai Business Review International*, *9*(2), 118–142. DOI: 10.1108/NBRI-01-2017-0003

Ding, Z.-C., Yan, J., & Fu, J. (2021). Internet and mobile phone addiction self-control mediate physical exercise and subjective well-being in young adults using IoT. *Mobile Information Systems, 2021*, 1–6. DOI: 10.1155/2021/9923833

Divya, L. R., & Sudhier, K. G. (2019). Use of social networking tools and services among research scholars at the University of Kerala. *International Journal of Information Dissemination and Technology*, *9*(1), 23. DOI: 10.5958/2249-5576.2019.00005.0

Gao, L., & Bai, X. (2014). A unified perspective on the factors influencing consumer acceptance of internet of things technology. *Asia Pacific Journal of Marketing and Logistics*, *26*(2), 211–231. DOI: 10.1108/APJML-06-2013-0061

George, A., & Kumar, G. S. G. (2013). Antecedents of customer satisfaction in internet banking: Technology Acceptance Model (TAM) redefined. *Global Business Review*, *14*(4), 627–638. DOI: 10.1177/0972150913501602

Gupta, V., & Duggal, S. (2021). How the consumer's attitude and behavioural intentions are influenced: A case of online food delivery applications in India. *International Journal of Culture, Tourism and Hospitality Research*, *15*(1), 77–93. DOI: 10.1108/IJCTHR-01-2020-0013

Hassan, A. O., Wang, L., Hasan, A. A., & Latif, S. (2022). Behaviour profile on social media: TikTok and QQ. In Lu, Y., & Cheng, C. (Eds.), *International Conference on Computer Application and Information Security (ICCAIS 2021)*. SPIE. DOI: 10.1117/12.2637412

Ismail, K. A., & Abdul Wahid, N. (2020). A review on technology readiness concept to explain consumer's online purchase intention. *International Journal of Information Management*, *6*, 49–57. DOI: 10.15282/ijim.6.0.2020.5629

Jarrar, Y., Awobamise, A. O., & Sellos, P. S. (2020). Technological Readiness Index (TRI) and the intention to use smartphone apps for tourism: A focus on inDubai mobile tourism app. *International Journal of Data and Network Science*, 297–304. DOI: 10.5267/j.ijdns.2020.6.003

Lam, S. Y., Chiang, J., & Parasuraman, A. (2008). The effects of the dimensions of technology readiness on technology acceptance: An empirical analysis. *Journal of Interactive Marketing*, *22*(4), 19–39. DOI: 10.1002/dir.20119

Lu, J., Mao, Z., Wang, M., & Hu, L. (2015). Goodbye maps, hello apps? Exploring the influential determinants of travel app adoption. *Current Issues in Tourism*, *18*(11), 1059–1079. DOI: 10.1080/13683500.2015.1043248

Mathew, P., & Krishnan, R. (2020). Impact of problematic internet use on the self-esteem of adolescents in the selected school, Kerala, India. *Archives of Psychiatric Nursing*, *34*(3), 122–128. DOI: 10.1016/j.apnu.2020.02.008 PMID: 32513461

Menon, V. A., Prasad, A., Puthur, L. A., K K, S., & Joseph, L. (2023). Social media dependency and Facebook usage among the older adults of Kerala. *Studies in Media and Communication*, *11*(4), 202. DOI: 10.11114/smc.v11i4.6060

Mohan, N., Zakkariya, & Bobby, R. R. (. (2023). Technology readiness motivators and Online Behavioural Advertising: A perceived benefits-risk assessment using Privacy Calculus Theory. *International Journal of Professional Business Review*, *8*(6), e02297. DOI: 10.26668/businessreview/2023.v8i6.2297

Muhideen, S., Jianxun, C., Akintunde, T. Y., Olayemi, R. H., Koroma, J., Amosum, T. T., & Shahani, R. (2021). Nexus between students' attitude towards self-learning, tencent app usability, mobile-learning, and innovative performance. SSRN *Electronic Journal*. DOI: 10.2139/ssrn.3926083

Munandar, J. M., & Munthe, R. C. F. (2019). How technology affects behavioral intention (case study of online transportation in Indonesia and Thailand). *The South East Asian Journal of Management*, *13*(2), 222–236. DOI: 10.21002/seam.v13i2.11343

Oh, J. C., Yoon, S. J., & Chung, N. (2014). The role of technology readiness in consumers' adoption of mobile internet services between South Korea and China. *International Journal of Mobile Communications*, *12*(3), 229. DOI: 10.1504/IJMC.2014.061460

Panchanathan, S., & Raj, K. (2022). A study on impact of social media among students of adolescent age group on individual performance. *International Journal of Professional Business Review*, *7*(3), e0505. DOI: 10.26668/businessreview/2022.v7i3.0505

Parasuraman, A., & Colby, C. L. (2015). An updated and streamlined Technology Readiness Index: TRI 2.0. *Journal of Service Research*, *18*(1), 59–74. DOI: 10.1177/1094670514539730

Pradhan, M. K., Oh, J., & Lee, H. (2018). Understanding travelers' behavior for sustainable smart tourism: A technology readiness perspective. *Sustainability (Basel)*, *10*(11), 4259. DOI: 10.3390/su10114259

Ranaeiy, S., Taghavi, M. R., & Goodarzi, M. A. (2015). The effect of Loneliness on Social Networking Sites use and its related behaviors. *Global Journal of Health Science*, *8*(8), 162. DOI: 10.5539/gjhs.v8n8p162 PMID: 27045407

Rosen, L. D., Whaling, K., Carrier, L. M., Cheever, N. A., & Rokkum, J. (2013). The Media and Technology Usage and Attitudes Scale: An empirical investigation. *Computers in Human Behavior, 29*(6), 2501–2511. DOI: 10.1016/j.chb.2013.06.006 PMID: 25722534

Saji, T. G., & Paul, D. (2018). Behavioural intention to the use of mobile banking in Kerala: An application of extended classical technology acceptance model. *Metamorphosis, 17*(2), 111–119. DOI: 10.1177/0972622518792802

Seo, J.-Y., Kim, S.-I., & Jeong, C. (2018). Effects of technology readiness on usage intention of smart-phone tourism applications: An application of the technology readiness and acceptance model. *The Tourism Sciences Society of Korea, 42*(8), 109–127. DOI: 10.17086/JTS.2018.42.8.109.127

Shareef, M. A., Kapoor, K. K., Mukerji, B., Dwivedi, R., & Dwivedi, Y. K. (2020). Group behavior in social media: Antecedents of initial trust formation. *Computers in Human Behavior, 105*(106225), 106225. DOI: 10.1016/j.chb.2019.106225

Shukla, S., & Sharma, P. (2018). Emotions and media multitasking behaviour among Indian college students. *Journal of Creative Communications, 13*(3), 197–211. DOI: 10.1177/0973258618790794

Stock, R., & Gross, M. (2016). How does knowledge workers' social technology readiness affect their innovative work behavior? *2016 49th Hawaii International Conference on System Sciences (HICSS).*

Sultana, A. (2021). Impact of online advertising and the use of cosmetic products: A study on the influence of online advertisements and change in the purchasing behaviour of women in Kerala. *International Journal of Communication and Society, 3*(2), 112–119. DOI: 10.31763/ijcs.v3i2.214

Thomas, L. P., Chaudhary, R., Thomas, J., & Menon, V. A. (2023). Assessing Instagram addiction and social media dependency among young adults in Karnataka. *Studies in Media and Communication, 11*(6), 72. DOI: 10.11114/smc.v11i6.6102

Thomas, L. P., Menon, V. A., Thomas, J., Ali, K. A. A., Soman, K. K., & Kumar, T. K. S. (2024). Towards a model: Exploring fatigue factors in ZOOM online classes. *2024 International Conference on Current Trends in Advanced Computing (ICCTAC).* DOI: 10.1109/ICCTAC61556.2024.10581300

Vahdat, A., Alizadeh, A., Quach, S., & Hamelin, N. (2021). Would you like to shop via mobile app technology? The technology acceptance model, social factors and purchase intention. [AMJ]. *Australasian Marketing Journal, 29*(2), 187–197. DOI: 10.1016/j.ausmj.2020.01.002

Waheed, A., Zhang, Q., Farrukh, M., & Khan, S. Z. (2021). Effect of mobile social apps on consumer's purchase attitude: Role of trust and technological factors in developing nations. *SAGE Open*, *11*(2), 215824402110067. DOI: 10.1177/21582440211006714

Xian, C., Wang, Z., & Wang, L. (2021). Multitasking habits of Chinese smartphone users: Under the influence of social media apps. *2021 International Conference on Information Science, Parallel and Distributed Systems (ISPDS)*. DOI: 10.1109/ISPDS54097.2021.00054

Yi, G., Zainuddin, N. M. M., & Bakar, N. A. B. A. (2021). Conceptual model on Internet Banking acceptance in China with social network influence. *JOIV: International Journal on Informatics Visualization*, *5*(2), 177–186. DOI: 10.30630/joiv.5.2.403

# Chapter 3
# "No Gree for Anybody": Internet Memes and the Framing of Resistance in Nigerian Online Discourse

**Matthew Alugbin**
https://orcid.org/0000-0003-2219-5155
*Edo State University, Uzairue, Nigeria*

## ABSTRACT

*This study examines how Internet memes serve as a tool for resistance in Nigerian online discourse, focussing on the 2024 New Year slogan "No gree for anybody." Using 40 purposively selected Internet memes gathered between January and March 2024, from Facebook and X, the analysis draws on Benford and Snow's Collective Action Frames and Kress and van Leeuwen's concept of visual grammar. Dominant issues expressed through the memes include social inequality, infrastructural challenges, political discontent, gender roles, and national identity. Through visual exaggeration, narrative framing and symbolic juxtaposition, the memes highlight people's daily struggles and frames of resistance. The memes' visual symbolism fosters resistance, critiques societal norms and amplifies marginalised voices. This research concludes that internet memes play a crucial role in shaping resistance discourse in Nigeria, serving as both a reflection of ongoing struggles and an active space for expressing defiance, identity, and solidarity in the digital age.*

DOI: 10.4018/979-8-3373-5297-8.ch003

## INTRODUCTION

The slogan "No gree for anybody" emerged as a 2024 New Year's resolution in the Nigerian online space, with people jointly and tacitly adopting the phrase as the hallmark to guide the New Year. New Year's resolutions, often personal, are common across cultures. However, the digital age has fostered collective forms of resolutions, where culturally significant slogans like "No gree for anybody" serve as a rallying point for social movements. The slogan evolved into a tool for shared resistance in the Nigerian online space, aligning with the "social media ritual" of New Year's resolution (Hallinan et al., 2023). Burgess et al. (2018: 10) see media rituals as "generic conventions and media practices", highlighting how people use media in response to planned and unplanned events, celebrations, or crises to communicate shared values. This means that while people build a sense of online community through social media rituals, the intentions behind these rituals are not fixed but negotiated based on established norms (Highfield, 2016). Notwithstanding the universal patterns of social media rituals (Trillò et al., 2022), there are cultural differences in the way people deploy them when they engage in online communication. This accounts for why the slogan could be perceived in a positive or negative sense, depending on how it is contextually deployed. Internet memes in online communication provide a unique way for people to relate together, with a shared understanding of how to forge ahead in the complex world.

In the Nigerian space, the earliest use of the expression is traced to Evangelist Agatha Moses' song, "I no go gree", written as a gospel song to inspire the Christian faithful to be resilient in their pursuit of expected miracles. The phrase embodies concerns about self-confidence and resistance against oppression (Nwabunwene and Waive-Aghante, 2024). Beyond reviving the almost-forgotten song, contemporary artists also composed new songs after the phrase became popular. Oludipe Oluwasanmi David, a Nigerian singer professionally known as Spyro, took advantage of the trend to release a single titled "No gree for anybody" in 2024. His song also reiterates self-assertion in daily dealings. Sequel to the diverse application of the phrase in different discourse situations, the Nigeria Police Force (NPF) tagged the expression a "message of rebellion" because of its revolutionary tendencies (The Guardian, 2024), fearing that the continuous use of the phrase may lead to societal chaos.

While existing research on New Year's resolutions focuses on individual behaviour change, such as the adoption of healthier lifestyles including eating habits, improved personal productivity through weight loss or the cessation of negative habits like smoking (Oscarsson et al., 2020), there has been limited exploration of how culturally significant slogans function as collective resolutions. These studies typically examine the psychological mechanisms underlying goal-setting and self-regulation, the success rates of individuals adhering to their resolutions, and the factors that influence the sustainability of these personal commitments over time. The primary emphasis has been on understanding how individuals set, pursue, and achieve personal goals, often within the frameworks of self-improvement and behavioural psychology. Despite the extensive research on personal resolutions, there is a noticeable gap in the scholarly exploration of how collective or cultural elements, such as slogans, can influence the broader societal and cultural dynamics of resolution-making. Specifically, there has been insufficient attention to how the use of culturally significant slogans within the context of New Year's resolutions can facilitate the sharing and construction of resistance culture among members of the same cultural environment in online communication platforms.

The present study examines the popular 2024 slogan "No gree for anybody" to understand how people think of and communicate their problems through Internet memes. The objectives of this study are twofold. Firstly, it aims to identify the dominant issues expressed through Internet memes, particularly those emanating from the popular 2024 New Year slogan "No gree for anybody," which became a widespread New Year's resolution for many Nigerians in the early months of 2024. It examines how these memes reflect the daily challenges faced by Nigerians. This involves a thorough examination of the content to uncover the themes that are prevalent in the selected memes. Secondly, the study seeks to analyse how visual and multimodal elements within these memes are employed to construct narratives of resistance. By applying Benford and Snow's Collective Action Frames and Kress and van Leuween's (2020) socio-semiotic approach to multimodality, the research examines the use of imagery to understand how memes convey messages of defiance and challenge dominant narratives. This study provides an understanding of the role of memes in Nigerian online discourse, highlighting their function as tools for social commentary and resistance. Understanding how slogans like "No gree for anybody" and memes are used as tools for resistance sheds light on how digital activism is reshaping Nigerian political discourse.

## LITERATURE REVIEW

This section starts by examining slogans and internet memes as powerful tools for mobilisation, identity formation and narrative construction, especially in protest movements. The literature review examines existing scholarship on slogans and memes as mechanisms of resistance, with particular attention to their use in online protest discourse.

## Slogans and Internet Memes as Tools for Protest Mobilisation in Online Discourse

The digital age has revolutionised communication and transformed how individuals engage in discourse, share cultural values and mobilise for collective action (Letamendia, 2017; Alugbin and Iyoha, 2024). Online communication platforms, such as social media and blogs, have become central arenas for public conversations, enabling rapid dissemination of information, the formation of virtual communities, and the amplification of social movements. Within these digital spaces, various discursive strategies emerge, including slogans and Internet memes, which serve as powerful tools to shape public opinion and reinforce group identities. Slogans and memes are related but distinct forms of communication that thrive in online spaces. A slogan is a short, memorable phrase used to convey a message, often in protests, advertising, or political campaigns. Internet memes, like slogans, spread across individuals, generations, and groups through imitation, evolving into shared cultural symbols. This study aligns with Dawkins' (1993:20) concept of memes as "mind-viruses", noting their persistence in society and the challenges associated with eradicating them once they take root in public consciousness. The present study considers Internet memes as digital cultural artefacts (Shifman, 2013), typically in the form of images, videos, or text that spread rapidly online, often through humour, satire or commentary. They serve various functions, including social critique, resistance, and identity formation, making them powerful instruments in online discourse and mobilisation (Pavlović, 2016).

The viral nature of slogans and memes allows them to facilitate shared understanding and coordinated action among individuals within the same cultural orientation. For instance, when a culturally loaded slogan is adopted as a New Year's resolution, it can quickly gain traction and become a viral meme, facilitating a shared understanding and collective action among individuals within the same cultural milieu. This process of cultural sharing and resistance-building through online platforms highlights the need for a deeper exploration of how digital communication influences cultural dynamics and social movements. Nigerian students have been at the forefront of incorporating information and communication technology into their daily lives, and this digital immersion has led to the development of unique phrases that reflect the influence of online platforms, social media, and digital trends (Folayan et al., 2018).

Similarly, slogans serve as powerful tools for protest mobilisation, encapsulating the sentiments, demands, and aspirations of a movement in a concise and memorable format. Whether they emerge online as viral memes or offline during protests, slogans convey complex social or political messages to wide audiences. During protests, slogans help unify participants around a common cause, fostering a sense of solidarity and collective identity. It also plays a crucial role in political settings, as it helps in mobilising voters and shaping political discourse. The example of "O To Ge" in Nigeria's Kwara State illustrates how a well-designed slogan can successfully capitalise on the gap between elites and the general populace, ultimately resulting in electoral success (Ahmed, 2021). In addition, during Hong Kong's Umbrella Movement, protesters created a textual public space through slogans and visual materials, asserting agency at various levels and mobilising diverse cultural repertoires (Veg, 2016). This discursive space attempted to build a new civic culture among younger generations. Udoudom et al. (2024) argue that the various languages and dialects spoken in Nigeria may influence how the slogan "No Gree for Anybody" is interpreted. While recognising the slogan as a means for expressing long-standing frustrations, the authors highlight the risk that its original meaning could be lost if used outside its cultural context or that its core message may be diluted through overuse or misuse. However, their study is limited by a lack of primary data and an insufficient examination of the slogan's practical application. In contrast, the present study offers a more comprehensive analysis of how visual representations and linguistic expressions work together to shape resistance.

Van De Velde (2024) explores the crucial role of protest slogans and writings in social movement research, emphasising their importance in understanding collective identities, emotions, and claims made during contemporary demonstrations. She urges researchers to regard these slogans as political performances that convey diverse messages to various audiences, encapsulating both individual and collective voices within social movements. To effectively capture this diversity, the article introduces a typology that categorises protest writings according to their primary functions—such as laying claims, proclaiming, mobilising, or witnessing—which shapes their form and support. However, this typology may be subjective, potentially leading to inconsistencies in application across different researchers and resulting in varied interpretations of the same material. Moreover, the article notes that cultural, social, and political contexts significantly influence the functions of protest writings. A slogan that resonates in one movement may serve entirely different purposes in another context. Thus, a rigid categorisation could overlook the fluidity and complexity inherent in protest rhetoric, necessitating a more nuanced approach to understanding the dynamic nature of these expressions in various sociopolitical landscapes.

The vibrancy of meme-sharing in public discourse extends far beyond the realm of political commentary. In their 2020 study, Moussa et al. examine the impactful role of Internet memes in a 2018 boycott campaign targeting three major corporate brands in Morocco, which were closely tied to the country's dominant power structures. The authors argue that these memes serve as critical "tactics" for marginalised groups striving for social and economic justice. By leveraging humour and satire, individuals are empowered to challenge powerful entities and influence public discourse, even in the absence of a centralised structure to consolidate their achievements (Moussa et al., 2020: 5290). This dynamic illustrates how memes not only foster collective action but also reshape conversations surrounding the intricate relationship between politics and business. Through this lens, memes become tools of resistance, enabling the marginalised to articulate their grievances and mobilise support in creative and accessible ways. Ultimately, the study highlights the potential of memes to disrupt established narratives, foster social awareness, and cultivate a more inclusive dialogue around issues of justice and equity in contemporary society.

The studies reviewed collectively highlight the transformative impact of digital communication on cultural values and resistance narratives across various contexts. Within social movements, slogans and memes serve as vital tools for protest mobilisation, encapsulating complex sentiments in succinct, memorable formats that resonate widely. Furthermore, Internet memes act as tactical instruments for marginalised groups, showcasing their capacity to challenge dominant power structures through humour and satire. Overall, these findings emphasise the importance of digital platforms in facilitating social discourse and shaping contemporary movements for justice and equity.

## Memes in Political Participation and Protest Movements

Internet memes have evolved into a versatile form of expression, serving as both entertainment and social commentary. Beyond their use in political participation, such as in election contexts (Adegoju & Oyebode, 2015; Bamgbose, 2021; Tella, 2018), memes also function as outlets for popular engagement across various contexts. For example, during public health crises or emergencies like the COVID-19 pandemic, memes were used to express opinions and emotions about mask-wearing (Dynel, 2021), to combat the pandemic (Adebomi, 2022) and to convey social responsibility in helping to curb the virus (Osisanwo & Falade, 2024). Just as memes have become a way to engage in fan culture (Osisanwo & Alugbin, 2024), they also reflect changing ideas about gender in society, helping to reinforce or challenge gender stereotypes (Gbadegesin, 2020). These various deployments show that memes act as channels through which people can respond to current events, critique societal norms, or spread awareness on important issues, making them powerful tools in shaping and reflecting popular narratives in modern society. In addition to their broader social and cultural roles, memes are also increasingly recognised as significant tools in political protest movements, particularly in online activism.

Makhortykh and González (2020), focusing on memes from protests in Ukraine and Venezuela, compare how pro-government protest memes often evoke negative emotions and reference dominant historical narratives to polarise and stigmatise the opposition, whereas anti-government protest memes typically avoid controversial memories and use less divisive narratives to criticise authorities. This highlights the distinct ways memes are used in protest situations. However, such binary categorisation may oversimplify the emotional deployment of memes capable of eliciting a complex range of emotions. Okesola and Oyebode (2023) look at how Nigerian social media users employed memes on WhatsApp and Twitter during the #EndSARS protest to express shared opinions on civil unrest and evaluate the roles of various stakeholders, such as the political class, government agencies, the older generation, and the youth. The study shows how memes became a tool for positive and negative evaluation of socio-political affairs in the country, allowing people to critique and evaluate societal issues and key actors, often using humour, visuals, and rhetorical strategies. Unuabonah and Oyebode (2021) focus on how Nigerian WhatsApp users used internet memes during the COVID-19 pandemic to engage in political protest. They note that the memes serve to resist an anti-welfare ideology and express dissatisfaction with the government's handling of public welfare and societal issues. The reviewed studies prioritise high-profile protests and events, which may neglect the significance of everyday forms of resistance inherent in an event such as the "No gree for anybody" meme.

In conflict situations such as protests, framing becomes a crucial strategy for highlighting key issues, identifying active agents, and ultimately defining the nature of the social conflict. Murphy et al. (2021) explore how reframing the Northern Ireland conflict and peace process can create a more favourable environment for change. Their study demonstrates that broadening the way a problem is framed facilitates cooperation and enables the collective actions necessary for effective transformation. The research identifies four essential framing mechanisms: frame contesting, reframing, frame reproduction, and frame defending. These mechanisms illustrate how frames are actively constructed and contested, often originating from grassroots movements, which can drive system-wide change. Importantly, the study emphasises that frames are not static but evolve over time, shaped by ongoing interactions and shifting contexts. The study stresses that understanding the historical background, context, and dynamics between different agents is key to decoding how change occurs. This approach reveals the complexity of framing processes and highlights their significance in shaping collective action and systemic change in conflict scenarios.

Ayodeji-Falade and Osunkunle (2021) explore how the Daily Dispatch Newspaper (DDN) framed the #FeeMustFall protests and the influence of this framing on readers' perceptions. Employing a mixed-method approach, the researchers conducted a quantitative content analysis of 31 protest stories published by DDN, followed by focus group discussions to assess the impact of these frames. The content analysis revealed that the most prominent frames were the conflict frame (45.16%), attribution of responsibility frame (29%), and human-interest frame (16%). The remaining stories fell under the economic consequence frame (6.45%) and morality frame (3.23%). Thematic analysis of the focus group discussions showed that DDN's framing significantly shaped readers' perceptions, with the news frames generating similar responses across the audience. As a result, readers tended to perceive the protesters negatively, viewing them as violent, while attributing the responsibility for free higher education and job creation to the government. This highlights how media framing can shape public opinion by emphasising certain aspects of a protest. Thus, framing in protest situations plays a powerful role in shaping public perceptions and narratives about the protest.

The reviews above suggest that framing and internet memes serve as powerful tools for shaping public perception, social commentary, and engagement in protest situations. Memes, in particular, have evolved beyond mere entertainment to become influential in political participation, public health messaging, and societal critique to express collective dissent, critique societal norms, and assess key actors. Framing, especially in media coverage of protests, also plays a critical role in influencing how events are perceived. While academic studies on memes have largely focused on their use in contexts of major protests and public agitations, such as the #EndSARS movement or global political demonstrations, this present study examines memes in the context of the unique 2024 New Year slogan "No gree for anybody", which is itself a new cultural phenomenon, marking a shift in how resistance is articulated in everyday Nigerian discourse. This study considers this kind of everyday resistance as subtle, dispersed, and found in common interactions. Unlike protest-orientated memes, which are tied to highly visible political movements, the "No gree for anybody" memes reflect the persistent, daily pushback against the socioeconomic and political pressures that shape Nigerian life.

## THEORETICAL ORIENTATION

This study combines Benford and Snow's Collective Action Frames (2000) with Kress and van Leeuwen's concept of visual grammar. Benford and Snow (2000: 614) note that framing as meaning construction refers to how social movements create and shape interpretations of reality through a process called "framing." This process is "active," meaning that participants are intentionally doing something to construct meaning. It is "dynamic," continually evolving over time. It is also "contentious" because the new frames they create often challenge or differ from the existing ways people understand issues. The outcome of this process is what is known as "collective action frames," which are the shared perspectives that frame activity. They build their notion of frame on Goffman's idea, which conceptualises frame as what gives meaning to events and organises how people experience and react to events. As such, collective action frames also focus on certain parts of reality to motivate action.

The success of collective action frames in mobilising people relies on effectively addressing three core tasks: diagnostic, prognostic, and motivational framing. Diagnostic framing identifies an issue within society or the government and attributes responsibility for it. Prognostic framing then proposes a solution, outlining how to address the problem and why alternative solutions may be inadequate. Finally, motivational framing provides the rationale for taking action, encouraging people to get involved by connecting the identified problem and proposed solution to a call for collective action (Snow, Vliegenthart & Ketelaars, 2019; Benford & Snow, 2000). The definition of situations during interactions plays a crucial role in shaping individuals' perceptions of reality (Ardevol-Abreu, 2015). This theoretical lens will be applied to analyse how memes use visual and textual elements to construct narratives of resistance and challenge dominant narratives within the Nigerian online discourse.

Kress and van Leeuwen's concept of visual grammar offers a framework for interpreting and analysing visual images across multiple forms of media. It is an extension of Michael Halliday's systemic functional grammar, focusing on the semiotic resources used to create meaning. This approach to multimodality ensures that the specific representations of different modes, such as text, images, and other visual elements, are considered within the cultural context or situation in which they are used. In this framework, the modal resources available in one culture are viewed as a coherent and integral field, even though they consist of distinct elements for making meaning. The theory emphasises how these modes work together to convey messages effectively, highlighting the interplay between cultural context and semiotic resources.

Their approach draws from Halliday's three metafunctions—ideational, interpersonal, and textual—to systematically examine how visual elements such as gestures, posture, colour and symbols create meaning. These functions can also be transferred to semiotic resources (Feng & O'Halloran, 2013). Kress and van Leeuwen (2020) propose that visual images, much like language, serve three key purposes. Representational meaning, which conveys what we see and experience, corresponds to Halliday's ideational metafunction; interactive meaning aligns with the interpersonal metafunction; and compositional meaning corresponds to the textual metafunction. Together, these functions highlight the complex ways in which images communicate meaning and engage audiences. Representational meaning arises from how processes (actions), participants (actors), and circumstances (locations) are organised. In contrast, interactive meaning is defined by four essential factors: symbolic contact, which pertains to the gaze of visual participants; social distance, which refers to the distance of the shot; power relations, influenced by the camera angle; and involvement, which is determined by the viewing angle (Moerdisuroso, 2014). Compositional meaning brings together both representational and interactive meanings to create a unified interpretation.

The combination of Benford and Snow's Collective Action Frames and Kress and van Leeuwen's concept of visual grammar provides a comprehensive approach to analyse how memes construct resistance narratives in Nigerian online discourse. Both theories emphasise how meaning is actively constructed. Benford and Snow's framing process highlights how social movements create collective action frames to shape reality, focusing attention on key issues and mobilizing people. Kress and van Leeuwen's visual grammar similarly explores how images use semiotic resources to create meaning through representational, interactive, and compositional elements. Combining these allows for an analysis that considers both the textual and visual framing of memes as tools of resistance. Kress and van Leeuwen (2020: 3) note that "visual language is not transparent and universally understood, but culturally specific." Thus, there is an emphasis on the cultural context of visual images which enriches Benford and Snow's analysis by situating memes within specific Nigerian socio-political realities.

## DATA AND METHODOLOGY

The study draws on 40 purposively selected Internet memes gathered between January and March 2024 from two major social media platforms: Facebook and *X*. The three-month period represents the first quarter of the year when experiences of the New Year are very high and the slogan was most popular and widely used. The two platforms used have always served useful purposes in the expression of dissent, as witnessed in the #EndSARS protests (Aboh, 2024). This makes information shared on these platforms effective in reaching a large audience. Memes were selected based on their direct reference to the 2024 New Year slogan "No gree for anybody", which was widely popular during this period. Out of 40 Internet memes gathered, a purposive sampling technique was used to select and analyse eleven memes that not only contained the phrase but also visually or textually conveyed resistance to adversity or societal challenges, aligning with the study's focus on resistance narratives. Only memes that explicitly used this phrase in posts and tweets were selected. A systematic search was conducted using keywords related to "No gree for anybody" and "#NoGreeForAnybody" to identify related memes. The data deploys Benford and Snow's core framing tasks, using diagnostic framing to interpret how memes diagnose social problems faced by Nigerians and prognostic framing to interrogate how the memes communicate strategies that people should take to address the problems. Through Kress and van Leeuwen's Socio-semiotic Approach to Multimodality, the study explores how visual elements and positioning within the memes communicate resistance through aggression, humour, and exaggerated depictions. The linguistic choices in the captions, where present, were also analysed.

## ANALYSIS

In the analysis, the dominant issues expressed through the memes include economic struggles and survival (2), social inequality and class struggles (2), infrastructural decay and public services (1), political discontent and leadership (1), gender roles (2), nation-building and national identity (1), and everyday hustle and resilience (2). The memes utilised irony, satire and exaggeration to juxtapose contrasting images and frame the narrative of inequality and resistance. Analysis reveals how the memes narrate resistance and reflect the daily challenges faced by the people. The findings underscore how memes function as powerful tools for social commentary and resistance in the digital age.

### Economic Struggles and Survival

Memes focus on the economic hardships Nigerians face – scarcity and food shortages – and how people resist or cope with these challenges. The memes' framing emphasises the theme of economic deprivation and the lengths to which people may go to survive in difficult circumstances. The scarcity of resources, as represented by the limited food supply, creates a sense of desperation and competition.

*Figure 1. Economic struggle*

The meme of one family attempting to close a door while another group is pushing it open highlights the desperation caused by economic hardship. In the meme, we identify the key participants: the family trying to close the door (representing those who have limited resources) and the group pushing it open (representing those seeking access to resources). The struggle to close the door illustrates the action of denial and concealment driven by economic hardship. The meme operates on a narrative structure, showing an unfolding action where the family is actively trying to hide their food while others are attempting to access it. The exaggerated physical struggle to deny cooking fried chicken while children from another house confront them highlights how scarcity leads to secrecy and dishonesty. The diagnostic frame presents the severe economic deprivation and mistrust in communal settings. The in-text accusations underscore mistrust in a society where resources are limited and people fight to survive. The in-text expression, "We didn't cook anything," and the bold accusation of "Na Lie!" (a Nigerian Pidgin phrase meaning "You're lying!") from the neighbours point to a deep-seated mistrust within the community.

The wall represents a boundary between those who have limited resources and those who perceive others as more fortunate. The effort by a group to gain access to what they believe to be food symbolises the widespread scarcity in the community. Economic deprivation is visually shown through this struggle, where food becomes a contested resource. Concealing resources as a survival tactic and resisting scarcity by developing survival strategies is a prognostic frame for families on both sides. For the first family on the left, there is a denial of food availability, which is not truly present in the meme. However, the irony of situation lies in the fact that the family inside denies having any food while the family outside can smell it. This contrast adds to the humour in the meme. The visual representation of division, through exaggerated physical struggle – pushing and pulling at the door – visualises the tension that can arise in deprived communities when there is suspicion of unequal access to food or other essentials. The refusal to share resources leads to isolation and an erosion of the communal spirit. The meme visually communicates that even perceived inequality can cause division in communities. The meme addresses the pervasive issue of dishonesty or betrayal. The characters on both sides of the wall represent opposing perspectives on truth and honesty.

Economic hardship also drives people to adopt creative and sometimes extreme measures to protect their limited resources, highlighting the economic deprivation faced by many Nigerians, who may be struggling to meet their basic needs.

*Figure 2. Economic hardship*

The image of the locked gas cylinder stands as a powerful representation of scarce essential resources, symbolising the economic deprivation and resource scarcity prevalent in many communities, particularly in Nigeria. By portraying the gas cylinder as the sole participant in this visual narrative, it highlights the urgency of protecting limited resources during times of extreme scarcity. This context reflects broader economic hardships, where the need to safeguard essential goods becomes paramount for survival.

The presence of the lock serves as both a practical and symbolic solution, illustrating how individuals resort to creative, and sometimes extreme, measures to defend their resources. It suggests that survival in difficult times necessitates careful management and protection of what little one possesses. This visual reinforces an awareness of vulnerability, encapsulating a sentiment of defiance against potential exploitation. The act of locking away a vital resource reflects a deeper narrative of resilience in the face of adversity, where individuals are determined not to allow their needs to be undermined or taken advantage of. The padlock itself becomes a potent tool within this conceptual structure. It signifies control and restriction, emphasising a defensive strategy that resonates with the collective experience of Nigerians who grapple with the ongoing struggle for basic necessities. In this light, the locked gas cylinder transcends its immediate function, becoming emblematic of a broader socio-economic reality. It conveys a poignant message: the fundamental aspects of life, including the means to prepare food, are now under constant threat, necessitating vigilance and proactive defence. Thus, the image suggests that survival is not merely about enduring the harsh realities of economic deprivation; it is an active struggle to maintain and protect one's resources against depletion or theft, underscoring the resilience and resourcefulness of individuals facing systemic challenges.

## Social Inequality and Class Struggles

The meme in this section highlights the disparities between different social classes, with an emphasis on how the marginalised or disadvantaged resist structural inequities. The meme frames coexistence as a solution to the crisis of resource sharing.

*Figure 3. Class struggle*

The meme shows multiple animals as participants in the visual narrative (a dog, a goat, a chicken, and what appears to be a cat), all gathered around the same plate of food, eating together. The animals, regardless of their natural hierarchy or dietary preferences, are all sharing the available resources to meet their basic needs. They feed from the same source without apparent conflict, reflecting harmony and the possibility of collaboration among diverse groups. The meme presents a diagnostic understanding of the scarcity of resources or opportunities, which many Nigerians face daily. It visually depicts how individuals/groups, despite their differences, are forced to share the same limited resources. The coming together of the animals to share the food bowl suggests a prognosis of collaboration and mutual survival in the face of adversity.

The absence of dominance or hierarchy in the image can be seen as a symbolic representation of equality. All the animals, irrespective of their species, seem to have equal access to food, suggesting that in certain situations, everyone deserves equal opportunities. The visual narrative implicitly attributes this issue to broader social or political inequalities that make access to resources difficult for many people. The collective experience of "scrambling" for resources is a shared problem in Nigeria, particularly in the context of economic hardship. The narrative invites viewers to consider their own social contexts and the potential for collaboration among different classes or groups. The action of the animals feeding together, regardless of species, suggests an alternative path of shared survival, indicating that in tough times, collaboration or mutual engagement becomes essential. The image metaphorically proposes that the solution to adversity may not lie in conflict or competition alone but in finding ways to "share the plate" in unconventional ways.

The visual narrative presented in the meme challenges the usual hierarchical structures that exist between animals (e.g., predators and prey) and, by extension, challenges societal norms or expectations. The animals are not competing but rather coexisting in a way that speaks to shared struggle and survival. This visual humour softens the critique of societal inequality. The different animals could symbolise different classes, ethnic groups, or social statuses in Nigerian society. The fact that they all gather around one plate of food despite their differences illustrates a shared plight or collective struggle. This reinforces the idea that, in the face of common challenges, individuals must find common ground for survival.

*Figure 4. Class struggle*

This image vividly captures a context of scarcity and resource competition, with two men engaging in a seemingly light-hearted contest over food. The visual exaggeration, especially in the oversized portions of food and their eager expressions, serves as a striking commentary on the prevailing inequality and struggle for resources that many Nigerians endure. This humorous depiction invites viewers to relate to the characters, highlighting the everyday realities of competition for limited resources in a nation where such struggles are all too familiar. Set against a rural backdrop, one might expect the environment to foster communal bonds and cooperation. Ironically, however, the anticipated spirit of unity is conspicuously absent, suggesting a profound disconnect between the ideal of communal existence and the harsh realities of life. The medium close-up shot effectively diminishes the social distance between the two men, creating an intimate relationship with the audience and positioning viewers to feel implicated in the scene of competition. This framing encourages a shared understanding of the social dynamics at play, drawing the audience into the narrative of scarcity. At a deeper level, this meme subtly critiques systemic failures within society. The image of individuals humorously competing for food—a fundamental human necessity—serves as a poignant indictment of governmental policies and economic mismanagement. It implies that the ruling elite has failed to ensure equitable resource distribution, fostering a societal landscape where survival competition has become normalised. The visual framing of both men engaged in equal struggle subtly encourages a collective consciousness among Nigerians, promoting the idea that the fight for resources should be directed not against one another but toward the systemic powers that perpetuate inequality.

The humour embedded in the meme serves a dual purpose. While it highlights the absurdity of competing over necessities, it also empowers Nigerians to remain defiant in the face of scarcity and injustice. The exaggerated rivalry over food underscores the daily survival struggles faced by many, but the comedic context suggests that such conditions should not be passively accepted. Instead, the image galvanises resistance, framing the quest for resources as a shared challenge that unites individuals against the status quo. The prominence of the large food portions and the men's outstretched arms strategically guides the viewer's attention, reinforcing the central theme of competition. This exaggeration not only symbolises the desperate scramble for essential resources—such as food, electricity, and healthcare—but also challenges dominant narratives surrounding wealth distribution and social inequality. By portraying the characters' eagerness, the meme underscores a critical truth: while there appear to be sufficient resources to satisfy everyone's needs, greed and selfishness have corroded the values of communality and shared prosperity. Moreover, the image invites viewers to reflect on the broader implications of resource allocation. The striking disparity depicted raises pressing questions about societal values: Why do some individuals possess more than they need while others face deprivation? This criticism not only addresses immediate economic concerns but also extends to ethical considerations about community responsibility and social justice. By using humour as a vehicle for commentary, the meme effectively challenges viewers to reconsider their perspectives on wealth, resource distribution, and the collective responsibility to resist the systems that perpetuate inequality.

This meme serves as a critique of scarcity, competition, and systemic failures in Nigeria. Through its humour and visual exaggeration, it invites viewers to engage with pressing societal issues while simultaneously motivating a collective resistance against the structures that sustain inequality. By framing the struggle for resources as a shared challenge, the meme fosters a sense of unity among Nigerians, encouraging a defiant stance against the pervasive forces of greed and economic mismanagement.

## Infrastructural Decay and Public Services

Memes also address the problem of infrastructural inequality in Nigeria, suggesting how self-reliance and innovation through technological integration are needed to motivate others to fight for progress and access to modernity. This mentality encourages people to resist technological marginalisation and actively seek access to what they need, no matter the circumstances. The meme presents the frustration of people with poor infrastructure, painting a picture of how this impacts daily life and showing how people combine humour or defiance in the face of inadequate public services.

*Figure 5. Infrastructure*

The meme features a rural Nigerian hut characterised by its thatched roof, prominently displaying modern technological elements such as a satellite dish and a solar panel. At the centre of this depiction is the rural hut, which serves as the primary participant. The juxtaposition of this traditional structure with contemporary technologies highlights a significant theme: adaptation. This imagery illustrates how rural communities are not merely passive victims of infrastructural neglect but actively respond to these challenges by integrating modern technology into their everyday lives. By framing the adoption of modern technology within the context of rural Nigeria, the meme positions this act as a form of resistance against systemic neglect. It suggests that rural populations are striving to improve their living conditions despite the limited support they receive from government infrastructure initiatives. This resistance is not just a reaction to adversity; it is an assertion of agency, highlighting the determination of these communities to take control of their own development. The diagnostic frame of the meme brings attention to the stark lack of access to essential services such as electricity and communication technologies in rural areas. This deficiency can be traced back to the broader societal and governmental neglect of these communities. The contrast illustrated in the meme suggests that rural areas have been systematically overlooked in governmental policies and infrastructural development efforts, which has dire implications for rural-urban migration. As opportunities in urban centres continue to draw people away from rural areas, this meme serves as a poignant reminder of the struggles faced by those left behind.

From an interactive perspective, the meme establishes a symbolic connection between the viewer and the depicted participants. The presence of modern technology prompts a shift in perception, inviting viewers to reflect on the resilience and resourcefulness of rural communities. While the visual juxtaposition of the traditional hut and modern technology creates a certain social distance, it also underscores a vital narrative of empowerment. This framing indicates a refusal by the rural community to be marginalised or left behind in a rapidly changing world. Flowing from this empowerment frame, the meme conveys a powerful sense of determination. It suggests that the rural community is proactively seeking ways to enhance their quality of life by embracing modern technologies. This self-initiative serves as a testament to their resolve to improve their living standards. The striking visual contrast between the traditional hut and modern technology encapsulates the tension between tradition and progress, illustrating the complex dynamics at play in rural Nigeria. Furthermore, the integration of these modern elements into the traditional structure creates a nuanced commentary on the evolving identity of rural communities, highlighting their ability to adapt and thrive amid adversity.

The meme not only depicts a physical space but also serves as a narrative vehicle that captures the essence of resilience, adaptation, and empowerment within rural Nigerian communities. Through its effective use of visual elements, it encourages viewers to reconsider their perceptions of rural life, acknowledging the strength and agency present in these often-overlooked areas.

## Political Discontent and Leadership

The meme analysed in this section also reflects the dissatisfaction of the people with the political system and governance issues. It represents the political leaders as "internal colonialists", associating their actions with the same experiences the people had during the colonial era. Struggle against oppression and survival resonates with the experiences of many Nigerians who face significant challenges in their daily lives.

*Figure 6. Struggle for survival*

The meme conveys a struggle for survival, with the frog refusing to give up despite being swallowed. The central theme is persistence in the face of overwhelming odds. This could represent Nigerians' perseverance against systemic challenges like corruption, unemployment, or poor governance. The physical struggle between the two animals visually denotes a resistance against overpowering forces. The frog's stretched limbs and determined grip on the stork's neck indicate a desperate but bold act of survival. This communicates an unwillingness to be defeated, even when the odds are stacked against one. The inclusion of the "LOL" emoticon suggests humour, but the irony of the frog's grim situation underlines the deeper message: laughing in the face of adversity. The positioning of the frog choking the stork mid-swallow is key to the meme's message of resistance. The frog is halfway into the bird's mouth, yet the focus on the outstretched hand gripping the stork's throat signals a refusal to surrender. The frog's bold move to fight back shows how individuals can resist even overwhelming situations. Visually, the upward position of the frog's arm choking the bird suggests that no matter how trapped or defeated people may seem, they can always push back, conveying the message of unyielding perseverance.

The stork represents oppression or a powerful force (government or systemic challenges), while the frog represents the oppressed (the marginalised group). The problem diagnosed here is the threat of being swallowed by larger, more powerful entities. The visual positioning of the frog (the oppressed) against the stork (the oppressive force) highlights the asymmetrical power dynamics in Nigerian society. The meme promotes an ethos of "never giving up" and pushing back against oppression. The slogan "No gree for anybody" aligns with the frog's resistance. The resistance is visualised through the frog's determination to choke the predator, stopping it from "swallowing" him, symbolising defiance in the face of suppression.

## Gender Roles

This heading captures a meme addressing resistance to gender norms, inequality, or societal expectations, particularly from women's perspectives or marginalised gender groups. The meme's framing suggests that economic hardship can exacerbate traditional gender roles, leading to an unequal distribution of responsibilities and resources within households. When faced with financial difficulties, women often take on a disproportionate share of domestic labour, while men may prioritise other activities or responsibilities.

*Figure 7. Gender balancing*

The meme features two primary participants: a woman and a man, representing traditional gender roles within a domestic setting. It uses humour to highlight domestic inequality by illustrating how traditional gender roles often lead to an unequal distribution of responsibilities and resources, with the woman burdened by household demands while the man remains unconcerned. The diagnostic frame meme critiques the common household power dynamics where financial inadequacies are managed through improvisation. This image plays into the stereotype of women being the caretakers, responsible for managing domestic affairs like food and budgeting, despite facing obstacles like inadequate financial support. The resistance here is subtle. The woman's demand for more money reflects economic hardship, and the man's passive response to "just improvise" reflects a normalisation of scarcity. The humour comes from the reversal of roles in the second frame, where the woman mimics the man's earlier apathy, turning his dismissiveness into an ironic commentary on male privilege in domestic settings. The reversal in the second panel amplifies the absurdity of the man's lack of engagement, reinforcing the message that domestic duties and financial decisions should be more equally shared.

The prognostic frame is driven by a role reversal as a coping mechanism. Role reversal is a key narrative device that highlights the absurdity and inequality of traditional gender roles within domestic spaces. By switching the man's and woman's positions in the second panel, the meme sheds light on how these roles are often unequally distributed and taken for granted. The role reversal points to a double standard in how household concerns are prioritised based on gender. By reversing the roles, the meme calls into question the legitimacy of the man's perceived authority in the household. His failure to adequately provide, coupled with his dismissive attitude, exposes the fragility of his role as the "head of the household". The visual framing acts as a tool of resistance by emphasising the equal footing of both characters in the household, despite their different gender roles. The exact replication of body positions and the domestic setting show that the woman's concerns are just as valid as the man's concerns. Contrasting body language and posture, facial expressions, and symmetrical framing all contribute to visual resistance in the meme. The woman's active stance in front of her passive partner, her passive, relaxed posture in the second panel, and the dialogues expose the unfairness of dismissing household struggles by men.

*Figure 8. Gender roles*

The meme features a man and a woman juxtaposed in a conceptual structure, creating a symbolic comparison between their bodies. This visual arrangement constructs a metaphorical parallel between the man's pronounced belly and the woman's pregnancy, effectively challenging traditional gender roles and societal expectations regarding masculinity and femininity. By placing these two figures side by side, the image encourages viewers to reconsider preconceived notions about body image and the distinct yet interconnected burdens each gender carries. Set in a relaxed beach environment, the scene evokes a sense of leisure and comfort, yet the parallel poses prompt a critical examination of societal norms concerning gendered bodies and roles. The humour embedded in this visual metaphor serves as a tool for subverting conventions, inviting the audience to reflect on the often-unspoken expectations imposed on men and women. The man's exaggerated belly, humorously framing him as "pregnant", prompts a playful critique of how societal perceptions of masculinity often overlook the vulnerabilities and challenges men face. Notably, neither participant directly engages with the viewer through gaze, creating a sense of detachment and objectivity. This compositional choice allows the audience to observe the scene and reflect on the visual metaphor without direct emotional engagement, fostering a space for introspection. By presenting the characters in this manner, the image encourages viewers to contemplate the broader societal implications of the juxtaposition. This portrayal points to the pervasive societal issue of imbalances between expectations and lived realities. While pregnancy in women is conventionally associated with the anticipation of a child, the man humorously positions himself in a similar light, inviting viewers to reconsider the notion that challenges and burdens are gender-specific.

The visual representation of both participants with protruding bellies serves as a powerful metaphor for the collective struggles experienced by people within society. The pregnant bellies symbolise the various burdens carried by individuals, highlighting that both genders and, by extension, all social classes, face unique challenges in different ways. The man's exaggerated belly, while not indicative of the same physical experience as the woman's pregnancy, signifies that he too grapples with personal and societal challenges. This shared visual presentation suggests that both genders, and indeed all social strata, are equally impacted by the socio-economic difficulties that pervade the nation. In essence, the image acts as a call to action, urging viewers to recognise their roles in confronting the challenges facing their society. By depicting the participants as both carrying a metaphorical burden, the image encourages individuals to reflect on their contributions to social change and collective problem-solving. The visual metaphor of pregnancy serves not only to challenge traditional gender roles but also to promote a sense of unity in addressing the pressing issues that affect all members of society.

## Nation-Building and National Identity

The meme draws on nationalistic elements to resist pressures, affirming a Nigerian identity and unity where all services are important in the face of adversity. There is the framing of nation-building and equality in several ways. The meme suggests social stratification and contrasts this with the potential for unequal opportunities or treatment based on one's role within the nation.

*Figure 9. Nation-building and equality.*

The meme features two main participants: a member of the National Youth Service Corps (NYSC) and a soldier. The processes represented involve the act of service, which is central to both participants. However, the visual distinction between their uniforms—simple khaki versus military camouflage—highlights the disparity in how society perceives their contributions. Given the contrast, the meme potentially frames nation-building and equality in several ways. It presents a diagnostic frame that contests disparities in national service. The meme uses visual elements (body positioning and attire) to communicate the unequal experiences of young Nigerians. While both individuals serve the country, their lived experiences differ vastly in terms of privilege and respect. This meme subtly reinforces the idea that all forms of service are equally valued by society. Hence, the motivation is to challenge societal norms that undervalue certain types of service, particularly civil service, through the visual juxtaposition of the NYSC uniform and the soldier's uniform. Additionally, the positioning of their legs adds another layer to the analysis. Struggling for leg space is a common issue in Nigerian buses, and in the meme, the corps member appears to be making an effort to secure adequate space for themselves. This positioning suggests an attempt to assert presence and visibility to ensure that the contributions of the corps member to national service are not overlooked or diminished. Visually, there is the juxtaposition of uniforms. The corps member's uniform consists of a simple khaki outfit, symbolic of the obligation required of all university graduates in Nigeria. The military camouflage uniform worn by the soldier is immediately associated with defence, combat, and a form of service that is often glorified or held in higher regard. This uniform embodies the prestige and seriousness often attached to military service. By placing the two individuals side by side in the same vehicle, the meme visually questions the societal norm that elevates military service above civil service.

The equal positioning, shared setting, and symbolic contrasts between the uniforms highlight the undervaluation of the NYSC's contributions while suggesting that both forms of service are equally important for the nation's progress. Through this visual and symbolic representation, the meme resists societal hierarchies that devalue youth-led civil service and underscores the shared national mission of both individuals. The positioning suggests that both individuals are serving their country in different ways. The shared space of the vehicle positions the corps member and the soldier on the same plane, both seated at the same level. This visual choice is significant because it physically places both individuals on equal footing, despite their different uniforms and roles. The setting within a vehicle suggests a journey, potentially denoting the national journey towards progress, unity, and development. As such, both the NYSC and the military are national institutions that embody service to the country.

## Everyday Hustle and Resilience

Memes here reflect the "hustle" culture, showcasing how Nigerians navigate daily challenges with perseverance and creativity, resisting defeat in tough circumstances. The precarious nature of the situation suggests the difficulties and near-impossible choices Nigerians often face in their daily lives. It resonates with the metaphor of navigating extreme pressure or danger, highlighting the challenges of survival in a harsh socio-economic environment. The meme diagnoses how the daily adversities faced by Nigerians represent a narrative of survival under intense pressure.

*Figure 10. Navigating narrow, dangerous political pathways.*

The meme expresses the navigation of life's challenges, particularly those that seem impossible to overcome. The car caught between two massive trucks represents the individual (citizen) trying to manoeuvre through narrow, dangerous pathways created by political, economic, or social obstacles. The process depicted here is one of navigation of the daily struggle to manoeuvre through overwhelming challenges. The image evokes a sense of being trapped between forces beyond one's control yet continuing to push forward. It reflects the precariousness of life in Nigeria, where danger (symbolised by the two large trucks) is ever-present. The view from the car's windscreen shows the average Nigerian's perspective – trapped between systemic challenges. The visual tension created by the trucks on a narrow road heightens the sense of danger and urgency. The positioning of the camera (from the driver's perspective) places the viewer in the centre of the action, inviting them to empathise with the daily struggles faced by many. The point-of-view perspective from the car's windscreen puts the viewer directly into the scene, implying that these challenges are something that people face head-on. It creates a sense of immersion for the viewer, inviting them to empathise with the challenges.

The size and mass of the trucks compared to the car represent the power imbalance between the citizen (the car) and external forces (the trucks), whether political or economic. Yet the car remains in its lane, pushing forward and showing resilience. The minimal space left for the car to move symbolises narrow survival margins. Despite the overwhelming danger, the image captures a forward-moving scenario, suggesting that survival is not a static endurance but an active, dynamic engagement with challenges. Nigerians need to carefully navigate daily risks, reinforcing the idea of resilience in difficult circumstances. The narrative constructed in the meme frames resistance against societal, systemic, or personal adversities. It suggests that resistance is not just about protesting or confronting power directly but also about resilience, innovation, and a refusal to be defeated by circumstances.

*Figure 11. Citizen survival.*

The meme features a central participant, a woman who is depicted engaging in a determined action, climbing through the window of a crowded bus. The woman's action of climbing through the window of a bus instead of using the door showcases resistance through her determination to find an alternative solution when the conventional path (the door) is blocked. The fact that she chooses to climb through the window suggests that there is some kind of blockage or inaccessibility to the door. Instead of accepting defeat or waiting for the door to open, she resists this limitation by finding another way in. In Nigeria's socio-economic contexts, the meme portrays survival as dependent on finding ways around barriers, and this action reflects everyday resistance to hardship. By climbing the window, the woman metaphorically resists being left behind or excluded.

The text mentions "no time to blame village people", a phrase that suggests the blame game that people often engage in. The meme portrays the futility of blaming external forces for one's misfortunes, implicitly diagnosing the problem as a need for more proactive action instead of excuse-making. The text-image visual representation addresses the cultural tendency to externalise blame for personal hardships. The prognostic framing in the meme signifies that when traditional paths to success are blocked, unconventional methods must be pursued. This image directly connects with the text and reinforces the idea that Nigerians sometimes take extreme measures to achieve their goals, while the bus setting is a relatable and everyday scene in Nigeria. The text gives meaning to the image, and the image, in turn, provides a visual representation of the text.

## CONCLUSION

The memes analysed in this study encapsulate narratives of resistance focusing on themes such as social inequality, infrastructural challenges, political discontent, gender roles, and national identity. The analysis demonstrates how memes function as powerful tools for social commentary and resistance, using a combination of visual, textual, and rhetorical elements to construct compelling narratives. Central to this discourse is the slogan "No gree for anybody", which symbolises a collective refusal to accept unfavourable conditions. Through this slogan, Nigerians express defiance and nonconformity, creating a sense of solidarity among those facing systemic challenges. The slogan "No gree for anybody" serves as a rallying cry, uniting individuals who share common frustrations with political and socio-economic hardships. It captures the spirit of resilience and determination, motivating individuals to resist oppression, corruption, and exclusion. By combining humour, irony, and relatable scenarios, memes serve as digital platforms for amplifying these resistance narratives. The memes reveal how ordinary Nigerians cope with and adapt to difficult circumstances, often through strategic improvisation and defiance of societal norms.

The study underscores that resistance is not only event-driven but an ongoing process embedded in everyday discourse. Memes serve as vehicles for expressing resistance against chronic adversities such as rising living costs, gender inequality, and corruption. Through visual exaggeration, narrative framing, and symbolic juxtaposition, memes highlight inequalities, criticise authority, and underscore the resilience of the Nigerian people. For instance, the contrasting imagery of the

NYSC uniform and military camouflage questions societal hierarchies, while role reversals in gender-related memes critique traditional domestic power dynamics. These findings suggest that memes, particularly those carrying slogans like "No gree for anybody", contribute to broader societal movements by making complex political and social issues more accessible and relatable. Memes do not merely reflect passive frustration but foster active resistance and resilience, providing a space for marginalised voices to challenge dominant narratives, assert their identities, and build solidarity.

By employing visual and linguistic strategies, these memes offer alternative avenues for voicing dissent, especially in digital spaces where traditional forms of protest may be restricted. As a result, memes play a critical role in sustaining a culture of resistance, allowing individuals to express defiance in subtle yet powerful ways. This study concludes that internet memes are integral to the framing of resistance in Nigerian online discourse, representing an ongoing negotiation of power, identity, and survival in the face of systemic challenges.

## REFERENCES


Aboh, S. C. (2024). 'It will never be well with SARS': A discourse analytic study of the# EndSARS protests on social media. *Discourse & Society*, *35*(2), 153–173. DOI: 10.1177/09579265231200994

Adebomi, O. O. (2022). Language in a pandemic: A multimodal analysis of social media representation of COVID-19. *Journal of African Media Studies*, *14*(1), 7–28. DOI: 10.1386/jams_00062_1

Adegoju, A., & Oyebode, O. (2015). Humour as discursive practice in Nigeria's 2015 presidential election online campaign discourse. *Discourse Studies*, *17*(6), 643–662. DOI: 10.1177/1461445615602378

Ahmed, I. L. (2021). The role of slogan in political mobilisation: A study on 'O To Ge'. *Journal of History and Social Sciences*, *12*(1), 36–44. DOI: 10.46422/jhss.v12i1.141

Alugbin, M., & Iyoha, O. (2024). Narratives of resistance: Discursive strategies in Nigeria's 2020 #EndSARS protest. *Àgídìgbo. ABUAD Journal of the Humanities*, *12*(1), 105–121. DOI: 10.53982/agidigbo.2024.1201.07-j

Ardèvol-Abreu, A. (2015). Framing theory in communication research. Origins, development and current situation in Spain. *Revista latina de comunicación social*, 70. 423-450.

Ayodeji-Falade, M. B., & Osunkunle, O. O. (2021). Framing of FeeMustFall students' protest by Daily Dispatch Newspaper and the effect on readers' perceptions. *Heliyon*, *7*(8), e07782. Advance online publication. DOI: 10.1016/j.heliyon.2021.e07782 PMID: 34430751

Bamgbose, G. (2021). Multimodal analysis of post-election memes in the Edo State (Nigeria) 2020 Gubernatorial Election. *Argentinian Journal of Applied Linguistics*, *9*(2), 91–107.

Benford, R. D., & Snow, D. A. (2000). Framing processes and social movements: An overview and assessment. *Annual Review of Sociology*, *26*(1), 611–639. DOI: 10.1146/annurev.soc.26.1.611

Burgess, J., Mitchell, P., & Munch, F. (2018). Social media rituals: The uses of celebrity death in digital culture. In Papacharissi, Z. (Ed.), *A networked self: birth, life, death* (pp. 223–239). Routledge. DOI: 10.4324/9781315202129-14

Dawkins, R. (1993). Viruses of the mind. In Dahlbohm, B. (Ed.), *Dennett and his critics: Demystifying mind* (pp. 13–27). Blackwell.

Dynel, M. (2021). COVID-19 memes going viral: On the multiple multimodal voices behind face masks. *Discourse & Society, 32*(2), 175–195. DOI: 10.1177/0957926520970385 PMID: 38603045

Feng, D., & O'Halloran, K. L. (2013). The visual representation of metaphor: A social semiotic approach. Review of Cognitive Linguistics. Published under the auspices of the Spanish *Cognitive Linguistics Association*, 11(2), 320-335.

Folayan, B. J., Omojola, O., Egharevba, M., Oyesomi, K., Yartey, D., & Adeyeye, B. (2018). The use of ICT-rooted communication codes and slangs among Nigerian students. *The Journal of Social Sciences Research, 4*(12), 633–641.

Gbadegesin, V. O. (2020). Gender ideology and identity in humorous social media memes. *Digital Scholarship in the Humanities, 35*(3), 529–546.

Hallinan, B., Kim, B., Mizoroki, S., Scharlach, R., Trillò, T., Thelwall, M., & Shifman, L. (2023). The value (s) of social media rituals: A cross-cultural analysis of New Year's resolutions. *Information Communication and Society, 26*(4), 764–785. DOI: 10.1080/1369118X.2021.1983003 PMID: 39973900

Highfield, T. (2016). *Social media and everyday politics*. Polity Press.

Kress, G., & van Leeuwen, T. (2020). *Reading images. The grammar of visual design* (3rd ed.). Routledge. DOI: 10.4324/9781003099857

Letamendia, A. (2017). Towards the aestheticisation of the resistances in the Digital Age? A critical approach. *Precarity within the Digital Age: Media change and social insecurity*, 135-149.

Letamendia, A. (2017). Towards the aestheticisation of the resistances in the digital age? A critical approach. In Heidkamp, B., & Kergel, D. (Eds.), *Precarity within the Digital Age. Prekarisierung und soziale Entkopplung – transdisziplinäre Studien*. Springer VS., DOI: 10.1007/978-3-658-17678-5_9

Letamendia, A. (2017). Towards the aestheticisation of the resistances in the digital age? A critical approach. In Heidkamp, B., & Kergel, D. (Eds.), *Precarity within the Digital Age* (pp. 135–149). Springer VS Wiesbaden., DOI: 10.1007/978-3-658-17678-5_9

Makhortykh, M., & González Aguilar, J. M. (2020). Memory, politics and emotions: Internet memes and protests in Venezuela and Ukraine. *Continuum (Perth), 34*(3), 342–362. DOI: 10.1080/10304312.2020.1764782

Moerdisuroso, I. (2014). Social semiotics and visual grammar: A contemporary approach to visual text research. *International Journal of Creative and Arts Studies, 1*(1), 80–91. DOI: 10.24821/ijcas.v1i1.1574

Moussa, M. B., Benmessaoud, S., & Douai, A. (2020). Internet memes as "tactical" social action: A multimodal critical discourse analysis approach. *International Journal of Communication, 14*, 5920–5940.

Murphy, J., Denyer, D., & Pettigrew, A. (2021). The Role of Framing Mechanisms in Explaining System-Wide Change: The Case of the Northern Ireland Conflict and Peace Process. *British Journal of Management, 32*(2), 322–341. DOI: 10.1111/1467-8551.12393

Nwabunwene, D., & Waive-Aghante, R. (2024). A pragmatic analysis of the slang expressions, no gree & oya in Nigerian English. *PREORC Journal of Arts and Humanities, 9*, 115–141.

Okesola, S., & Oyebode, O. (2023). "The soro-soke [speak up] generation": Multimodality and appraisal choices in selected #EndSars civil protest-related memes in Nigeria. *Language and Semiotic Studies, 9*(2), 290–312. DOI: 10.1515/lass-2022-0016

Oscarsson, M., Carlbring, P., Andersson, G., & Rozental, A. (2020). A large-scale experiment on New Year's resolutions: Approach-oriented goals are more successful than avoidance-oriented goals. *PLoS One, 15*(12), e0234097. DOI: 10.1371/journal.pone.0234097 PMID: 33296385

Osisanwo, A., & Alugbin, M. (2024). Metaphorical constructs and semiotic expressions in the BBC Yoruba Internet memes of English Premier League match results. *Language and Semiotic Studies, 10*(3), 415–436. DOI: 10.1515/lass-2024-0032

Osisanwo, A., & Falade, T. (2024). Directives and references in selected coronavirus-motivated internet memes. *Language and Semiotic Studies, 10*(2), 245–266. DOI: 10.1515/lass-2024-0008

Pavlović, L. M. (2016). Internet memes as a field of discursive construction of identity and space of resistance. *AM Časopis za studije umetnosti i medija*, (10), 97-106.

Shifman, L. (2013). *Memes in digital culture*. The MIT Press. DOI: 10.7551/mitpress/9429.001.0001

Snow, D. A., Vliegenthart, R., & Ketelaars, P. (2019). The framing perspective on social movements: Its conceptual roots and architecture. In Snow, D. A., Soule, S. A., Kriesi, H., & McCammon, H. J. (Eds.), *The Wiley Blackwell Companion to Social Movements* (2nd ed., pp. 392–410). Wiley Blackwell., DOI: 10.1002/9781119168577.ch22

Tella, A. (2018). Humour generation and multimodal framing of political actor in the 2015 Nigerian presidential election campaign memes. *The European Journal of Humour Research*, *6*(4), 95–117. DOI: 10.7592/EJHR2018.6.4.tella

The Guardian. (2024, January 15). 'No gree for anybody' slang could be message of rebellion, Nigerian police claim. https://www.theguardian.com/world/2024/jan/15/no-gree-for-anybody-slang-message-rebellion-nigerian-police-claim

Trillò, T., Hallinan, B., & Shifman, L. (2022). A typology of social media rituals. *Journal of Computer-Mediated Communication*, *27*(4), zmac011. DOI: 10.1093/jcmc/zmac011

Udoudom, U., Obong, U. A., Etifit, S., & Idiong, E. (2024). Social media activism and sloganeering in Nigeria: Examining the socio-political contexts in the "no gree for anybody" mantra. *International Journal of Diverse Discourses*, *1*(2), 12–27.

Unuabonah, F. O., & Oyebode, O. O. (2021). 'Nigeria is fighting Covid-419': A multimodal critical discourse analysis of political protest in Nigerian coronavirus-related internet memes. *Discourse & Communication*, *15*(2), 200–219. DOI: 10.1177/1750481320982090

Van De Velde, C. (2024). The power of slogans: Using protest writings in social movement research. *Social Movement Studies*, *23*(5), 569–588. DOI: 10.1080/14742837.2022.2084065

Veg, S. (2016). Creating a textual public space: Slogans and texts from Hong Kong's Umbrella movement. *The Journal of Asian Studies*, *75*(3), 673–702. DOI: 10.1017/S0021911816000565

# Chapter 4
# Multimodal Communication Strategies in Digital Protests of Selected August 1, 2024 Nigeria Protest

**Esther Adeagbo**
*Ajayi Crowther University, Oyo, Nigeria*

## ABSTRACT

*This study investigates the multimodal discourse of the August 1, 2024, Nigeria protest on TikTok and Facebook, addressing a gap in understanding its application in digital protests on these platforms. Using a qualitative methodology and eight data samples, the research employs Kress and van Leeuwen's Multimodal Discourse Analysis and Halliday's Social Semiotic Theory. Findings reveal strategic use of colour, visual symbols, and interactive features to enhance protest impact, highlighting the transformative potential of digital communication in contemporary social movements. Conclusions underscore the importance of digital platforms in modern protests and suggest further research into multimodal strategies.*

DOI: 10.4018/979-8-3373-5297-8.ch004

## BACKGROUND TO THE STUDY

The proliferation of digital media has revolutionised the landscape of protest movements globally, and Nigeria is no exception. On 1 August 2024, Nigeria witnessed a significant digital protest, a manifestation of the populace's dissatisfaction with socio-political issues. This protest, notable for its extensive use of digital platforms, offers a rich site for analysing multimodal communication strategies. The intricacies of such communication can be effectively examined through the lens of Multimodal Discourse Analysis (MDA) as conceptualised by Kress and van Leeuwen (2001), combined with Halliday's Social Semiotic Approach. Digital protests have emerged as powerful tools for collective action in the 21st century, leveraging the ubiquity and connectivity of social media platforms to mobilise participants, disseminate information, and shape public discourse (Gerbaudo, 2012). Unlike traditional protests, digital protests utilise a variety of semiotic resources, including text, images, videos, and hashtags, to create compelling narratives and foster solidarity among participants. The digital space provides a relatively low-cost and accessible platform for activists to reach a global audience, thereby amplifying their messages and potentially influencing policy decisions (Castells, 2012). The digital protest in Nigeria on 1 August 2024 was characterised by the strategic use of social media to highlight grievances, coordinate activities, and generate international awareness. Platforms such as Twitter, Facebook, Instagram, and TikTok were instrumental in spreading information rapidly and engaging a diverse audience. TikTok, in particular, played a crucial role in this protest by allowing protesters to create and share short, impactful videos that quickly garnered widespread attention. The use of hashtags like #EndSARSNow and #ReformNigeria exemplifies how digital activists create and utilise succinct, memorable phrases that encapsulate the essence of their movements and facilitate the aggregation of related content (Bruns & Burgess, 2011).

Multimodal Discourse Analysis, as developed by Kress and van Leeuwen (2001), provides a comprehensive framework for examining the various semiotic resources employed in communication. MDA posits that meaning is constructed not only through language but also through other modes such as images, gestures, and spatial arrangements. In the context of digital protests, this approach facilitates an understanding of how protesters utilise a combination of textual, visual, and auditory elements to articulate their messages and mobilise support. The 1 August digital protest in Nigeria, characterised by the deployment of hashtags, memes, videos, and infographics, exemplifies the multifaceted nature of contemporary protest communication. TikTok and Facebook videos, with their dynamic combination of visual and auditory elements, provided a powerful medium for protesters to convey their messages succinctly and persuasively. Halliday's Social Semiotic Theory, on the other hand, emphasises the social functions of language and other semiotic modes.

According to Halliday (1978), every semiotic resource carries specific ideational, interpersonal, and textual meanings. This theoretical perspective underscores the role of semiotic choices in shaping social realities and identities. In the digital protest under study, Halliday's framework allows for an exploration of how different semiotic modes are strategically employed to construct and disseminate ideologies, forge collective identities, and negotiate power dynamics. The short, impactful videos shared on TikTok and Facebook, often accompanied by text overlays and soundtracks, illustrate how multiple semiotic modes converge to enhance the clarity and emotional appeal of protest messages.

The integration of MDA and Halliday's Social Semiotic Approach provides a robust analytical toolkit for dissecting the complex interplay of semiotic resources in digital protests. This combined framework facilitates a nuanced analysis of how protesters in Nigeria on 1 August 2024 orchestrated multimodal communication strategies to achieve their objectives. For instance, the strategic use of hashtags such as #EndSARSNow and #ReformNigeria highlights the interplay of textual and visual elements in creating resonant and mobilising narratives. Furthermore, the dissemination of protest videos and infographics illustrates how visual and auditory modes complement textual elements to enhance the protest's reach and impact. TikTok and Facebook, with their emphasis on video content, served as crucial mediums for these multimodal messages, demonstrating how different semiotic modes can be orchestrated to maximise engagement and impact. Understanding the multimodal communication strategies in digital protests is crucial for several reasons. Firstly, it sheds light on the evolving dynamics of political activism in the digital age. Secondly, it provides insights into how various semiotic resources are harnessed to construct persuasive and resonant messages. Lastly, it contributes to the broader discourse on the role of digital media in shaping contemporary socio-political landscapes. In conclusion, the analysis of the 1 August 2024 digital protest in Nigeria through the combined lens of Multimodal Discourse Analysis and Halliday's Social Semiotic Approach offers valuable insights into the complex semiotic strategies employed in digital activism. This study not only enhances our understanding of contemporary protest communication but also underscores the critical role of multimodal analysis in capturing the multifaceted nature of digital discourse. To this end, the study aims to critically examine the multimodal discourse employed by protesters during the 1 August 2024 Nigeria protest on TikTok and Facebook, elucidating how these multimodal resources contribute to the overall meaning and impact of the protest. Specifically, it seeks to identify and analyse the multimodal resources utilised by protesters on these platforms, examine how verbal and non-verbal elements were combined to construct and convey messages, and explore the ways in which multimodal discourse contributed to the protest's overall meaning and impact.

## LITERATURE REVIEW AND THEORETICAL FRAMEWORK

### Concept of Digital Communication

Digital communication has evolved into a critical tool for contemporary social engagement, enabling the rapid dissemination of information and the mobilisation of collective action across geographic boundaries. It is defined by the integration of various semiotic modes—including text, images, audio, and video—used to produce layered and context-sensitive messages. Scholars such as Kress and van Leeuwen (2001) have emphasised that digital texts demand multimodal reading competencies due to their complex semiotic configurations. The proliferation of mobile internet technologies and social networking platforms has transformed the terrain of political participation and grassroots activism, particularly in the Global South (Tufekci, 2017; Bosancianu et al., 2020). In this light, digital communication cannot be studied outside the socio-cultural realities it both reflects and reshapes. Within the Nigerian context, the intersection of digital communication and political expression has gained heightened scholarly attention. Recent studies have explored how digital platforms such as Twitter, Facebook, and TikTok have enabled youth-led movements to challenge socio-political inequalities and government accountability (Adeiza, 2021; Ogunyemi, 2022). The #EndSARS protests of 2020 and the August 1, 2024 protests represent paradigmatic examples of how Nigerian citizens employ digital tools not merely to express dissent but also to curate counter-narratives to dominant state discourses. Egbunike (2018) and Uche and Ngwu (2023) argue that digital activism in Nigeria is strongly shaped by cultural values, power asymmetries, and vernacular practices, which must be critically understood to decode the semiotics of protest communication.

Digital activism in Nigeria also exhibits a strong participatory and affective component. As Adebanwi (2020) observes, the emotional appeal embedded in memes, short-form videos, hashtags, and symbolic imagery enables activists to galvanise public sentiment and forge collective identities. TikTok, in particular, allows for visually saturated and emotionally resonant storytelling, which contributes to the viral spread of protest messages. These platforms afford users the ability to embed layered meanings within multimodal content, thereby enhancing the reach and efficacy of political communication (Opeibi, 2020). Additionally, researchers such as Akinbobola (2021) and Okunade and Aduloju (2023) have highlighted the affordances of digital platforms in fostering transnational solidarities and reframing local struggles within global discourses of justice and rights. The theoretical framing of this study draws upon Kress and van Leeuwen's (2001)*Grammar of Visual Design*, which foregrounds the interrelation between visual structure and communicative intent. Multimodal Discourse Analysis (MDA), as developed in this framework, elucidates how meaning is co-constructed through the interplay of visual, textual, and auditory elements. This approach is especially pertinent for interpreting protest materials shared via platforms like TikTok and Facebook, where visual symbolism, sound, and linguistic choices work synergistically to enhance message impact. Complementarily, Halliday's (1978) Social Semiotic Theory emphasises the socio-functional dimensions of semiotic resources—namely, their ideational, interpersonal, and textual functions—which inform how meanings are constructed and circulated within specific social contexts. In sum, recent scholarship underscores that digital communication is not a neutral or homogenous phenomenon. Rather, it is shaped by contextual parameters such as cultural norms, political structures, and technological access. In Nigeria, where structural inequality and political discontent persist, digital platforms serve both as arenas of resistance and as spaces where alternative forms of civic agency are articulated. This study situates itself within this critical tradition, aiming to offer a nuanced understanding of the multimodal strategies employed in Nigeria's August 1, 2024, protest and the socio-political meanings they generate.

## Empirical Works on Digital Communication

Extant studies have worked on digital communication from different linguistic standpoints. Androutsopoulos (2011) examined the role of language in digital communication, particularly how language use varies across different social media platforms. Employing a sociolinguistic framework, the study provided substantial insights into language variation. However, it did not delve deeply into the role of visual and multimodal elements in shaping online discourse, thus leaving a significant research gap. Herring (2013) employed Computer-Mediated Discourse Analysis (CMDA) to investigate the linguistic and interactional features of computer-mediated communication (CMC), focusing on both asynchronous and synchronous modes of communication. Despite its comprehensive analysis, the study overlooks the impact of newer, evolving platforms such as TikTok and how they alter discourse structures, indicating a gap in the literature. Tagg (2015) explored the pragmatic functions of language in text messaging, analysing how users manage conversations and relationships through this medium using a pragmatic theoretical approach. Although comprehensive in its exploration of text messaging, the study does not extend its analysis to other forms of digital communication like social media posts or comments, highlighting a need for broader investigation. Barton and Lee (2013) utilised Multimodal Discourse Analysis (MDA) to investigate how different semiotic resources (text, image, layout) are utilised in blogs and social networking sites. The research is robust in its analysis of these platforms but does not consider emerging platforms such as Facebook and TikTok, which integrate complex multimodal elements, presenting a clear research gap. Jones and Hafner (2012) applied New

Literacies Theory to examine digital literacies within the context of participatory culture, focusing on how individuals engage with digital media. While the study is thorough, it does not adequately address how digital literacy practices vary across different cultural and socio-economic contexts, which is a critical aspect that remains underexplored. Crystal (2006) analysed how the internet is changing language, focusing on new forms of written language in online communication through a linguistic lens. Despite its in-depth examination of written forms, the study does not address the role of spoken language in digital communication, especially on video-centric platforms like Facebook or TikTok, thereby identifying another gap in the literature. Therefore, most research focuses predominantly on textual elements, with insufficient attention given to the multimodal nature of digital communication. The interplay of text, images, videos, and sound is crucial for a holistic understanding of digital discourse, necessitating further exploration. Also, Platform-specific analysis remains underdeveloped in the literature. While many studies provide insights into specific platforms, there is a lack of comprehensive analysis across diverse and emerging platforms such as TikTok, Facebook, and other video-centric social media. This gap highlights the need for research that encompasses a broader range of digital communication environments. Thus, Research into cross-platform dynamics is lacking. There is a need for more research into how communication strategies and practices transfer across different digital platforms and how users navigate these multi-platform environments. Such studies would provide valuable insights into the interconnected nature of digital communication.

## Theoretical Framework

The theories considered suitable for the analysis of this chapter are Kress and Leeuwen's (2001) Multimodal Discourse Analysis approach and Halliday's (1978) Socio-semiotic theory.

Multimodal Discourse Analysis (MDA) represents a comprehensive approach to analysing communication that transcends traditional linguistic boundaries, incorporating a range of semiotic resources such as text, images, gestures, and sound. Rooted in the work of scholars like Gunther Kress and Theo van Leeuwen, MDA provides a framework for understanding how these diverse modes interact to create meaning in contemporary communication contexts. At its core, MDA is predicated on the notion that meaning is constructed through multiple semiotic modes, each contributing to the overall communicative act. Kress and van Leeuwen (2001) argue that traditional linguistic analysis, which focuses solely on textual elements, is insufficient for capturing the full spectrum of meaning-making processes in modern discourse. Instead, MDA considers how visual, auditory, and spatial elements interact with textual components to produce complex, multimodal texts. One of the fundamental principles of MDA is the concept of "mode." According to Kress (2010), a mode is a socially and culturally shaped resource for meaning-making, encompassing not only language but also visual, gestural, spatial, and aural forms of communication. Each mode has its own affordances, or potentials for meaning, which shape how it can be used in discourse. For instance, images can convey spatial relationships and emotional nuances that text alone may struggle to represent. Kress and van Leeuwen's (1996) framework of visual grammar provides a detailed methodology for analysing the visual components of multimodal texts. This framework examines elements such as composition, framing, colour, and perspective, highlighting how visual elements contribute to the overall meaning. For example, the placement of elements within an image can guide the viewer's attention and create a sense of hierarchy or importance. In addition to visual grammar, MDA also draws on Halliday's (1978) social semiotic theory, which emphasises the social functions of language and other semiotic resources. Halliday's framework posits that all communicative acts are inherently social, serving to construct and negotiate relationships, identities, and social norms. By integrating this perspective, MDA not only examines the formal properties of multimodal texts but also their social and cultural contexts. Another critical aspect of MDA is the concept of "intersemiosis," which refers to the interaction between different semiotic modes within a single text (O'Halloran, 2008). This interaction is not merely additive; rather, the combination of modes can create new meanings that are not present in any single mode alone. For instance, the combination of text and image in a political cartoon can produce a satirical meaning that neither the text nor the image could achieve independently.

The application of MDA extends to various domains, including education, media studies, and social media analysis. In educational contexts, MDA has been used to examine how textbooks and other instructional materials employ multimodal resources to facilitate learning (Jewitt, 2008). In media studies, MDA has provided insights into the complex interplay of text, image, and sound in film, television, and online media (Machin, 2007). Social media platforms, with their rich multimodal content, offer fertile ground for MDA, revealing how users employ various semiotic resources to construct identities, convey messages, and engage with audiences (Zappavigna, 2012). Despite its strengths, MDA also faces several challenges. One significant challenge is the development of consistent and rigorous methodologies for analysing multimodal texts, given the vast diversity of semiotic resources and their potential combinations (Norris, 2004). Additionally, the rapidly evolving nature of digital media poses a continual challenge for MDA scholars, requiring ongoing adaptation and refinement of analytical frameworks. In conclusion, Multimodal Discourse Analysis provides a robust framework for understanding the complex, multimodal nature of contemporary communication. By integrating insights from visual grammar, social semiotics, and intersemiosis, MDA offers a holistic approach to analysing how meaning is constructed across different semiotic modes. As digital and multimedia texts continue to proliferate, the relevance and applicability of MDA are likely to grow, offering valuable insights into the evolving landscape of communication.

## METHODOLOGY

This study adopts a qualitative case study design to explore how digital communication strategies were deployed during the 1 August 2024 protest in Nigeria. A case study approach is well-suited for examining socio-political phenomena within their real-world digital contexts (Yin, 2014). The focus on TikTok and Facebook, two widely used platforms in Nigeria, enables a nuanced understanding of how multimodal elements operate in constructing protest messages. Data were purposively sampled from both platforms using relevant hashtags and keywords associated with the protest. Eight videos—four from TikTok and four from Facebook—were selected for their strong interplay of visual and verbal elements. Screenshots were extracted at significant moments where multimodal features such as text overlays, colour schemes, and symbolic imagery were most prominent. These screenshots constitute the primary data for the multimodal discourse analysis.

The analysis draws on Kress and van Leeuwen's (2001) Multimodal Discourse Analysis (MDA) and Halliday's (1978) Social Semiotic Theory. While MDA outlines four strata of meaning—discourse, design, production, and distribution—this study intentionally focuses on two aspects within the design level: colour and visual symbols. This decision is based on the centrality of these elements in protest visuality, particularly in digital environments where quick cognition, affective appeal, and visual resonance are crucial (Opeibi, 2020; Ogunyemi, 2022). Colours and symbols are readily accessible, instantly recognisable, and ideologically loaded, making them powerful tools for mobilisation and collective identity formation. Analysis proceeded in three stages. First, screenshots were examined to identify semiotic resources—textual slogans, colours, icons, emojis, and other symbols. Second, the interaction between these resources was scrutinised to uncover how they collectively construct protest narratives. Third, contextual interpretation was applied, considering the socio-political circumstances and audience reception within Nigeria's protest ecology. By foregrounding colour and visual symbolism, the study provides insight into how selective multimodal choices perform persuasive and emotive functions in digital protest discourse. The combination of theoretical frameworks from Kress and van Leeuwen (2001) and Halliday (1978) offers a robust analytical lens for examining how semiotic elements are orchestrated in digital protest messages to evoke solidarity, resistance, and urgency.

## PRESENTATIONS OF DATA AND ANALYSIS

*Figure 1. Analysis of Data 1: August 1, 2024, Nigeria Protest Video on TikTok*

The analysis of the August 1, 2024, Nigeria protest video on TikTok, using Kress and van Leeuwen's Multimodal Discourse Analysis (MDA) and Halliday's Social Semiotic Theory, provides a comprehensive understanding of the multimodal elements at play. This video serves as an excellent example of how digital communication strategies are employed to convey potent messages during social movements. The use of colours in the video is particularly noteworthy. The text "TWO DAYS TO RAGE" and "WE ARE NOT SLAVES" is written in red, placed prominently on the right-hand side. The choice of red, a colour associated with urgency, anger, and passion, underscores the protest's call for immediate action and highlights the protesters' intense dissatisfaction. Similarly, the video title "END BAD GOVERNMENT IN NIGERIA 2024", also in red, reinforces this urgency and serves as a direct call to action against the current government. In contrast, the text "NATION WIDE PROTEST" is written in white, symbolising purity and truth. This colour choice suggests the legitimacy and righteousness of the protest, framing it as a necessary and just action. The visual representation of two people, a male and female, depicted as ready to fight, symbolises resistance and determination. This imagery aligns with the textual elements, enhancing the overall message of readiness and confrontation. The male painted in red further amplifies the sense of aggression and passion, visually reinforcing the textual calls for action. The inclusion of the Nigerian flag at the bottom right-hand side is a significant visual element. It symbolises national identity and solidarity, indicating that the protest is a collective action of Nigerian citizens. Beneath the flag, the caption "soro soke 11" (translated as "speak up 11") further encourages vocal resistance and active participation in the protest. This combination of national symbols and rallying cries fosters a sense of unity and shared purpose among the viewers. The textual messages in the video are clear and impactful. "TWO DAYS TO RAGE" and "WE ARE NOT SLAVES" are powerful declarative statements that highlight the urgency and rejection of subjugation. These messages are designed to evoke a strong emotional response from the audience, encouraging them to join the protest. The title "END BAD GOVERNMENT IN NIGERIA 2024" clearly states the protest's objective, leaving no ambiguity about the target of the protesters' dissatisfaction. The phrase "NATION WIDE PROTEST" emphasises the scale of the movement, suggesting widespread support and participation. Additionally, the text "END ANTI-PEOPLE POLICIES OVER TAXING AND ELECTORAL FRAUD" provides specific grievances, linking the protest to concrete issues that affect the populace. This specificity lends legitimacy to the protest, presenting it as a response to tangible injustices. The combination of these textual elements creates a compelling narrative that aligns the protest with the broader public discontent over these issues.

According to Halliday's framework, the ideational function is evident in how the visual and textual elements construct the protest's content. The urgency conveyed through the red text and the readiness for confrontation depicted by the individuals in the video illustrate the protesters' preparedness to challenge the status quo. The mention of specific grievances such as "over taxing" and "electoral fraud" grounds the protest in real issues, providing clear reasons for the movement. The use of colour and imagery creates a strong emotional appeal, connecting with the audience on a personal level. The declarative statements and the visual of people ready to fight establish a sense of solidarity and collective identity among the protesters. The caption "soro soke 11" acts as a call to action, urging viewers to speak up and participate, thereby fostering a sense of active engagement. The multimodal composition, including the strategic placement of text and images, guides the viewer's interpretation of the protest message. The use of bold colours and prominent positioning creates a cohesive and persuasive narrative that reinforces the protest's objectives. This careful arrangement ensures that the messages are not only seen but also felt, enhancing their impact. This analysis of the August 1, 2024, Nigeria protest video on TikTok reveals the strategic use of multimodal discourse to amplify the protest's message. By combining visual and textual elements, the protesters effectively convey urgency, solidarity, and specific grievances, creating a compelling narrative that encourages public participation and vocal resistance. Integrating Kress and van Leeuwen's Multimodal Discourse Analysis with Halliday's Social Semiotic

Theory provides a nuanced understanding of how different semiotic modes interact to construct meaning in digital protest communications. This comprehensive approach demonstrates the potency of multimodal resources in shaping public discourse and mobilising social movements in the digital age.

*Figure 2. Analysis of Data 2: August 1, 2024, Nigeria Protest Video on TikTok*

This data 2 visual and textual elements interact to convey a powerful message of resistance and mobilisation against poor governance in Nigeria. The use of colour in this video is particularly strategic. The phrase "END BAD" is written in red, a colour typically associated with urgency, danger, and a call to action. This choice highlights the critical nature of the protest's message, urging immediate attention and action. In contrast, the word "GOVERNANCE" is written in white, symbolising purity and a call for transparency and integrity in leadership. The stark contrast between the red and white text enhances the visibility and impact of the message, drawing the viewer's attention to the demand for an end to bad governance. The visual composition includes a raised hand with folded fingers, a potent symbol of solidarity, resistance, and unity. This gesture is emblematic of collective defiance and the shared resolve of the protesters. The image of the hand, central to the video's visual rhetoric, amplifies the message of readiness and determination conveyed through the text. The text “OSUN STATE IS READY” sets a regional context, indicating that the mobilisation is not limited to a single area but is part of a broader, nationwide movement. This regional specificity underscores the widespread discontent and the collective readiness to participate in the protest. It serves to rally individuals from Osun State, creating a sense of localised commitment within the larger national framework. The core message “END BAD GOVERNANCE” is visually segmented into “END BAD” in red and “GOVERNANCE” in white, reinforcing the urgency of ending poor governance and the aspiration for pure and truthful leadership. The segmentation and colour differentiation break down the message into more digestible and impactful components, making it easier for viewers to grasp and internalise the protest’s objectives.

The detailed schedule provided by the text “Days of Rage AUG. 1-10 8:00am Daily” specifies the duration and timing of the protest, contributing to the organisational aspect of the movement. This information is crucial for mobilisation, as it allows potential participants to plan their involvement. The inclusion of a clear timeline underscores the sustained nature of the protest, indicating that this is not a one-off event but a prolonged campaign for change.

With Halliday’s framework, the ideational function is evident in how the visual and textual elements construct the protest's content. The urgency conveyed through the red text “END BAD” and the symbol of the raised hand illustrate the protesters' preparedness to challenge the status quo. The mention of “OSUN STATE IS READY” situates the protest within a specific regional context, highlighting the widespread nature of the movement and its deep-rooted support across different parts of Nigeria. The use of colour and imagery creates a strong emotional appeal, connecting with the audience on a personal level. The declarative statements and the visual of the raised hand establish a sense of solidarity and collective identity among the protesters. The specific call to action and detailed protest schedule act as rallying points, urging viewers to participate actively and continuously. This fosters a sense of ongoing engagement and commitment to the protest’s cause. The multimodal composition, including the strategic placement of text and images, guides the viewer's interpretation of the protest message. The use of bold colours and prominent positioning of the text creates a cohesive and persuasive narrative that reinforces the protest’s objectives. This careful arrangement ensures that the messages are not only seen but also felt, enhancing their impact. The visual segmentation of the text into “END BAD” and “GOVERNANCE” ensures that each component of the message receives attention, making the call for action clear and compelling.

*Figure 3. Analysis of Data 3: August 1, 2024, Nigeria Protest Video on TikTok*

Data 3 of the August 1, 2024, Nigeria protest video on TikTok presents a compelling interplay of visual and textual elements designed to evoke strong emotional responses and mobilise public sentiment against political corruption and police brutality. The multimodal composition of this datum provides a rich site for analysis through the frameworks of Multimodal Discourse Analysis (MDA) by Kress and van Leeuwen, and Halliday's Social Semiotic Theory. The visual representation in this video is particularly striking. The depiction of many people lying down on the road where vehicles are supposed to pass, as if they are dead, creates a powerful and morbid visual metaphor for the state of Nigeria. This imagery conveys the message that the country is metaphorically 'dying' due to hunger, corruption, and bad governance. The static car further enhances this metaphor, symbolising the paralysis and stagnation of the nation due to systemic failures. The placement of the Nigerian flag next to the word "Nigeria" serves as a visual anchor, linking the textual message to the national identity. The flag's presence underscores the patriotic nature of the protest and the protesters' desire to reclaim their country from corrupt political parties. This use of national symbols aims to foster a sense of unity and shared purpose among viewers. The text "Nigeria is dying in hunger" succinctly summarises the dire situation and sets a grim tone for the message. The use of the present continuous tense "is dying" indicates an ongoing crisis, making the call for action more urgent. The subsequent text, "end all political parties stealing our money for their own selfish interest," directly accuses political parties of corruption and theft. This explicit condemnation serves to galvanise public outrage and direct it towards a clear target: the political elite.

The phrase "We are protesting happening now August 1" provides immediate temporal context, emphasising the urgency and real-time nature of the protest. This immediacy aims to spur viewers into action, highlighting that the protest is not a distant or abstract event but a current and pressing issue. The additional text, "Today is the day to liberate Nigeria. End bad government is now or never. Come out let us end police brutality," serves as a rallying cry. It frames the protest as a pivotal moment in the nation's history, a critical juncture where action must be taken. The imperative "Come out let us end police brutality" directly addresses the audience, encouraging physical participation and collective action. The juxtaposition of liberation from bad government and ending police brutality links the two issues, suggesting that they are interconnected and must be addressed simultaneously.

Halliday's ideational function is evident in the way the video constructs the narrative of a nation in crisis. The textual and visual elements work together to depict Nigeria as being in a state of emergency, with corruption and police brutality being the primary culprits. The metaphor of people lying on the road as if dead, coupled with the static car, visually represents the country's stagnation and decline. The emotional appeal of this video is significant. The imagery of people lying down, symbolising death, evokes a sense of urgency and desperation. The text directly addresses the audience, fostering a sense of involvement and responsibility. The call to action is clear and urgent, aiming to mobilise viewers into joining the protest and taking a stand against the injustices highlighted. The multimodal composition effectively guides the viewer's interpretation of the protest message. The strategic use of colour, imagery, and text creates a cohesive narrative that emphasises the gravity of the situation and the necessity of immediate action. The integration of the Nigerian flag reinforces national identity and solidarity, while the explicit accusations against political parties and calls to end police brutality provide clear targets for the protest.

*Figure 4. Analysis of Data 4: August 1, 2024, Nigeria Protest Video on TikTok*

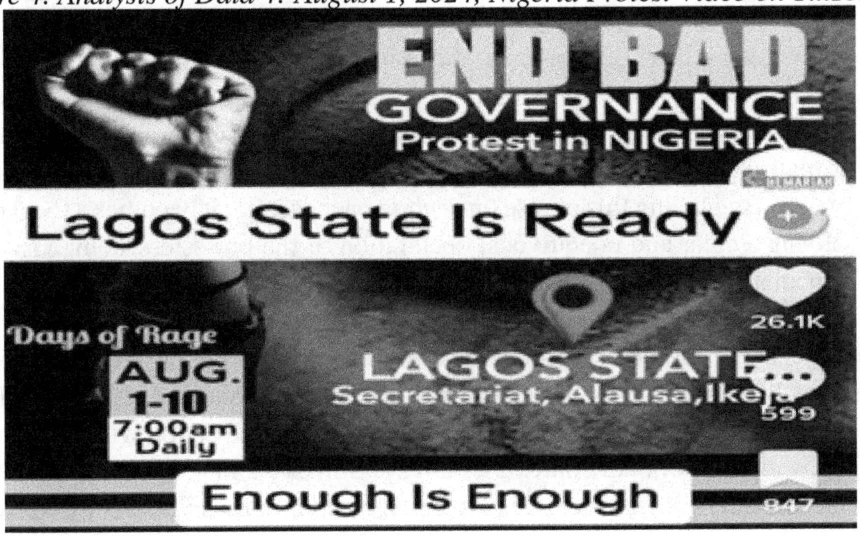


Data 4 from the August 1, 2024, Nigeria protest video on TikTok presents a multimodal composition that strategically employs both visual and textual elements to communicate the urgency and resolve of the protest movement. This analysis utilises Kress and van Leeuwen's Multimodal Discourse Analysis (MDA) and Halliday's Social Semiotic Theory to examine how these elements interact to convey a compelling protest message. The visual components in this datum are meticulously designed to amplify the protest's message. The text "END BAD GOVERNANCE" is prominently displayed in yellow, a colour that symbolises caution and urgency. This colour choice ensures that the message stands out, drawing immediate attention and signalling the critical nature of the demand. The emphasis on the word "END" underscores the definitive and uncompromising stance of the protesters. The background features two phrases, "Lagos State is Ready" and "Enough is Enough," both written in black on a white surface. This stark contrast enhances readability and underscores the gravity of the messages. Black signifies seriousness and determination, while the white background provides a clean, unobstructed canvas, ensuring that the messages are clear and impactful. Additionally, the visual representation includes a hand raised up with folded fingers. This gesture, commonly associated with solidarity and resistance, symbolises the unity and collective strength of the protesters. It conveys a powerful image of defiance and readiness to fight against bad governance. The visual of the raised hand complements the textual elements, reinforcing the message of collective action and resolve. The text "LAGOS STATE Secratarial, Alausa, Ikeja" specifies the protest location, providing clear logistical information for participants. This specificity aids in organising the protest effectively, directing participants to a central and politically significant location in Lagos. The use of uppercase letters for "LAGOS STATE" further accentuates the importance of the location, signalling that the protest is a major and organised event. The phrase "Enough is Enough" serves as a rallying cry, encapsulating the collective frustration and determination of the protesters. The repetition of this phrase across various protest materials reinforces the shared sentiment of exasperation with the current governance. By placing this phrase on a white background, it becomes a focal point, symbolising a clear and unequivocal declaration of the protesters' demands.

From an ideational perspective, the datum constructs a narrative of urgency and readiness. The combination of "END BAD GOVERNANCE" and "Lagos State is Ready" suggests that the protesters are prepared and organised, ready to take decisive action against corrupt governance. The specification of "LAGOS STATE Secratarial, Alausa, Ikeja" as the protest venue situates the action within a concrete geographical and political context, lending legitimacy and seriousness to the protest. Interpersonally, the video seeks to engage and mobilise viewers by conveying a sense of immediacy and collective resolve. The use of yellow for the main message draws viewers' attention, signalling caution and urgency. The straightforward and commanding nature of the text, coupled with the visual clarity, fosters a sense of involvement and responsibility among the audience. The message "Enough is Enough" directly appeals to shared frustrations, encouraging viewers to join the protest and contribute to the collective action. The visual of the raised hand with folded fingers further personalises the protest, invoking a sense of solidarity and collective empowerment. The textual function of this datum is to guide viewers through the protest's key messages and logistical details seamlessly. The strategic use of colour and contrast ensures that each element of the message is clear and impactful. The cohesive visual design allows the audience to quickly understand the core demand ("END BAD GOVERNANCE"), the readiness of the protest location ("Lagos State is Ready"), and the specific logistical details ("LAGOS STATE Secratarial, Alausa, Ikeja"). The visual of the raised hand with folded fingers integrates with the text to provide a powerful, unified call to action.

*Figure 5. Analysis of Data 5 from Facebook Platform*

In this instance, Data 5, the digital protest strategy involves a screenshot derived from Facebook, depicting a significant visual and textual combination designed to convey a potent political message. The visual composition features two individuals prominently holding a banner with the text "BRING BACK FUEL SUBSIDY," while a multitude of supporters stand behind them. The strategic use of colour and composition in this digital artefact is critical in underscoring the protest's demands and enhancing its impact on the audience.

The text on the banner employs a deliberate colour scheme, with "BRING" written in red and "BACK FUEL SUBSIDY" in black. The choice of red for the word "BRING" is emblematic, as red is often associated with urgency, warning, and attention. This colour choice effectively draws immediate attention to the demand for the reinstatement of the fuel subsidy, signalling its critical importance to the audience. In contrast, the use of black for the remainder of the message, "BACK FUEL SUBSIDY," adds a sense of gravity and seriousness to the plea, underscoring the protesters' resolve and the importance of their demand. At the bottom of the banner, the text "End bad governance in Nigeria" further amplifies the protest's core message. This additional textual element broadens the scope of the protest, linking the specific issue of fuel subsidy with the broader context of governmental reform. This holistic framing serves to connect the immediate grievance with a larger call for systemic change, thereby enhancing the persuasive power of the protest message. The visual elements are equally compelling. The two individuals holding the banner serve as the focal point of the image, symbolising leadership and direct action. Their position at the forefront, coupled with their assertive posture, suggests determination and a readiness to challenge the status quo. The presence of a larger crowd behind them signifies widespread support and solidarity, amplifying the collective voice of the protesters. This backdrop of supporters enhances the legitimacy of the protest, suggesting that the demand for the return of the fuel subsidy is not isolated but rather a shared concern among many.

Further analysis of the visual composition reveals a person standing in front of the banner holders, facing the interactive participants with folded arms and wearing a black top. This individual's stance—arms folded and facing forward—can be interpreted as a gesture of defiance and determination. The black attire may symbolise mourning or a sombre reflection of the hardships faced by the populace due to the removal of the fuel subsidy. This visual metaphor effectively communicates a narrative of resistance and resilience. The integration of both visual and textual elements in this digital protest artefact exemplifies the principles of Multimodal Discourse Analysis (MDA) as articulated by Kress and van Leeuwen (2001), and the functional semantics outlined in Halliday's (1978) Social Semiotic Theory. The banner's textual elements provide clarity and directness to the protest message, while the visual components add layers of emotional and contextual meaning, enhancing the overall communicative impact. The utilisation of Facebook as the platform for disseminating this protest image further exemplifies the strategic use of digital media in contemporary activism. Facebook's wide reach and interactive capabilities enable the message to spread rapidly and engage a broad audience, thus amplifying the protest's visibility and influence. This aligns with the broader trend of leveraging digital platforms for political mobilisation, allowing for the efficient organisation and dissemination of protest messages.

In conclusion, Data 5 exemplifies a sophisticated use of multimodal resources in digital protest communication. The strategic deployment of colour, visual symbolism, and textual clarity effectively conveys the protesters' demands and mobilises support. This analysis underscores the importance of integrating visual and textual elements to create compelling and impactful digital protest content, leveraging the affordances of social media platforms to amplify the message and galvanise collective action.

*Figure 6. Analysis of Data 6 from Facebook Platform*

Data 6 presents a digital protest artefact from Facebook, where two individuals hold a banner or sticker with the text "Hungry Dey Everyday in this Country," written in blue. This visual and textual combination is designed to capture the audience's attention and convey a potent message about the daily struggles faced by citizens. The use of blue for the text signifies a sense of calmness and reliability, but in this context, it also conveys a somber reality, contrasting sharply with the urgency of the protest. The phrase "Hungry Dey Everyday in this Country" is a poignant expression of the pervasive hunger and economic hardship experienced by the populace. This colloquial phrasing adds an element of authenticity and relatability, resonating deeply with those who are directly affected by these issues. The use of everyday language ensures that the message is accessible and impactful, effectively communicating the protesters' grievances.

Behind the banner holders, a crowd of individuals reinforces the message of the protest. Their presence signifies collective discontent and solidarity, essential elements in amplifying the protest's impact. The background includes a partially visible person holding another banner with the text "end bad governance," linking the issue of hunger to broader systemic problems. This connection underscores the argument that poor governance is at the root of economic hardships, creating a more comprehensive narrative of the protest. The presence of an individual holding a white megaphone in the background further emphasises the active nature of the protest. The megaphone, a symbol of amplification and voice, suggests that the protesters are not only gathering but also actively communicating their demands to a broader audience. This element highlights the dynamic and vocal aspects of the protest, reinforcing the urgency and the need for immediate attention and action.

The movement of the protesters, as depicted in the visual, suggests a march or rally, indicating continuous and active engagement in the protest. This dynamic visual element adds to the narrative of resilience and determination, portraying the protesters as persistent in their fight against economic and political injustices. The strategic use of Facebook as the platform for sharing this protest image plays a crucial role in its dissemination and impact. Facebook's extensive user base and interactive features enable rapid sharing and engagement, amplifying the protest's visibility. This use of digital platforms aligns with contemporary trends in activism, where social media serves as a powerful tool for mobilisation and advocacy. In conclusion, Data 6 effectively utilises multimodal resources to convey a powerful message about economic hardship and systemic governance issues. The combination of relatable text, supportive crowd, and symbolic elements like the megaphone creates a compelling and impactful protest narrative. This analysis underscores the importance of integrating visual and textual elements in digital protest communication to maximise reach and resonance. The strategic use of social media platforms like Facebook further enhances the protest's visibility and engagement, demonstrating the significant role of digital communication in modern activism.

*Figure 7. Analysis of Data 7 from Facebook Platform*

Data 7 presents a digital protest artefact from Facebook, depicting a significant scene where numerous individuals are obstructed by a barbed wire barrier. This visual narrative effectively captures the physical and symbolic barriers faced by the protesters, conveying a powerful message of suppression and resistance. The barbed wire serves as a metaphor for the systemic obstacles and repressive measures that hinder the movement and freedom of the populace. The prominent visual of individuals being blocked by the barbed wire evokes a sense of entrapment and struggle. The depiction of people unable to move forward underscores the severity of the hindrances they face, both physically and metaphorically. This barrier symbolises the oppressive structures and policies that stifle progress and restrict the voices of the people. The visual representation of the barbed wire adds a layer of urgency and desperation to the protest narrative, highlighting the need for immediate change and liberation.

Among the individuals, one person is seen raising the Nigerian flag, a powerful symbol of national identity and solidarity. The flag's presence signifies the protesters' patriotic sentiments and their demand for a better Nigeria. It serves as a reminder of their right to protest and their collective aspiration for a nation free from oppression and misgovernance. The flag acts as a unifying symbol, rallying the protesters under a common cause and reinforcing their sense of national pride and resilience. Additionally, another individual holds a banner with the text "TINUBU" written on a black surface in white colour, followed by "Let Nigeria Breathe!" in red colour. The stark contrast between the black background and white text for "TINUBU" highlights the central figure of contention, drawing attention to the person perceived as responsible for the current state of affairs. The phrase "Let Nigeria Breathe!" written in red conveys a sense of urgency and distress, emphasising the dire need for political and social reform. The use of red in this context symbolises the critical and alarming nature of the situation, calling for immediate action and intervention.

The strategic use of Facebook as the platform for disseminating this protest image is significant. Facebook's vast reach and interactive features facilitate the rapid spread of protest messages, enabling wide-scale mobilisation and engagement. The platform allows for the creation of a digital community where individuals can share their grievances, rally support, and organise collective action. This digital engagement is crucial for amplifying the protest's visibility and impact, demonstrating the power of social media in contemporary activism. The depiction of people hindered by the barbed wire, coupled with the symbolic elements of the Nigerian flag and the banner, creates a compelling and evocative narrative of struggle and resistance. This multimodal approach effectively communicates the protesters' plight and their demand for liberation and reform. The visual and textual elements work together to convey a powerful message, resonating with the audience and eliciting empathy and support. In conclusion, Datum 8 utilises multimodal resources to convey a vivid and impactful protest narrative. The visual of the barbed wire barrier, the symbolic raising of the Nigerian flag, and the pointed message on the banner collectively highlight the protesters' struggles and their call for change. The strategic use of Facebook enhances the protest's reach and engagement, illustrating the significant role of digital communication in modern activism. This analysis underscores the importance of integrating visual and textual elements in digital protest communication to effectively convey messages and mobilise support.

*Figure 8. Analysis of Data 8 from Facebook Platform*

Data 8 showcases a protest scene from Facebook, where a multitude of individuals are depicted standing with their hands raised and fingers folded, a gesture symbolising solidarity and defiance. This visual representation effectively captures the collective resolve and unity among the protesters, presenting a powerful image of resistance against perceived injustices. The presence of numerous individuals reinforces the magnitude of the movement, signifying widespread discontent and a unified call for change. At the forefront, seven individuals hold a prominent banner with the text "End Bad Governance in Nigeria" written in black colour. The use of black text is stark and authoritative, conveying a serious and urgent message. The clear and bold demand for an end to bad governance serves as a focal point of the protest, encapsulating the primary grievance of the protesters. This central message is crucial in rallying support and highlighting the core issue driving the movement.

Beneath this main message, the banner further declares, "Enough is Enough to Hunger and Hardship," written in yellow colour on a black background. The contrasting colours draw attention to the statement, emphasising the critical and dire nature of the protesters' situation. The use of upper case letters adds to the urgency and intensity of the plea, underscoring the immediate need for alleviating hunger and hardship. This appeal highlights the socio-economic dimensions of the protest, linking the call for better governance with tangible issues affecting the populace. Additionally, the banner includes the text "Reverse all Anti Poor Policies," written in white colour and upper case. This demand targets specific policies perceived as detrimental to the poor, advocating for a reversal of such measures. The use of white text on a dark background ensures visibility and clarity, making the message stand out. The call to reverse anti-poor policies aligns with the broader theme of social justice and equity, further strengthening the protest's appeal to a wider audience.

The visual scene also features several smaller banners held by other protesters. The first short banner reads, “Reverse all anti-people MRI liberal policies of privatisation, deregulation, and devaluation.” This detailed message addresses specific economic policies, critiquing their impact on the populace. The explicit mention of privatisation, deregulation, and devaluation indicates a nuanced understanding of the issues and a targeted critique of neoliberal economic reforms. This banner adds depth to the protest narrative, highlighting the protesters' awareness of and opposition to complex economic policies. The second short banner states, “The hunger is too much,” succinctly encapsulating the protesters' plight. This straightforward message resonates with a broad audience, emphasising the immediate and tangible impact of governance on daily life. The simplicity and directness of this banner make it a powerful addition to the protest's visual rhetoric.

The third short banner proclaims, “One day, the poor will have nothing else to eat but the rich oppressors.” This provocative statement serves as a stark warning, suggesting a potential uprising against systemic inequalities. The metaphorical language underscores the severity of the socio-economic divide and the growing frustration among the poor. This banner adds a dramatic and urgent tone to the protest, evoking a sense of impending crisis if the issues are not addressed. The strategic use of Facebook as the platform for disseminating this protest image is significant. Facebook's extensive reach and interactive features enable the rapid spread of protest messages, facilitating broad engagement and mobilisation. The platform allows for the creation of a digital community where individuals can share their grievances, organise collective action, and amplify their voices. This digital engagement is crucial for enhancing the protest's visibility and impact, demonstrating the power of social media in contemporary activism. In conclusion, Datum 9 employs multimodal resources to convey a compelling and multifaceted protest narrative. The visual of raised hands, the prominent and detailed banners, and the strategic use of Facebook collectively highlight the protesters' unity, grievances, and demands. The integration of visual and textual elements effectively communicates the urgency and complexity of the issues, resonating with a wide audience and galvanising support. This analysis underscores the importance of multimodal communication in digital protests, illustrating how different semiotic modes can be leveraged to create a powerful and impactful narrative.

## FINDINGS AND CONCLUSION

The analysis of the August 1, 2024, Nigeria protest, based on multimodal data drawn from TikTok and Facebook, reveals how digital communication significantly enhances the visibility, reach, and emotional force of contemporary social movements.

The integration of verbal and visual elements across the protest content generates a layered, persuasive narrative that underscores the potency of multimodal discourse in shaping public consciousness. Strategic use of colour emerges as a particularly powerful semiotic tool—red and yellow are employed to signal urgency and distress, while black and white convey seriousness and solemnity. These colour choices are not arbitrary; they function as meaning-making resources that intensify the affective impact of protest messages, in line with Kress and van Leeuwen's (2001) emphasis on the semiotic affordances of visual grammar and Halliday's (1978) social semiotic theory. Moreover, the deployment of visual symbols—such as raised fists, individuals lying on roads, and national icons like the Nigerian flag—serves to reinforce themes of resistance, solidarity, and national identity. These non-verbal cues are central to the communicative intent of the protest, operating not merely as illustration but as vital modes of engagement that deepen the resonance of the verbal text.

The participatory affordances of TikTok and Facebook also prove crucial in fostering a sense of immediacy and collective agency. Through real-time sharing, commenting, and interaction, these platforms function as digital arenas of mobilisation and solidarity. They enable protesters to build communities across geographic divides, amplifying the movement's impact and sustaining engagement beyond the immediate context of physical protest. The content further reveals a sophisticated critique of state governance and socio-economic hardship. Protesters articulate their discontent through textual elements that reference issues such as taxation, electoral malpractice, and neoliberal economic reforms. These expressions are far from emotive outbursts; they represent deliberate, informed critiques of systemic challenges, dispelling reductive assumptions about the intellectual content of protest cultures. In sum, the August 1 protest demonstrates how digital media, through multimodal forms of communication, empower citizens to challenge dominant narratives, assert agency, and participate actively in civic discourse. The findings reinforce the central role of digital platforms in contemporary activism, illustrating how colours, symbols, and interactive media coalesce to shape compelling and impactful protest communication in Nigeria's socio-political landscape.

## REFERENCES

Adebanwi, W. (2020). The affective infrastructures of digital activism in Nigeria. *African Studies Review*, *63*(4), 654–673. DOI: 10.1017/asr.2020.50

Adeiza, A. (2021). Social media, protest repertoires, and the evolving structure of political participation in Nigeria. *Media Culture & Society*, *43*(5), 921–938. DOI: 10.1177/0163443720957882

Akinbobola, Y. (2021). Reframing African struggles: Transnational digital activism and the reimagining of political agency. *Information Communication and Society*, *24*(10), 1458–1473. DOI: 10.1080/1369118X.2020.1716035

Androutsopoulos, J. (2011). Language change and digital media: A review of conceptions and evidence. In Kristiansen, T., & Coupland, N. (Eds.), *Standard Languages and Language Standards in a Changing Europe* (pp. 145–163). Novus Press.

Barton, D., & Lee, C. (2013). *Language Online: Investigating Digital Texts and Practices*. Routledge. DOI: 10.4324/9780203552308

Barton, D., & Lee, C. (2013). *Language Online: Investigating Digital Texts and Practices*. Routledge. DOI: 10.4324/9780203552308

Bosancianu, C. M., Hilbig, H., & Humphreys, M. (2020). *Political protest in times of crisis: The role of digital media*. WZB Berlin Social Science Center. https://doi.org/DOI: 10.2139/ssrn.3582125

Bruns, A., & Burgess, J. (2011). The use of Twitter hashtags in the formation of ad hoc publics. In *Proceedings of the 6th European Consortium for Political Research General Conference* (pp. 1-9). University of Iceland.

Bruns, A., & Burgess, J. (2011). The use of Twitter hashtags in the formation of ad hoc publics. In *Proceedings of the 6th European Consortium for Political Research General Conference* (pp. 1-9). University of Iceland.

Castells, M. (2012). *Networks of outrage and hope: Social movements in the Internet age*. Polity Press.

Castells, M. (2012). *Networks of outrage and hope: Social movements in the Internet age*. Polity Press.

Crystal, D. (2006). *Language and the Internet*. Cambridge University Press. DOI: 10.1017/CBO9780511487002

Egbunike, N. (2018). Beyond hashtags and retweets: Twitter as a space of participation in Nigerian politics. In Dumova, T. (Ed.), *Social interaction and the Internet: A study of social media use in Nigeria* (pp. 75–92). IGI Global.

Gerbaudo, P. (2012). *Tweets and the streets: Social media and contemporary activism*. Pluto Press.

Halliday, M. A. K. (1978). *Language as Social Semiotic: The Social Interpretation of Language and Meaning*. Edward Arnold.

Herring, S. C. (2013). Discourse in Web 2.0: Familiar, reconfigured, and emergent. In Tannen, D., & Trester, A. M. (Eds.), *Discourse 2.0: Language and New Media* (pp. 1–25). Georgetown University Press.

Jenkins, H. (2006). *Convergence Culture: Where Old and New Media Collide*. New York University Press.

Jewitt, C. (2008). Multimodality and literacy in school classrooms. *Review of Research in Education, 32*(1), 241–267. DOI: 10.3102/0091732X07310586

Jones, R. H., & Hafner, C. A. (2012). *Understanding Digital Literacies: A Practical Introduction*. Routledge. DOI: 10.4324/9780203095317

Kress, G. (2010). *Multimodality: A Social Semiotic Approach to Contemporary Communication*. Routledge.

Kress, G., & van Leeuwen, T. (1996). *Reading Images: The Grammar of Visual Design*. Routledge.

Kress, G., & van Leeuwen, T. (2001). *Multimodal Discourse: The Modes and Media of Contemporary Communication*. Arnold.

Machin, D. (2007). *Introduction to Multimodal Analysis*. Hodder Arnold.

Norris, S. (2004). *Analyzing Multimodal Interaction: A Methodological Framework*. Routledge. DOI: 10.4324/9780203379493

O'Halloran, K. L. (2008). Systemic functional-multimodal discourse analysis (SF-MDA): Constructing ideational meaning using language and visual imagery. *Visual Communication, 7*(4), 443–475. DOI: 10.1177/1470357208096210

Ogunyemi, B. (2022). Digital activism and civic engagement in Nigeria: A study of the #RevolutionNow and #EndSARS movements. *African Journalism Studies, 43*(2), 37–55. DOI: 10.1080/23743670.2022.2035692

Okunade, S. K., & Aduloju, A. A. (2023). Hashtag activism and youth political engagement in Nigeria: A study of the #EndSARS protest. *Journal of African Media Studies*, *15*(1), 45–62. DOI: 10.1386/jams_00059_1

Opeibi, T. (2020). Multimodal discourse in digital protest communication: An analysis of #EndSARS online activism in Nigeria. *Discourse & Society*, *31*(6), 680–698. DOI: 10.1177/0957926520939674

Tagg, C. (2015). *Exploring Digital Communication: Language in Action*. Routledge. DOI: 10.4324/9781315727165

Tufekci, Z. (2017). *Twitter and tear gas: The power and fragility of networked protest*. Yale University Press.

Uche, L. U., & Ngwu, C. C. (2023). Media activism and digital resistance in Nigeria: A study of youths' engagement during the #EndSARS protest. *Communication and the Public*, *8*(1), 23–39. DOI: 10.1177/20570473221141891

Van Dijk, J. (2005). *The Deepening Divide: Inequality in the Information Society*. Sage Publications.

Yin, R. K. (2014). *Case study research: Design and methods* (5th ed.). SAGE Publications.

Zappavigna, M. (2012). *Discourse of Twitter and Social Media: How We Use Language to Create Affiliation on the Web*. Bloomsbury Academic. DOI: 10.5040/9781472541642

## ADDITIONAL READING

Androutsopoulos, J. (2011). Language change and digital media: A review of conceptions and evidence. In Kristiansen, T., & Coupland, N. (Eds.), *Standard Languages and Language Standards in a Changing Europe* (pp. 145–160). Novus Press.

Halliday, M. A. K. (1978). *Language as Social Semiotic: The Social Interpretation of Language and Meaning*. Edward Arnold.

Jewitt, C. (2009). *The Routledge Handbook of Multimodal Analysis*. Routledge.

Kress, G., & van Leeuwen, T. (2001). *Multimodal Discourse: The Modes and Media of Contemporary Communication*. Arnold.

Machin, D. (2010). *Analysing Popular Music: Image, Sound and Text*. Sage Publications. DOI: 10.4135/9781446280027

Scollon, R., & Scollon, S. W. (2003). *Discourses in Place: Language in the Material World*. Routledge. DOI: 10.4324/9780203422724

Thurlow, C., & Mroczek, K. (2011). *Digital Discourse: Language in the New Media*. Oxford University Press. DOI: 10.1093/acprof:oso/9780199795437.001.0001

van Leeuwen, T. (2005). *Introducing Social Semiotics*. Routledge.

# Chapter 5
# Exploring Socio-Cultural Challenges in Online Movements

**Olusegun Jegede**
https://orcid.org/0000-0002-0169-2331
*Lead City University, Ibadan, Nigeria*

## ABSTRACT

*This paper argues that digital activism relies on pragmatic language strategies to explore and address the socio-cultural challenges inherent in online spaces. Digital activism, defined as the use of digital platforms to mobilize for social and political causes, relies on pragmatic language strategies to foster engagement, address cultural sensitivities, and represent diverse voices. Pragmatics, the study of language in context, offers insight into how speech acts, politeness, and implicature are employed to enhance the persuasiveness and inclusivity of activist messages. Theoretical frameworks of pragmatics and sociocultural identity are discussed, revealing the role of language in shaping collective identities within movements. Case studies illustrate how each movement overcame linguistic barriers and cultural tensions through pragmatic approaches. The paper concludes by emphasizing the importance of further research into the evolution of language in digital activism and the need to better understand how online communication impacts social change.*

DOI: 10.4018/979-8-3373-5297-8.ch005

# I. INTRODUCTION

## A. Background and Relevance of Digital Activism in Global Discourse

Activism encompasses the deliberate actions and efforts of individuals or collectives to bring about change in societal, political, economic, or environmental spheres (Jegede, 2024). From historical contexts such as the civil rights movement and women's suffrage to contemporary labour rights campaigns, activism has long been a driving force for justice and transformation. These traditional forms of activism relied heavily on physical mobilisation, demonstrations, and other on-the-ground tactics that required substantial resources and coordination. As noted by Jegede (2024), these movements often utilised advocacy strategies such as strikes, petitions, and legal battles to challenge authority and raise awareness.

The advent of digital technologies has significantly transformed the context of activism. Social media platforms, mobile apps, and other digital tools now serve as essential channels for mobilisation and message dissemination. This contemporary mode of activism, often referred to as "clicktivism" or "hashtag activism," relies on platforms like Twitter, Facebook, and Instagram to propagate causes and foster global engagement. Through digital activism, grassroots movements can achieve widespread visibility and exert influence without relying on mainstream media or substantial financial backing. Movements like #BlackLivesMatter, #MeToo, and climate change advocacy campaigns have successfully used the internet's reach to promote justice and challenge systemic issues on a global scale.

Digital activism involves the use of digital technologies—especially social media—to organise, mobilise, and advocate for political, social, or cultural transformation. According to Gerbaudo (2017), the ideological framework of digital activism has evolved from cyber-autonomism to cyber-populism, reflecting a shift towards using digital spaces for collective identity formation and coordinated action. While earlier forms of digital engagement focused on minimal-effort actions such as liking or sharing posts (George & Leidner, 2019), the scope of digital activism has expanded. Activists now employ more sophisticated methods like hacktivism and cyber-conflict to disrupt established power structures (Karatzogianni, 2015).

Infrastructures supporting sustained digital campaigns have also emerged. Scholz (2010) argues that digital activism is not confined to momentary actions but includes long-term strategies that build digital communities and support networks. However, this evolution has prompted critical reflection. The initial optimism about the democratizing potential of digital activism is increasingly tempered by concerns regarding its actual impact and effectiveness (Kaun & Uldam, 2018). The continuously shifting digital environment demands that activists adapt their tactics while maintaining their focus on systemic change (Joyce, 2010). Digital activism remains a crucial mechanism for collective expression and mobilisation, offering unprecedented opportunities for dissent and advocacy in the digital age.

Pragmatics, the study of language in use and context, is central to understanding communication in digital activism. Ishihara and Cohen (2010) and Xie and Yus (2018) describe pragmatics as the intersection between language and culture, which is essential in conveying meaning across diverse digital communities. Online communication lacks non-verbal cues such as gestures, tone, and facial expressions, increasing the risk of misinterpretation. Pragmatic competence, therefore, becomes vital in tackling digital interactions and ensuring messages are culturally appropriate and clearly understood.

The application of speech acts—expressions that perform actions, such as apologising or suggesting—is influenced by cultural and contextual factors (Kondo, 2010; Yus, 2019). For example, Martinez-Flor (2010) explains that suggestions in digital spaces are framed by social norms, requiring thoughtful language choices. Likewise, Eslami (2013) observes that students' online pragmatic behaviour often reflects their awareness of context and audience, indicating a learning process in digital communication. Waugh (2014) and Tatsuki and Houck (2010) argue that fostering pragmatic awareness enhances intercultural understanding, which is crucial in global digital activism. As activists communicate across diverse linguistic and cultural contexts, pragmatic strategies help them build bridges, promote inclusivity, and avoid conflict.

Despite its potential, digital activism encounters multiple socio-cultural challenges. One major obstacle is the digital divide, where unequal access to digital tools and internet connectivity excludes marginalised communities from active participation (González-Bailón et al., 2011). This disparity results in underrepresentation of certain voices, weakening the democratic promise of digital activism. Language diversity and cultural differences further complicate cross-border activism, as shared meanings can be elusive in culturally heterogeneous networks (Treré et al., 2017).

Additionally, platform design and algorithms can reinforce exclusion. Garrett (2006) reveals how digital infrastructures often prioritise content from dominant groups, marginalising others. Online activism also struggles with translating digital enthusiasm into tangible outcomes. Critics like Wolfson (2014) describe this phenomenon as "slacktivism," where low-effort participation replaces deeper engagement. Furthermore, cultural and political contexts influence the reception of digital activism. In repressive environments, digital activists face censorship, surveillance, and potential persecution, making their efforts more precarious (Yang, 2016). These socio-cultural challenges necessitate flexible and inclusive strategies that account for linguistic, cultural, and systemic variations in digital activism.

Digital activism depends significantly on the strategic use of pragmatic language to overcome these challenges. Through context-sensitive communication, activists can engage diverse audiences, explore cultural boundaries, and foster inclusivity. Pragmatic tools such as politeness, inference, and speech acts allow messages to align across different communities. These tools also contribute to the formation of collective identities and shared goals, enabling movements to attract broader support and achieve cohesion. Pragmatic language use thus plays a fundamental role in ensuring the effectiveness and sustainability of digital activism.

## B. Statement of the Problem and Research Questions

The increasing reliance on digital technologies in activism has redefined how social and political causes are communicated and mobilised. However, this transformation introduces critical challenges related to communication effectiveness and inclusivity. Socio-cultural factors such as language, cultural norms, digital access, and platform dynamics can obstruct meaningful participation and limit the success of online movements. In this context, the role of pragmatics—how language functions in social interactions—becomes increasingly important.

This chapter seeks to investigate how digital activism employs pragmatic language strategies to address socio-cultural challenges in online environments. It will explore the ways in which activists adapt their language to various cultural and linguistic contexts, foster inclusive dialogue, and manage identity construction in digital spaces. The chapter will also examine how pragmatic competence affects the persuasiveness and clarity of activist messages.

The primary research questions guiding this inquiry are:

a) How do socio-cultural challenges impact the effectiveness of digital activism?
b) In what ways do pragmatic language strategies facilitate communication in online activist movements?
c) How do digital activists explore linguistic and cultural differences to promote inclusion and collective identity?

## C. Scope and Objectives of the Chapter

This chapter focuses on the intersection of digital activism and pragmatics, particularly the socio-cultural challenges that affect communication and mobilisation in online movements. It does not seek to provide an exhaustive account of all forms of activism but concentrates on the pragmatic aspects of digital activism in varied cultural contexts. While examples may be drawn from global movements such as

#BlackLivesMatter and #MeToo, the emphasis will be on the linguistic strategies employed to overcome cultural and communicative barriers.

The main objectives of the chapter are:

a) To examine the role of pragmatics in shaping digital activism discourse
b) To analyse how activists employ language strategically to address socio-cultural challenges
c) To assess the effectiveness of pragmatic strategies in fostering inclusion and promoting collective identity
d) To contribute to the academic discourse on digital communication and activism from a pragmatic perspective

Through this focus, the chapter aims to reveal the importance of linguistic awareness and cultural sensitivity in enhancing the impact and reach of digital activist movements.

### D. Structure and Outline of the Chapter

The chapter is organised into six main sections. Following this introduction, the second section provides a comprehensive literature review on digital activism and pragmatics, revealing key theoretical and empirical contributions. The third section discusses the socio-cultural challenges that impact online activism, including the digital divide, linguistic diversity, and platform dynamics. The fourth section explores the pragmatic strategies employed by activists to explore these challenges. It draws on case studies and examples to illustrate how speech acts, politeness, and inference are used in digital communication. The fifth section analyses the role of pragmatic language in building collective identity and promoting inclusivity within activist networks. The final section concludes the chapter with a summary of key findings, theoretical implications, and suggestions for future research. It emphasises the significance of pragmatics in understanding and enhancing digital activism in a culturally diverse and interconnected world.

## II. CONCEPTUAL FRAMEWORK AND LITERATURE REVIEW

### A. Definition and Scope of Digital Activism

Digital activism, also referred to as cyberactivism or online activism, encompasses the strategic use of digital technologies—such as the internet, social media, and mobile platforms—to promote, organise, and enact social, political, or cultural change. This form of activism has evolved significantly since its inception in the 1980s, transitioning from basic information dissemination to sophisticated forms of online protest and mobilisation (Encyclopaedia Britannica, 2025). The advent of social media platforms like Twitter, Facebook, and Instagram has revolutionised the context of activism. These platforms enable rapid information sharing, real-time organisation, and the amplification of marginalised voices, thereby facilitating grassroots mobilisation on a global scale (TrendMind, 2025). Movements such as #MeToo and Black Lives Matter exemplify the power of digital activism to transcend geographical boundaries and effect tangible societal change (Papa, 2025).

Digital activism manifests in various forms, ranging from low-effort activities like sharing posts (often termed "clicktivism") to more intensive actions such as "hacktivism," where individuals disrupt digital systems to protest or draw attention to specific issues (George & Leidner, 2019). While clicktivism has been criticised for its perceived lack of depth, it plays a crucial role in raising awareness and fostering initial engagement. Conversely, hacktivism represents a more confrontational approach, aiming to directly challenge and disrupt existing power structures. The scope of digital activism extends beyond mere online engagement; it encompasses the creation of virtual communities, the shaping of public discourse, and the potential to influence policy and societal norms. However, challenges such as the digital divide, algorithmic biases, and online harassment pose significant obstacles to the inclusivity and effectiveness of digital activism (González-Bailón et al., 2011; Garrett, 2006).

## B. Overview of Pragmatics: Speech Acts, Politeness, Contextual Meaning

Pragmatics, a subfield of linguistics, examines how context influences the interpretation of meaning in language. Unlike semantics, which focuses on the literal meaning of words and sentences, pragmatics is concerned with the implied meaning—how speakers use and understand language in real-life situations based on context, shared knowledge, and the intentions of the participants (Word Gate, 2025). One foundational concept in pragmatics is the theory of speech acts, introduced by philosopher J.L. Austin. Austin categorised speech acts into three types: locutionary (the act of saying something), illocutionary (the intended meaning or function of the utterance), and perlocutionary (the effect the utterance has on the listener) (Britannica, 2025). For instance, the statement "It's cold in here" can serve as a mere observation (locutionary), a request to close a window (illocutionary), or prompt someone to take action (perlocutionary).

Politeness theory, developed by sociolinguists Penelope Brown and Stephen Levinson, explores how individuals manage and maintain face-saving acts in communication. According to this theory, speakers adjust their language based on social factors, such as power dynamics, social distance, and the degree of imposition. For example, saying "Could you please pass the salt?" is a polite request that considers the listener's autonomy, whereas "Pass the salt" is more direct and may be perceived as impolite (Word Gate, 2025).

Context plays a crucial role in pragmatics. It encompasses various factors, including the physical setting, the relationship between speakers, cultural norms, and shared knowledge. Understanding these contextual elements is essential for interpreting the intended meaning behind utterances. For example, the phrase "Nice job" can be interpreted as sincere praise or sarcasm, depending on the speaker's tone, facial expressions, and the situational context (Fiveable, 2025). In digital communication, the absence of non-verbal cues such as tone of voice and facial expressions presents unique challenges for pragmatic interpretation. Users rely heavily on textual cues, emojis, and shared digital norms to convey and interpret meaning. Misunderstandings can easily arise if these cues are misinterpreted or absent, revealing the importance of pragmatic competence in online interactions (Media Theory, 2023).

## C. Sociocultural Theory: Language, Identity, and Online Discourse

Sociocultural theory posits that language is both a product and a shaper of social and cultural contexts. It emphasises the role of social interaction and cultural tools in the development of cognitive functions. In the field of digital activism, language serves as a vehicle for constructing and expressing identities, forming communities, and negotiating power dynamics. Online discourse allows individuals to craft and project identities through language choices, participation in specific communities, and alignment with particular causes. For instance, the use of specific hashtags, memes, or linguistic styles can signal membership in a movement or adherence to certain values. This identity construction is dynamic and context-dependent, influenced by the affordances of digital platforms and the interactions within them (Treré et al., 2017).

Language also plays a critical role in shaping collective identities within digital activism. Shared narratives, terminologies, and discursive practices foster a sense of belonging and solidarity among participants. These linguistic elements help define the boundaries of the community, delineate in-group and out-group members, and establish the movement's goals and values. However, the diversity of participants' cultural backgrounds and linguistic repertoires can lead to challenges in achieving mutual understanding and cohesion (Treré & Mattoni, 2015). Moreover, the global nature of digital activism necessitates tackling linguistic diversity and cultural differences. Activists must consider how language choices align with diverse audiences and how cultural norms influence the interpretation of messages. Failure to account for these factors can result in miscommunication, exclusion, or the reinforcement of existing power imbalances. Therefore, a sociocultural perspective is essential for understanding the dynamics of language use in digital activism and for developing inclusive and effective communication strategies.

## D. Interdisciplinary Approaches to Digital Communication

The study of digital communication, especially in the context of activism, necessitates an interdisciplinary approach that integrates insights from linguistics, sociology, media studies, political science, and information technology. Each of these disciplines contributes unique perspectives that help explain the dynamics of how people use digital tools to influence public discourse, organise communities, and promote change. From a linguistic perspective, the focus lies on how language is used to construct meaning, persuade audiences, and establish credibility online. Pragmatics, discourse analysis, and sociolinguistics offer tools for understanding how messages are crafted and interpreted within specific digital contexts. For example, hashtags like #EndSARS or #MeToo serve as both linguistic and cultural signifiers that embody collective sentiment and rally support for specific causes (George & Leidner, 2019).

Media studies contribute an understanding of the platforms themselves—their design, affordances, and limitations. The concept of the "architecture of participation" (Scholz, 2010) illustrates how certain platforms are more conducive to activism because they enable user-generated content, facilitate community building, and provide mechanisms for viral dissemination. At the same time, scholars also interrogate the role of algorithms, moderation policies, and platform governance, noting how these can both empower and constrain activist efforts (Garrett, 2006). Sociology offers insights into the dynamics of collective identity, power relations, and social change. It helps explain how online communities are formed, how social capital is built and maintained, and how digital networks replicate or challenge existing hierarchies. Concepts such as networked individualism and connective action (Bennett & Segerberg, 2012) reveal how individuals collaborate within loosely structured networks, often without centralised leadership.

Political science contributes to understanding the relationship between digital activism and governance. It examines how digital movements influence policy, mobilise voters, and challenge authoritarian regimes. In contexts where traditional forms of protest are suppressed, online activism becomes a vital avenue for dissent, making digital communication a powerful tool for democratisation and resistance (Yang, 2016). Finally, information technology provides the technical infrastructure and tools that enable digital activism. It addresses issues such as cybersecurity, data privacy, and the development of tools for anonymous communication and secure organising. The rise of encryption technologies, blockchain platforms, and decentralised networks reveals the ongoing intersection between technical innovation and political resistance.

These interdisciplinary perspectives emphasise the diverse nature of digital communication. Understanding digital activism, therefore, requires not only examining the messages being shared but also the technological, cultural, and political ecosystems in which they circulate. A comprehensive approach reveals the interplay between human agency and technological structure, enabling a deeper appreciation of both the potential and the limitations of digital activism.

## E. Review of Recent Scholarly Works

Recent scholarship on digital activism and pragmatics has expanded the field significantly, particularly in response to evolving technologies and shifting global political climates. Scholars have explored the intersection of digital discourse, identity, and social mobilisation, offering subtle analyses of how online communication shapes public consciousness and political engagement. Gerbaudo (2018) examined the performative aspect of digital activism, arguing that social media users engage in identity work through digital performances that align with political causes. His work demonstrates how online expressions, even those as brief as tweets, contribute to the broader spectacle of protest. Treré (2019) further explored digital activism in the Global South, emphasising the importance of context in understanding how technology is appropriated by activists facing economic, political, and linguistic barriers.

Kaun and Uldam (2018) critiqued the commercialisation of activism on corporate platforms, revealing the tension between visibility and vulnerability. They argued that activists must explore platform logics that reward sensationalism while risking surveillance or censorship. This duality complicates the sustainability and authenticity of online movements. Papacharissi (2020) introduced the concept of affective publics—networks of individuals connected through shared feelings and digital expression. Her research illustrated how emotional expressions online help build solidarity and shape political discourse, particularly in movements like #BlackLivesMatter and climate activism. This emotional dimension of digital activism ties closely with pragmatic strategies that appeal to empathy and shared experience.

Further contributions from Xie and Yus (2018) focused on digital pragmatics, exploring how users construct meaning in asynchronous, text-based environments. Their research shed light on how politeness, humour, irony, and inference function in digital spaces, emphasising the cultural variability of pragmatic norms. Similarly, Eslami (2020) investigated the role of pragmatic competence among university students in online interactions, finding that awareness of social norms significantly affects communication efficacy. Martínez-Flor (2019) revisited speech acts in online discourse, noting how advice, requests, and criticism are managed through a balance of directness and politeness. Her findings confirmed the importance of cultural sensitivity in digital spaces where tone and intent are often difficult to discern.

Recent work has also addressed the implications of language in algorithmic environments. Gillespie (2018) discussed how algorithms act as gatekeepers of visibility, shaping what content is amplified or suppressed. This dynamic affects not only what messages are seen but also how movements define themselves and frame their narratives. In turn, activists increasingly tailor their language to appeal to algorithmic preferences, using keywords, timing, and engagement strategies to maximise reach. Treré and Mattoni (2021) argued for a decolonial approach to digital activism, calling attention to the epistemic and linguistic injustices present in global digital discourse. Their work pointed to the dominance of English and Western-centric frameworks in online activism, urging scholars to examine how local languages and knowledge systems contribute to alternative activist epistemologies.

These recent contributions emphasise a shift towards a more subtle, critical understanding of digital activism—one that acknowledges the importance of language, emotion, and technological structure. Scholars continue to call for interdisciplinary, inclusive, and context-sensitive frameworks to address the challenges of contemporary digital movements.

## F. Rationale for Study

This chapter responds to a growing need for integrated perspectives on the relationship between language use, pragmatic strategies, and digital activism. While much has been written about the technical and political aspects of online activism, fewer studies address the central role that language and pragmatics play in shaping the success and inclusivity of these movements. Pragmatic competence influences not only how messages are interpreted but also how collective identities are negotiated and maintained across diverse cultural and linguistic backgrounds. Furthermore, this chapter addresses the socio-cultural challenges that limit participation in digital activism, such as linguistic exclusion, the digital divide, and algorithmic bias. This study aims to offer practical insights for activists, educators, and scholars through an exploration of how pragmatic strategies—such as politeness, contextual framing, and inference—enhance communication. Basically, the goal is to contribute to a more equitable and effective model of digital engagement, one that bridges cultural divides and amplifies marginalised voices.

## III. PRAGMATIC LANGUAGE STRATEGIES IN DIGITAL ACTIVISM

### A. Speech Acts in Digital Activism

Pragmatic language strategies hold significant importance in digital activism, especially when considered through the lens of speech acts. Philosophers such as J.L. Austin and John Searle have contributed foundational concepts in the study of pragmatics. Austin introduced the idea of performative utterances, where language doesn't just convey information but performs an action. For instance, statements like "I promise" or "I command" are performative because they enact what they state. Searle built on this idea by categorising speech acts into three primary types: locutionary acts (the utterance itself), illocutionary acts (the intended function of the utterance), and perlocutionary acts (the effect the utterance has on the listener). In the field of digital activism, speech acts are employed to mobilise support, express dissent, and build solidarity within online movements. A tweet, such as "We must unite against climate change!", serves as an illocutionary act that not only communicates urgency but also calls for collective action. This strategic use of language contributes to galvanising activists and shaping public discourse on social issues.

Illocutionary acts within digital activism can take various forms across social media platforms, revealing the dynamic nature of online communication. Activists frequently use directives, such as "Sign this petition!" or "Join our protest!" to rally individuals and encourage participation. These directives are specifically designed to provoke immediate responses, showcasing the power of language in driving action. In addition, expressive acts, which communicate the speaker's emotions or attitudes, play a crucial role in fostering community among activists. Statements like "We are in this together!" or "Your voice matters!" create a sense of belonging and collective identity, reinforcing shared objectives. Declarations of solidarity or commitment, such as "We stand with [cause]," further align individuals with broader movements, solidifying shared values and aspirations. As Eslami (2013) points out, choices made in online communication reflect not only linguistic considerations but also the socio-cultural context in which they arise. These pragmatic choices are central to shaping the narrative of digital activism, mobilising individuals, and nurturing a shared sense of purpose in confronting societal challenges.

### B. Politeness Strategies and Cultural Sensitivity

Politeness strategies play an essential role in digital activism, especially in encouraging persuasion and engagement across diverse audiences. In online environments, where messages can be easily misinterpreted, using polite language helps mitigate potential conflict and promotes cooperation among people with varying viewpoints. Employing politeness strategies—such as hedging, indirectness, and respectful addressing—allows activists to create a more inviting space for dialogue, which is crucial for persuasive communication. Martinez-Flor (2010) suggests that social norms significantly influence pragmatic behaviour, noting that an understanding of these norms enables activists to tailor their language effectively. Such tailored communication fosters participation, as individuals feel respected and valued, thereby enhancing their engagement with the movement's goals. Consequently, politeness does not only help facilitate cooperation but also strengthens a sense of community and solidarity among participants.

Several case studies showcase how politeness strategies contribute to the success of digital activism campaigns. For example, during the global climate strikes initiated by youth activists, social media posts often featured polite requests, such as "We kindly ask you to join us in making a difference." This approach appealed to a broad audience, fostering a sense of collective responsibility. Similarly, the #MeToo campaign utilised polite yet assertive language to encourage individuals to share their experiences without fear of judgement. These strategies helped create an inclusive space where voices could be amplified, demonstrating how politeness can increase both the effectiveness of communication and the overall impact of activism. Examining these successful campaigns reveals that strategically using polite language can significantly enhance engagement and attract greater support for a cause.

## C. Implicature and Inference in Online Messaging

The concepts of implicature and inference are critical for understanding the dynamics of activist messages in digital contexts. Context is essential, as it provides the necessary background for interpreting the intended meaning behind explicit statements. Activist messages frequently contain implicit meanings that depend heavily on shared cultural knowledge and situational awareness. For example, a tweet saying, "We need to talk about our future," may implicitly convey a sense of urgency about climate change, prompting followers to engage in the discussion without explicitly identifying the issue. Tatsuki and Houck (2010) stress the importance of inferring meaning from context, particularly in situations where direct communication may be less effective or suitable. The impact of such messages relies on the audience's ability to understand these implicit cues, influencing the reach and effectiveness of the activism campaign.

Examples of implicit messages in campaigns further reveal the importance of context in digital activism. In the "Black Lives Matter" movement, phrases like "I can't breathe" serve as potent implicatures, sparking a wider conversation about systemic racism and police brutality. These statements align within the context of societal injustices, drawing attention to the issue without detailing every aspect. Similarly, the phrase "Silence is complicity" suggests that inaction in the face of injustice supports the status quo. Eslami (2013) reveals how online communication shapes pragmatic decisions, indicating that activists often use implicit messages to engage their audience more effectively. The strategic deployment of implicature allows movements to communicate challenging ideas succinctly, fostering deeper connections and mobilising support for their causes. Thus, understanding the role of context, implicature, and inference is essential for comprehending the realities of digital activism.

## D. The Role of Context and Relevance Theory

Pragmatics plays a crucial role in shaping language use in activism, as it emphasises the context in which communication takes place and the various factors that influence meaning beyond the literal interpretation of words. Activism often relies on language to mobilise support, articulate grievances, and foster solidarity among individuals with shared goals. Grasping the pragmatic aspects of language enables activists to craft messages that align with their audiences, taking into account cultural backgrounds, social norms, and emotional responses. This subtle approach empowers activists to communicate more effectively, tailoring their language to fit specific contexts and thereby strengthening their persuasive power. The ability to explore the subtleties of language and meaning is particularly critical in digital activism, where messages can be rapidly disseminated and interpreted in diverse ways.

Moreover, pragmatics encompasses various speech acts used in activist communication, such as requests, commands, and declarations. These acts are not merely about conveying information but also about creating social realities and influencing behaviour. For example, when activists issue a call to action, the language used may not only inform but also inspire individuals to join the movement, revealing the intention behind the words. The effectiveness of these speech acts often depends on their appropriateness within the context and the relationships between the speaker and the audience. The use of strategies like politeness, indirectness, and assertiveness allows activists to frame their messages in ways that encourage participation and foster a sense of community among supporters. Understanding the pragmatic implications of these speech acts can equip activists to explore the dynamics of social interaction, making their campaigns more impactful.

Furthermore, pragmatics helps activists understand the role of power and identity in online activism. Language is a key tool for constructing and negotiating identities, and activists frequently use pragmatic strategies to assert their positions, challenge dominant narratives, and amplify marginalised voices. This interplay of power dynamics is particularly evident in online activism, where language can serve as both a tool of empowerment and a means of resistance against oppression. Activists must be mindful of how their language choices reinforce or challenge societal norms, shaping the perceptions of their causes. For example, inclusive language can foster solidarity across diverse groups, while exclusionary language may alienate potential allies. Critically engaging with the pragmatic aspects of language use enables activists to articulate their messages in ways that align with broader audiences, ultimately enhancing the effectiveness of their movements. In this sense, pragmatics is integral to the language of activism, facilitating meaningful communication that drives social change.

## E. Pragmatic Strategies in Multi-Lingual/Multi-Cultural Spaces

In multi-lingual and multi-cultural digital spaces, pragmatic strategies must be carefully employed to foster understanding and build solidarity. Digital activism often takes place in diverse online environments where participants come from various linguistic and cultural backgrounds. Consequently, activists must explore these differences, using language that is sensitive to the cultural norms and values of their audience. Pragmatic strategies, such as code-switching, accommodation, and careful consideration of cultural references, play an essential role in ensuring that messages are accessible and align with a wide range of people. In multilingual contexts, activists may use multiple languages or adapt their messaging to suit different linguistic groups, fostering inclusivity and broadening the reach of their campaigns.

One key strategy in multilingual spaces is code-switching, where activists alternate between languages or dialects depending on the context and audience. This technique not only ensures clarity but also signals solidarity with different linguistic groups. Additionally, accommodation involves adjusting one's language to match the communicative style of the audience, promoting engagement and reducing the risk of misunderstandings. Activists who are sensitive to cultural references and social norms are better positioned to create messages that align with diverse groups, avoiding potential pitfalls that could alienate people or derail the message. For instance, in campaigns addressing global social justice issues, activists might use culturally relevant symbols, metaphors, or historical references that hold significance for different communities, ensuring that the message is meaningful and impactful across cultural boundaries. Understanding and applying pragmatic strategies in multilingual and multicultural contexts allows digital activists to overcome linguistic barriers, foster inclusivity, and build a unified, global movement for change.

## IV. SOCIOCULTURAL CHALLENGES IN ONLINE MOVEMENTS

### A. Language Barriers and Inclusivity

Language barriers significantly affect the inclusivity and reach of online movements, often excluding non-native speakers or those who speak less widely known languages. Sorce and Dumitrica (2022) reveal how the predominance of global languages, such as English, can alienate individuals who are not fluent, making it harder for them to actively participate in digital activism. This issue is particularly prevalent in international movements where activists may expect a shared linguistic framework, unintentionally sidelining the voices of linguistic minorities. The result is a reduction in the diversity of perspectives that can influence activism, undermining the broad-based solidarity essential for the effectiveness of such movements. Furthermore, Dobrin (2020) notes that specific terms, such as hashtags, are often coined to define movements, creating a shared language that may be unintentionally inaccessible to speakers of other languages. When language becomes a gatekeeper, the movement risks excluding those who are most affected by the issues at hand, thus weakening the movement's inclusivity and its potential to create a truly global change.

Overcoming these language barriers is critical for enhancing the accessibility of online activism. One effective strategy involves the use of translation tools and multilingual content to cater to diverse linguistic groups. Vlavo (2017) suggests that incorporating multiple languages into activist communications can help broaden the reach of campaigns while simultaneously validating the identities and experiences of different communities. Additionally, using visual communication, such as infographics and videos with subtitles, can transcend language limitations, making the message more accessible. Mohammed (2019) argues that recognising linguistic diversity is key to inclusive activism; by adopting multilingual approaches, movements can create spaces where people from different cultural backgrounds feel empowered to participate. This approach not only broadens the scope of digital activism but also enriches the collective narrative by ensuring that various perspectives are included. The integration of these strategies would help to create a more inclusive and participatory online space, facilitating a collective, global response to social issues.

### B. Cultural Sensitivity and Representation

Cultural sensitivity plays an essential role in online movements, particularly when it comes to the representation of diverse communities. Stornaiuolo and Thomas (2017) assert that incorporating diverse cultural perspectives into digital activism strengthens the movement, offering a more subtle understanding of social issues.

Cultural representation can help activists challenge dominant narratives, ensuring that the voices of marginalized communities are heard and respected. However, cultural sensitivity also requires activists to be mindful of cultural appropriation, a risk that arises when activists adopt symbols or practices from cultures they do not fully understand. Karatzogianni, Miazhevich, and Denisova (2017) note that cultural appropriation can commodify the very traditions and identities that activists aim to support, diminishing the authenticity of the movement. When done incorrectly, the misrepresentation of cultures can alienate the very communities that activists seek to empower, reducing trust and hindering collaboration. Thus, it is vital for digital activists to engage with cultural practices and symbols with respect and awareness of their historical and social contexts.

To prevent cultural appropriation and ensure genuine representation, activists must establish authentic partnerships with the communities they aim to support. This includes listening to and amplifying the voices of those directly affected by the issues being addressed. Aguilar Forero and Cifuentes Álvarez (2019) stress the importance of activists educating themselves about the histories and cultural contexts of the communities they represent. Such knowledge can help avoid misrepresentation and foster an atmosphere of mutual respect. Furthermore, encouraging dialogue and collaboration with affected groups enables activists to create more inclusive and culturally sensitive advocacy strategies. This practice not only strengthens the credibility of the movement but also cultivates a sense of solidarity among diverse participants. Ultimately, cultural sensitivity is crucial for the success of digital activism, as it ensures that the movement remains authentic, inclusive, and truly representative of the issues it seeks to address.

## C. The Digital Divide and Access to Technology

The digital divide is a significant barrier to the full participation of certain groups in online activism. As noted by George and Leidner (2019), individuals from economically disadvantaged backgrounds often face challenges accessing the necessary technology and infrastructure to engage with digital platforms. This inequality can prevent these individuals from participating in online movements, thus reinforcing existing social inequalities. Additionally, Kaun and Uldam (2018) point out that digital literacy itself can be a hurdle, as not all individuals possess the skills required to explore the dynamics of online platforms effectively. As a result, movements that rely exclusively on digital tools risk excluding those who are not digitally literate or who lack reliable internet access. This digital exclusion undermines the core democratic principles of many activism efforts, preventing the voices of those most affected by social injustices from being heard and limiting the ability of these groups to mobilise for change.

Addressing the digital divide is crucial to ensure that online activism is inclusive and accessible to all. One strategy is to provide access to technology through community centres, public libraries, and internet hubs. These spaces can help individuals from underserved communities access the internet, thus enabling them to participate in digital activism. Furthermore, initiatives aimed at promoting digital literacy, such as workshops or online courses, can equip people with the skills needed to explore and contribute to online movements. Joyce (2010) advocates for a culture of digital literacy that goes beyond basic technical skills to include an understanding of how to engage meaningfully in online activism. Additionally, alternative communication methods, such as SMS campaigns or community radio, could provide viable platforms for those without internet access to participate in activism. These strategies not only facilitate participation but also ensure that the voices of marginalized groups are included in the broader conversation. Ultimately, bridging the digital divide is essential for fostering more equitable and representative online movements.

## D. Identity Politics and Online Anonymity

The intersection of identity politics and online anonymity presents both opportunities and challenges in digital activism. On one hand, the relative anonymity provided by online platforms can empower individuals to express their identities without fear of immediate retaliation. This anonymity allows people to speak out on issues such as race, gender, and sexuality, which might otherwise expose them to social, professional, or even physical risks. However, as Vlavo (2017) notes, this anonymity can also lead to the misrepresentation of identities and a lack of accountability. Without clear accountability, some individuals may engage in harmful behaviour, such as trolling or spreading misinformation, under the guise of anonymity. This can undermine the goals of digital activism, creating an environment where individuals are unable to trust one another and thus reducing the movement's efficacy.

At the same time, identity politics in online spaces often leads to challenging and sometimes contradictory discussions around the authenticity of voices and experiences. As revealed by Mohammed (2019), digital platforms can offer a space for individuals to engage in intersectional activism, where they explore how various aspects of their identity, such as race, gender, and class, intersect and influence their experiences of injustice. However, these discussions can also spark tensions, especially when individuals or groups contest whose voices and experiences should be prioritised. The online anonymity that allows people to speak freely can sometimes encourage the prioritisation of individual experiences over collective goals, making it challenging to foster unity within the movement. To mitigate these challenges, digital activists must work to create spaces where open dialogue and accountability are valued. This involves balancing the need for anonymity with the need for transparency and trust among participants, ultimately ensuring that identity politics enrich the movement rather than fragmenting it.

In sum, addressing the socio-cultural challenges in online activism is vital to ensuring that these movements remain inclusive, representative, and effective. Overcoming language barriers, fostering cultural sensitivity, bridging the digital divide, and tackling the dynamics of identity politics and online anonymity are all essential tasks for digital activists. Addressing these challenges enables activists to ensure that their movements are truly global and inclusive, allowing diverse voices to contribute to collective efforts for social change. These considerations emphasise the importance of culture and identity in shaping digital activism and reveal the need for thoughtful, inclusive strategies in online movements.

## V. THE ROLE OF DIGITAL LANGUAGE TECHNOLOGIES

### A. Emojis, Memes, GIFs: Semiotic Expansion in Activist Discourse

The advent of emojis, memes, and GIFs has significantly expanded the semiotic possibilities in digital activism, enabling a more dynamic and expressive form of communication. These visual and semiotic icons serve as powerful tools in online discourse, enhancing the emotional and symbolic impact of activism. Emojis, for example, offer a condensed way to convey challenging emotions, solidarity, and messages within a compact visual form. According to Sorce and Dumitrica (2022), the use of emojis in digital activism has the potential to transcend linguistic barriers, making it easier for people from different cultural backgrounds to understand and engage with the messages being communicated. Emojis can serve to reinforce hashtags, drawing attention to specific issues while providing an emotional context that words alone may fail to convey. For instance, the use of the raised fist emoji in solidarity movements like #BlackLivesMatter communicates both defiance and empowerment, enriching the visual language of protest and making it more accessible to a global audience. Memes, similarly, carry a heavy cultural load, often embedding political and social commentary into humour, which can increase the viral potential of activism.

Memes and GIFs have also become important tools in spreading activist messages, as they allow for a humorous, often irreverent way of critiquing social issues. According to Vlavo (2017), these elements of digital language allow for the subversion of mainstream narratives and are particularly effective in targeting younger audiences. Memes and GIFs are shared widely on social media platforms, creating a ripple effect that magnifies the reach of the message. Their visual nature also aids in quick comprehension, allowing users to engage with challenging political issues in an easily digestible format. Memes, often crafted in response to news events or trending topics, can rapidly shape public discourse by making serious topics more relatable and approachable. This capacity for semiotic expansion, wherein images, symbols, and text converge, enhances the reach of digital activism and fosters a deeper connection with audiences, particularly in the context of movements that require mass mobilisation and engagement. The rise of such visual forms of communication signifies a shift towards more informal, yet highly potent, methods of advocacy that align across cultural and linguistic divides.

## B. Hashtag Activism: Meaning Construction and Message Amplification

Hashtag activism represents a significant shift in how social movements construct meaning and amplify their messages. According to Dobrin (2020), hashtags have become powerful linguistic tools that serve both as a rallying cry for solidarity and as a means to construct shared identities within digital movements. Hashtags not only help to categorise content but also create a form of digital solidarity, allowing activists to unify under a common banner. The simple act of attaching a hashtag to a post can signify an individual's support for a cause while also contributing to a broader, collective narrative. For example, the #MeToo movement, which gained international traction through the use of the hashtag, was able to build a shared discourse around sexual harassment and assault. The hashtag acted as a catalyst, creating a space where people could publicly discuss their experiences and draw attention to widespread social issues, thereby constructing new meanings around gender equality and sexual violence.

Moreover, hashtags are vital in amplifying messages within social media algorithms. According to Sorce and Dumitrica (2022), hashtags increase the visibility of content, allowing activists to reach wider audiences beyond their immediate networks. This amplification effect is particularly crucial in the digital age, where information is rapidly disseminated, and messages can be easily lost in the vast expanse of online content. Hashtags allow digital movements to maintain momentum by categorising posts and creating searchable, accessible content. They also serve as a form of digital indexing, which enables users to locate and engage with specific issues more efficiently. As a result, hashtag activism not only helps in the construction of meaning but also in the strategic visibility of campaigns, making it easier for individuals to connect with causes and participate in larger, global discussions. The role of hashtags in amplifying messages reveals their potential to mobilise individuals on a massive scale, transforming isolated acts of resistance into collective, coordinated efforts for change.

## C. Algorithmic Influence on Message Visibility and Virality

The algorithmic structures of social media platforms have a critical influence on the visibility and virality of activist messages. Algorithms, which determine which content appears in a user's feed, often prioritise content based on engagement metrics such as likes, shares, and comments. As George and Leidner (2019) point out, these algorithms tend to favour sensational or emotionally charged content, often elevating messages that are more likely to generate high engagement. In the context of digital activism, this can be both beneficial and problematic. On one hand, the algorithmic amplification of content can help movements gain wider visibility, bringing attention to social justice issues that may have been previously overlooked. Movements such as #BlackLivesMatter and #MeToo have benefited from algorithmic visibility, with high engagement leading to greater mainstream awareness of racial injustice and sexual harassment. However, algorithms are not neutral; they can also distort the reach of messages by promoting content that conforms to certain emotional or sensational patterns rather than substantive discussions. This can lead to oversimplification or the prioritisation of viral content that may not always align with the core goals of activism.

Moreover, the manipulation of algorithms by individuals or groups with political interests can impact the trajectory of online movements. As Kaun and Uldam (2018) observe, social media algorithms are often shaped by corporate interests that may not align with the values of grassroots movements. This creates a tension between the need for visibility and the risk of co-option or dilution of activist messages. In this sense, activists must explore the dynamics of algorithmic influence, using strategies such as timing, engagement, and hashtag trends to maximise the impact of their messages while remaining aware of the ways in which their content may be filtered or obscured. As a result, understanding the algorithmic dynamics of social media platforms has become an essential skill for digital activists who seek to maintain control over their narratives and ensure that their messages reach the widest possible audience without being co-opted or lost in the noise of online discourse.

## D. Case Examples of Language-Related Tech Tools in Movements (#BLM, #EndSARS, #MeToo)

Case studies of language-related tech tools in prominent social movements provide insight into the ways digital language technologies shape the course of activism. The #BlackLivesMatter (BLM) movement, for instance, has effectively harnessed the power of hashtags, emojis, and memes to amplify its message of racial justice. The hashtag #BlackLivesMatter, created in 2013, quickly became a global symbol of resistance against police violence and systemic racism. Through the use of strategic language and digital tools, BLM activists have been able to create a shared discourse around racial inequality, challenging traditional media representations and drawing attention to issues that disproportionately affect Black communities. Memes and GIFs featuring powerful images of resistance, such as those depicting protests and police brutality, have also been integral in communicating the emotional and political stakes of the movement. Additionally, the use of the raised fist emoji has become an iconic symbol of solidarity, further expanding the visual vocabulary of the movement. These tools not only reinforce the central message of racial justice but also enable activists to engage a wide and diverse audience, making the movement more accessible and relatable.

Similarly, the #EndSARS movement in Nigeria, which called for the disbandment of the Special Anti-Robbery Squad (SARS) due to widespread allegations of police brutality, relied heavily on digital language technologies to mobilise support and amplify its message. Hashtags such as #EndSARS and #EndPoliceBrutality served as rallying cries for protesters, while the use of emojis and memes helped convey the emotional weight of the issue. The hashtag #EndSARS, for instance, quickly gained traction on social media platforms, becoming a focal point for discussions about police violence and governance in Nigeria. The movement also utilised videos, memes, and GIFs to capture police brutality and protest actions, creating a visual narrative that alignd with both local and international audiences. These digital tools played a crucial role in circumventing traditional media censorship, allowing activists to bypass state control and disseminate their message to a global audience. Through the strategic use of hashtags and visual content, the #EndSARS movement was able to build a powerful global coalition calling for justice and reform.

The #MeToo movement, which gained global attention in 2017, also leveraged digital language technologies to amplify its message about sexual harassment and assault. The use of the #MeToo hashtag allowed individuals to share their personal experiences, creating a collective narrative around the pervasive nature of gender-based violence. The hashtag quickly went viral, and through its widespread use, it sparked global conversations about the need for systemic change in how sexual harassment is addressed in various industries. In addition to the hashtag, the movement utilised memes, GIFs, and emojis to reinforce messages of solidarity and empowerment, making the campaign more relatable and engaging. These tools were instrumental in shifting public discourse, encouraging individuals to speak out against abuse and demand accountability. The combination of hashtags, visual media, and emotional symbols played a crucial role in the success of the #MeToo movement, demonstrating the power of digital language technologies in shaping contemporary activism.

In sum, the role of digital language technologies in online activism cannot be overstated. Emojis, memes, GIFs, and hashtags have all contributed to the semiotic expansion of activist discourse, enabling activists to communicate challenging ideas in more accessible, relatable, and impactful ways. The use of algorithms to amplify messages and enhance visibility further emphasises the importance of understanding the digital dynamics of social media. Case examples from movements such as #BlackLivesMatter, #EndSARS, and #MeToo illustrate the practical application of these digital tools in promoting social change. As digital activism continues to evolve, the interplay between language, technology, and social movements will remain a key factor in shaping the future of global activism.

## VI. CASE STUDIES IN DIGITAL ACTIVISM

### A. #BlackLivesMatter

#### 1. Pragmatic Strategies Used in Messaging

The #BlackLivesMatter movement, which emerged in response to systemic racism and police violence against Black individuals, utilized a variety of pragmatic language strategies to convey its message. Speech acts such as demands for justice, calls to action, and expressions of solidarity became central to the movement's messaging, both online and offline. The hashtag "#BlackLivesMatter" itself served as a powerful illocutionary act, asserting the dignity and humanity of Black lives in a political and social context that often devalues them. This performative aspect of language in activism, as Sorce and Dumitrica (2022) explain, helps reinforce the urgency of social change by framing the message as a non-negotiable assertion rather than a mere request. Additionally, the movement utilized politeness strategies to engage a wider audience, crafting messages that appealed to empathy and inclusivity, even while discussing challenging and often polarizing issues. Through implicit messages, such as coded language and indirect references to historical injustices, the movement managed to invoke shared cultural memories and values, enhancing its appeal across various social and racial groups.

#### 2. Socio-Cultural Challenges Faced and Overcome

The socio-cultural challenges faced by the #BlackLivesMatter movement were significant. The movement needed to overcome entrenched racial biases, systemic inequalities, and a political climate that often dismissed their concerns as overblown or divisive. One of the key challenges was the linguistic framing of "Black

Lives Matter" as opposed to "All Lives Matter," with opponents of the movement attempting to dilute its message by suggesting the latter. The pragmatic strategy of carefully framing the movement's core message was crucial in maintaining its focus and legitimacy. According to Vlavo (2017), digital activism must explore these sociocultural dynamics, ensuring that messages remain clear, focused, and inclusive despite opposition. The #BlackLivesMatter movement successfully addressed these challenges by using language that not only focused on the immediate issues of police brutality but also spoke to the larger, ongoing struggle for racial equality. Incorporating speech acts that conveyed both solidarity and resistance allowed the movement to maintain its relevance and strengthen its resolve in the face of opposition.

## B. #MeToo Movement

### 1. Role of Language in Shaping Collective Identity

The #MeToo movement, which began as a campaign against sexual harassment and assault, relied heavily on language to shape a collective identity among survivors and allies. The phrase "Me Too" became an illocutionary act of solidarity and shared experience, as survivors of sexual violence came forward to share their stories, often for the first time. The simple but powerful utterance of "Me Too" transformed individual experiences of trauma into a collective narrative of resistance and empowerment. As Dobrin (2020) notes, digital activism often relies on symbolic language to create a shared sense of identity among participants, and in the case of #MeToo, this symbolic language helped build a global community of survivors who felt empowered to break their silence. The movement also utilized inclusive and accessible language to ensure that its message reached as many people as possible, transcending cultural and national boundaries to create a universal dialogue about sexual violence.

### 2. Responses to Socio-Cultural Challenges Through Language

The #MeToo movement faced several socio-cultural challenges, including victim-blaming, the stigmatization of survivors, and systemic power imbalances that made it difficult for victims to speak out. To address these challenges, the movement employed pragmatic strategies that focused on reframing the narrative around sexual violence. Utilizing speech acts that emphasized empowerment and resilience, the movement challenged existing socio-cultural norms that frequently silence victims. As Aguilar Forero and Cifuentes Álvarez (2019) point out, digital activism can be a powerful tool for challenging entrenched social hierarchies by creating new spaces for marginalized voices. In the case of #MeToo, the movement used language not only to share individual stories but also to demand systemic change, calling for greater accountability in workplaces, schools, and other institutions. The movement also responded to critiques of exclusion by expanding its messaging to address issues of intersectionality, ensuring that the voices of women of colour, LGBTQ+ individuals, and other marginalized groups were included in the conversation.

## C. #EndSARS Campaign

### 1. Pragmatic Approaches in Communication Strategies

The #EndSARS campaign in Nigeria, which aimed to end police brutality and hold the Special Anti-Robbery Squad (SARS) accountable for human rights abuses, utilized various pragmatic approaches in its communication strategies. Like #Black-LivesMatter and #MeToo, the #EndSARS movement used speech acts such as demands for justice, calls for systemic reform, and expressions of solidarity to communicate its goals. However, what set #EndSARS apart was its use of local languages and cultural references, which allowed it to align more deeply with Nigerian audiences. As Karatzogianni, Miazhevich, and Denisova (2017) explain, digital activism is most effective when it adapts to the cultural and linguistic norms of its target audience, and #EndSARS did this by incorporating Nigerian Pidgin and traditional proverbs into its messaging. This use of culturally relevant language helped galvanize a diverse coalition of Nigerians, from youth activists to older generations, ensuring that the message was accessible and compelling to a wide audience.

### 2. Addressing Local Socio-cultural Issues in a Global Context

While #EndSARS was primarily focused on Nigerian issues, it also gained global attention, with activists and supporters from around the world lending their voices to the cause. This created a unique set of socio-cultural challenges, as the movement had to explore both local and global expectations. On one hand, the use of local languages and references helped to ensure that the movement remained grounded in Nigerian realities. On the other hand, the movement also needed to communicate its message in ways that would align with international audiences. Mohammed (2019) emphasizes the importance of centering marginalized voices in activist work, and #EndSARS achieved this by ensuring that the stories of Nigerian victims of police brutality were front and center in its messaging. Employing speech acts that appealed to universal values of justice and human rights allowed the movement to bridge the gap between local concerns and global solidarity, effectively advocating for reform both in Nigeria and internationally. The pragmatic strategies employed by #EndSARS, therefore, demonstrate the power of language to address challenging socio-cultural challenges in both local and global contexts.

## VII. IMPLICATIONS FOR DIGITAL ACTIVISM IN COOPERATIVE MOVEMENTS

### A. Online Mobilisation of Co-Operative and Grassroots Movements

The advent of digital technologies has significantly transformed the ways in which co-operative and grassroots movements operate, particularly in terms of mobilisation and advocacy. Online platforms, social media, and digital communication tools have allowed grassroots organisations to reach wider audiences and engage in collective action in unprecedented ways. For co-operatives, the digital space provides an avenue for visibility, outreach, and collaboration that was previously unavailable. According to Munoz and Navas (2020), online mobilisation has become a key tool for grassroots movements seeking to address social issues, raise awareness, and initiate change. The use of digital platforms such as Facebook, Twitter, and Instagram has allowed these movements to build online communities, mobilise resources, and activate supporters on a large scale. For example, co-operatives focused on environmental sustainability can use social media to share their mission, engage with potential members, and advocate for policies that align with their goals. These digital tools enable rapid communication, allowing co-operatives to react swiftly to emerging issues and capitalise on the viral potential of social media.

Moreover, digital mobilisation has facilitated the creation of global networks that can strengthen the impact of local and regional co-operatives. Through the use of online petitions, crowdfunding platforms, and social media campaigns, co-operatives can extend their reach beyond geographical boundaries. As Smith and Jansson (2019) note, online mobilisation tools have enabled co-operatives to form transnational alliances that amplify their advocacy efforts. For instance, a cooperative focused on fair trade can mobilise support from consumers across the globe who are interested in ethical purchasing practices. The collective power generated through these digital tools enhances the ability of co-operatives to advocate for policy change, engage in consumer education, and promote social justice initiatives. This global dimension of digital mobilisation not only increases the visibility of co-operatives but also strengthens their collective voice in addressing challenging socio-economic issues. Furthermore, the interactivity offered by digital platforms fosters greater collaboration between co-operatives, allowing them to share knowledge, resources, and strategies for success.

## B. Sociocultural Constraints in Digital Co-Operative Advocacy

While the digital field offers vast opportunities for mobilisation, it also presents unique sociocultural challenges for co-operative movements, particularly those in developing countries or marginalised communities. The digital divide, which refers to the unequal access to digital technologies and the internet, remains a significant barrier for many co-operatives. As noted by Johnson and Williams (2018), in rural areas or low-income communities, internet access is often limited, and the digital literacy required to effectively engage with online platforms is lacking. For co-operatives that depend on local engagement and community-based practices, this digital gap can impede their ability to connect with members and potential supporters. The digital divide exacerbates existing inequalities, particularly when co-operatives seek to advocate for socio-economic change in areas where access to technology is minimal or non-existent. Without access to digital tools, these movements struggle to gain traction in an increasingly online world where much of the public discourse and activism take place.

Cultural factors also play a critical role in shaping the effectiveness of digital co-operative advocacy. In many regions, especially in non-Western societies, digital activism may clash with traditional practices and values. As Roberts and Taylor (2020) argue, digital advocacy that is rooted in individualism or Western values may not align with communities where collective action and community-based decision-making are central. In these contexts, co-operative movements may face resistance or scepticism towards online mobilisation efforts that prioritise individual engagement over collective action. Additionally, the language of digital activism, often characterised by hashtags, emojis, and memes, may not always align with the linguistic and cultural norms of grassroots movements. The challenge, therefore, lies in adapting digital tools and strategies to fit the cultural and social dynamics of different communities. This requires an understanding of local values, norms, and practices, as well as the need to incorporate community-led, bottom-up approaches in digital co-operative advocacy. Digital activists must also recognise that not all co-operatives have the same access to the resources required for effective online mobilisation, including the financial means to hire digital experts or the time needed to manage online campaigns.

## C. Educational and Entrepreneurial Co-operatives in the Digital Era

In the digital age, educational and entrepreneurial co-operatives have found new avenues for growth and development through digital technologies. These co-operatives, which often focus on providing services, resources, and training to their members, are increasingly using digital platforms to reach broader audiences, offer online courses, and create virtual spaces for collaboration. As Gupta and Patel (2021) note, educational co-operatives that operate in fields such as vocational training, community education, and entrepreneurship can use the internet to offer remote learning opportunities, webinars, and digital resources that support skill development. These online platforms provide an opportunity for co-operatives to scale their offerings and attract members who may not have previously had access to in-person training sessions. Through the creation of online communities, educational co-operatives can engage in peer-to-peer learning, share resources, and collaborate on projects in ways that were not possible before the rise of digital technologies.

The entrepreneurial potential of co-operatives has also been enhanced by digital tools, which facilitate online business ventures, e-commerce platforms, and digital marketing strategies. According to Hossain and Rahman (2020), co-operatives that are involved in small-scale production or service provision can use the internet to reach global markets, create online shops, and expand their customer base. For example, a cooperative producing handmade crafts or organic food products can utilise social media platforms like Instagram or Etsy to sell their products directly to consumers, bypassing traditional intermediaries. Furthermore, digital technologies provide co-operatives with access to tools for market research, customer feedback, and product development, which are crucial for growing a sustainable business. In this sense, the digital era offers entrepreneurial co-operatives the tools they need to compete in the global marketplace while maintaining their cooperative principles of shared ownership, democratic governance, and community empowerment.

However, the integration of digital technologies into educational and entrepreneurial co-operatives also presents challenges. As Barnett and Lee (2022) argue, there is a risk that digital tools may exacerbate inequalities within co-operatives, particularly when certain members or communities lack the necessary skills or access to participate fully. For example, while digital platforms provide opportunities for expanding educational reach, they may also alienate members who are not digitally literate or do not have access to reliable internet connections. Moreover, entrepreneurial co-operatives may struggle to compete with larger, more established companies that have greater financial resources and access to sophisticated digital marketing tools. In this context, co-operatives must ensure that their use of digital technologies is inclusive and equitable, providing training and support to members who may be less familiar with these tools. Additionally, entrepreneurial co-operatives must adopt a cooperative business model that balances profit-making with social and environmental goals, ensuring that their digital ventures do not undermine their ethical commitments.

Thus, the digital era offers both opportunities and challenges for co-operative and grassroots movements. While online mobilisation has enabled co-operatives to expand their reach and visibility, sociocultural constraints such as the digital divide and cultural barriers must be addressed in order to ensure that these movements remain inclusive and relevant. Educational and entrepreneurial co-operatives have benefitted from digital technologies, which allow them to expand their offerings and engage with a global audience. However, these advances must be accompanied by a recognition of the challenges that come with digital inclusion, ensuring that all members can fully participate in the digital context. As co-operatives continue to explore the digital era, it will be essential for them to balance the potential of digital tools with their core values of solidarity, equality, and mutual aid.

## VIII. IMPLICATIONS FOR FUTURE RESEARCH

### A. Integration of Artificial Intelligence and Machine Learning in Activism Language

The integration of artificial intelligence (AI) and machine learning (ML) into the analysis and development of activism language presents an exciting frontier for future research. As activists increasingly leverage digital platforms, the use of sophisticated AI tools to analyse linguistic patterns, trends, and sentiment in activist discourse could provide valuable insights into how messages align with different audiences. AI and ML technologies have already demonstrated their potential in analysing vast amounts of data from social media, online petitions, and other digital content. Future research could focus on how these technologies can be used to understand and predict the impact of particular phrases, hashtags, or memes on public opinion, helping activists refine their messages and outreach strategies. Utilising AI-driven analysis allows activists to more effectively tailor their language to diverse audience groups, thereby improving engagement and mobilisation efforts.

Moreover, the role of AI in shaping the content of activist messages could open new possibilities for the creation of persuasive narratives and impactful campaigns. AI-driven tools like natural language processing (NLP) can be used to generate content that is contextually relevant and emotionally resonant. This could be particularly useful in movements that rely heavily on emotional appeal and persuasion, such as those related to social justice or human rights. For example, AI could assist activists in crafting compelling narratives based on an analysis of trending topics, public sentiments, and the language used in successful campaigns. Machine learning algorithms could identify the linguistic features that have the most potential for generating empathy and solidarity, enabling activists to enhance the effectiveness of their messaging. As such, future research could explore the ethical considerations of using AI in activism, particularly regarding issues of bias, manipulation, and the potential for AI-generated content to unintentionally perpetuate harmful stereotypes or misinformation.

## B. Expanding Semiotic and Pragmatic Research into Emojis, Memes, and Visual Icons

One of the most significant developments in the language of digital activism has been the use of semiotic resources such as emojis, memes, and other visual icons. These forms of communication transcend traditional language barriers, allowing activists to express challenging ideas and emotions in a highly condensed and visually appealing format. Emojis, in particular, have become a central feature of online activism, allowing users to communicate solidarity, protest, and empathy in ways that are easily shareable and accessible across diverse social media platforms. Future research could delve deeper into the semiotic and pragmatic functions of these visual elements, exploring how they complement or subvert traditional linguistic forms in activist discourse. Scholars could investigate how emojis, memes, and other icons are not merely symbols but actively shape the meaning of activist messages, influencing the way they are perceived and interpreted by different audiences.

Research could also explore the evolution of visual communication within the context of activism, examining how memes and emojis have become vehicles for cultural commentary and political critique. Unlike traditional text-based activism, which often relies on linear narrative structures, memes and emojis can convey layered meanings in a fragmented, often humorous manner. This mode of communication may offer activists the opportunity to reach younger, digitally native audiences who are more accustomed to visual and digital forms of communication. Future studies could investigate how the pragmatics of memes and emojis vary across different social, political, and cultural contexts, identifying the ways in which these symbols gain power and significance within specific activist movements. Additionally, research could examine how these visual forms of communication contribute to the construction of collective identity within digital spaces, helping to strengthen community ties and mobilise supporters in pursuit of shared goals.

## C. Need for Localized Digital Communication Studies in the Global South

While much of the research on digital activism has focused on Western contexts, there is a growing need for localized studies that focus on the Global South. Activism in the Global South often operates within unique socio-political and cultural contexts that differ significantly from those in more developed nations. Future research should address the specific challenges faced by activists in these regions, including issues related to digital literacy, access to technology, and the political environment in which online activism takes place. For example, many activists in the Global South rely on mobile platforms as their primary means of engagement due to limited access to desktop computers or high-speed internet. Understanding the dynamics of mobile-based activism in these regions could help scholars and practitioners design more effective digital campaigns tailored to local conditions. Research could also explore how activists in the Global South explore digital spaces that may be heavily surveilled or censored by authoritarian regimes, uncovering strategies for resistance and subversion.

Furthermore, localized studies could address the linguistic and cultural variations in digital activism. While Western activists often use English as a lingua franca in digital spaces, activists in the Global South may rely on local languages, dialects, and idioms that carry specific cultural connotations. This reveals the importance of understanding the pragmatics of language use within different linguistic communities and how meaning is negotiated within these contexts. Future research could explore the role of localised language and digital symbols in fostering activism in the Global South, examining how regional movements use their own unique semiotic resources to engage audiences and communicate their messages. Such studies would contribute to a more subtle understanding of global digital activism, emphasising the need for context-specific strategies that account for local realities, resources, and cultural norms.

## D. The Impact of Digital Inequality on Activism in the Global South

One of the most pressing issues for activists in the Global South is the digital divide, which limits access to digital technologies and the internet. While digital activism offers new avenues for mobilisation, the reality is that many individuals in developing countries face significant barriers to participating in online movements. These barriers include limited access to reliable internet, high costs associated with digital devices, and a lack of digital literacy among certain populations. Research in this area could focus on how these inequalities affect the ability of grassroots movements in the Global South to fully participate in the digital public sphere. Understanding the impact of digital inequality on activism could shed light on the limitations of online mobilisation in these regions and inform the development of more inclusive strategies that bridge the gap between the digitally connected and disconnected.

Future research could also investigate how digital inequality intersects with other forms of social, economic, and political marginalisation in the Global South. For instance, women, rural communities, and ethnic minorities may face compounded challenges in accessing digital tools, thereby limiting their ability to engage in online activism. Studies could explore the ways in which these groups are excluded from digital platforms and the implications this has for the inclusivity and diversity of online movements. Additionally, research could examine how digital advocacy efforts can be made more accessible to these underserved populations, perhaps by leveraging low-tech solutions or community-based initiatives that promote digital literacy. As such, addressing digital inequality should be a central focus of future research on activism in the Global South, ensuring that all voices have the opportunity to be heard in the digital age.

## E. Cultural and Linguistic Diversification in Global Digital Movements

As digital activism continues to grow globally, there is a pressing need for research that explores how cultural and linguistic diversity shapes online movements. In many cases, global digital campaigns are led by actors from specific cultural contexts, often prioritising Western ideals and languages, which can marginalise non-Western perspectives. Future research should examine how activists from diverse cultural backgrounds utilise digital platforms to promote their causes while maintaining cultural authenticity and relevance. For example, how do non-Western movements adapt global digital tools and platforms to fit their local needs and cultural norms? How do they explore the dynamics of multilingualism in online spaces, where language barriers can hinder the effectiveness of cross-cultural communication? Investigating these issues would provide insights into the ways in which global movements can become more inclusive, ensuring that digital activism reflects the diverse cultural and linguistic realities of all participants.

Moreover, research could focus on the role of local languages in the success of digital campaigns. While English dominates many digital spaces, activists in non-English-speaking regions often use their native languages to engage with their communities, ensuring that their messages align on a deeper level. Research could explore how linguistic choices influence the success of digital movements, examining the subtleties of language use, translation issues, and the importance of preserving local dialects in online activism. This area of study could also include an exploration of how language shapes collective identity within movements, as activists use language not just to communicate messages but to assert cultural and political power. Such research would contribute to a more equitable understanding of digital activism that embraces linguistic diversity and cultural specificity in its strategies and goals.

## VII. CONCLUSION

The findings of this research reveal the challenging interplay between language, culture, and technology in the context of online activism. Digital platforms have become crucial spaces for activism, offering opportunities for individuals to engage in collective action and voice their concerns on a global scale. The use of language, both verbal and visual, plays a crucial role in shaping activist movements. Language, through the strategic use of hashtags, emojis, memes, and other digital symbols, allows activists to craft messages that align with diverse audiences. This linguistic and semiotic expansion facilitates the construction of collective identities, enabling movements to transcend geographical boundaries and unite people from various cultural contexts around shared causes. However, challenges such as language barriers, digital inequality, and cultural sensitivity remain significant obstacles to the inclusivity and effectiveness of these movements. These challenges reveal the importance of a subtle understanding of the sociocultural dynamics that shape digital activism.

In terms of contributions to theory and practice, this research emphasises the importance of integrating sociocultural theories into the study of digital activism. It illustrates how the online space functions as a site where identities, cultural values, and power dynamics are negotiated and contested. The role of language as both a tool for mobilisation and a marker of collective identity has been explored, offering valuable insights into how activists craft messages that align with the values of their target audiences. This research contributes to the growing body of literature on the pragmatics of digital communication, particularly in the context of activism. It also reveals the need for a more inclusive approach to digital activism, one that takes into account the linguistic, cultural, and technological barriers that many groups face. From a practical standpoint, the findings suggest that activists should employ strategies that incorporate multilingual and culturally sensitive content to reach a wider audience. Additionally, they should be mindful of the digital divide, ensuring that their campaigns are accessible to those who may lack the necessary technological resources.

The evolving nature of pragmatic strategies in online activism reflects the rapid advancements in digital technologies and the changing dynamics of global social movements. As new communication tools emerge, activists continuously adapt their strategies to effectively engage their audiences and explore the dynamics of digital platforms. The use of AI, machine learning, and other technological advancements will likely shape the future of online activism, enabling activists to refine their messages and enhance their reach. Furthermore, as the world becomes increasingly interconnected, the need for cross-cultural collaboration in digital activism will grow. Activists will need to find innovative ways to address the challenges of language, cultural sensitivity, and digital access in order to foster more inclusive and impactful movements. Ultimately, the study of pragmatic strategies in online activism is an ongoing process that will continue to evolve as new technologies and social issues emerge, requiring scholars and practitioners to remain responsive to the changing context of digital activism.

## REFERENCES


Aguilar Forero, N., & Cifuentes Álvarez, G. A. (2019). Education, activism and digital technologies: A systematic review. *Education in the Knowledge Society, 20*, 1–14. DOI: 10.14201/eks2019_20_a14

Barnett, S., & Lee, S. (2022). Digital inclusion and co-operatives in the 21st century. *Journal of Co-operative Studies, 40*(1), 45–59.

Bennett, W. L., & Segerberg, A. (2012). The logic of connective action. *Information Communication and Society, 15*(5), 739–768. DOI: 10.1080/1369118X.2012.670661

Dobrin, D. (2020). The hashtag in digital activism: A cultural revolution. *Journal of Cultural Analysis and Social Change, 5*(1), 3–14. DOI: 10.20897/jcasc/8298

Dobrin, S. (2020). Hashtag activism: Exploring digital discourse and social change. *Journal of Digital Activism, 12*(3), 122–135.

Encyclopaedia Britannica. (2025). *Digital activism*. https://www.britannica.com

Eslami, Z. R. (2013). Online communication and students' pragmatic choices in English. *Lodz Papers in Pragmatics, 9*(1), 71–92. DOI: 10.1515/lpp-2013-0005

Eslami, Z. R. (2020). Pragmatic competence in online learning environments. *Intercultural Pragmatics, 17*(2), 245–264.

Garrett, R. K. (2006). Protest in an information society: A review of literature on social movements and new ICTs. *Information Communication and Society, 9*(2), 202–224. DOI: 10.1080/13691180600630773

George, D., & Leidner, B. (2019). The algorithmic impact on digital activism: Visibility, virality, and influence. *Digital Media Studies, 15*(4), 98–110.

George, J. F., & Leidner, D. E. (2019). Digital activism and its effectiveness. *The Journal of Strategic Information Systems, 28*(4), 1–13.

George, J. J., & Leidner, D. E. (2019). From clicktivism to hacktivism: Understanding digital activism. [page numbers missing]. *Information and Organization, 29*(3), 100249. DOI: 10.1016/j.infoandorg.2019.04.001

Gerbaudo, P. (2017). From cyber-autonomism to cyber-populism: An ideological history of digital activism. *TripleC, 15*(2), 478–491. DOI: 10.31269/triplec.v15i2.773

Gerbaudo, P. (2018). *The digital party: Political organisation and online democracy*. Pluto Press. DOI: 10.2307/j.ctv86dg2g

Gillespie, T. (2018). *Custodians of the internet: Platforms, content moderation, and the hidden decisions that shape social media*. Yale University Press.

González-Bailón, S., Borge-Holthoefer, J., Rivero, A., & Moreno, Y. (2011). The dynamics of protest recruitment through an online network. *Scientific Reports, 1*(1), 197. DOI: 10.1038/srep00197 PMID: 22355712

Gupta, R., & Patel, M. (2021). Digital platforms for educational co-operatives: Opportunities and challenges. *Journal of Cooperative Education, 12*(3), 104–118.

Hossain, M., & Rahman, M. (2020). Entrepreneurial co-operatives in the digital era: A new paradigm for social enterprises. *Social Business, 10*(2), 88–101.

Ishihara, N., & Cohen, A. D. (2010). *Teaching and learning pragmatics: Where language and culture meet*. Longman.

Jegede, O. O.Olusegun Oladele Jegede. (2024). Pragmatic implicature and the articulation of protest in Femi Osofisan's plays. *Creative Saplings, 3*(9), 21–40. DOI: 10.56062/gtrs.2024.3.9.712

Johnson, C., & Williams, A. (2018). The digital divide in co-operative movements: Challenges and solutions. *Global Co-operative Review, 7*(4), 120–134.

Joyce, M. (Ed.). (2010). *Digital activism decoded: The new mechanics of change*. International Debate Education Association.

Karatzogianni, A. (2015). *Firebrand waves of digital activism 1994–2014: The rise and spread of hacktivism and cyberconflict*. Palgrave Macmillan. DOI: 10.1057/9781137317933

Karatzogianni, A., Miazhevich, G., & Denisova, A. (2017). A comparative cyberconflict analysis of digital activism across post-Soviet countries. *Comparative Sociology, 16*(1), 102–126. DOI: 10.1163/15691330-12341415

Kaun, A., & Uldam, J. (2018). Digital activism: After the hype. *New Media & Society, 20*(6), 2099–2106. DOI: 10.1177/1461444817731924

Kaun, A., & Uldam, J. (2018). The digital divide and its impact on activism in the 21st century. *Journal of Social Media and Society, 6*(2), 47–65.

Kondo, S. (2010). Apologies: Raising learners' cross-cultural awareness. In Martinez-Flor, A., & Usó-Juan, E. (Eds.), *Speech act performance: Theoretical, empirical and methodological issues* (pp. 145–162). John Benjamins. DOI: 10.1075/lllt.26.09kon

Martinez-Flor, A. (2010). Suggestions: How social norms affect pragmatic behavior. In Martinez-Flor, A., & Usó-Juan, E. (Eds.), *Speech act performance: Theoretical, empirical and methodological issues* (pp. 257–274). John Benjamins. DOI: 10.1075/lllt.26.15mar

Martínez-Flor, A. (2019). Speech acts in online discourse. *Journal of Pragmatics, 143*, 92–104.

Mohammed, W. F. (2019). Online activism: Centering marginalized voices in activist work. *Ada: A Journal of Gender. New Media, and Technology, 15*, 1–11.

Munoz, P., & Navas, L. (2020). Social media and grassroots mobilisation: The case of co-operatives. *Social Media Studies, 18*(2), 75–88.

Norrick, N. R., & Ilie, C. (Eds.). (2018). *Pragmatics and its interfaces*. John Benjamins.

Papacharissi, Z. (2020). *Affective publics: Sentiment, technology, and politics.* Oxford University Press.

Roberts, D., & Taylor, P. (2020). Sociocultural barriers to digital activism in co-operatives. *Journal of Social Media and Activism, 8*(3), 33–48.

Scholz, T. (2010). Infrastructure: Its transformations and effect on digital activism. In Joyce, M. (Ed.), *Digital activism decoded: The new mechanics of change* (pp. 17–31). Idebate Press.

Scholz, T. (2010). *Digital labor: The internet as playground and factory*. Routledge.

Smith, G., & Jansson, A. (2019). Transnational advocacy through digital tools: Case studies of co-operative movements. *International Journal of Digital Activism, 15*(1), 12–27.

Sorce, G., & Dumitrica, D. (2022). Transnational dimensions in digital activism and protest. *The Review of Communication, 22*(3), 157–174. DOI: 10.1080/15358593.2022.2107877

Sorce, S., & Dumitrica, D. (2022). Emojis and memes as tools of digital activism. *New Media & Society, 24*(6), 825–843.

Stornaiuolo, A., & Thomas, E. E. (2017). Disrupting educational inequalities through youth digital activism. *Review of Research in Education, 41*(1), 337–357. DOI: 10.3102/0091732X16687973

Tatsuki, D. H., & Houck, N. R. (Eds.). (2010). *Pragmatics: Teaching speech acts.* TESOL.

TrendMind. (2025). *How social media is transforming protest culture.* TrendMind Report.

Treré, E. (2019). *Hybrid media activism: Ecologies, imaginaries, algorithms.* Routledge.

Treré, E., Jeppesen, S., & Mattoni, A. (2017). Comparing digital protest media imaginaries: Anti-austerity movements in Greece, Italy & Spain. *TripleC, 15*(2), 405–424. DOI: 10.31269/triplec.v15i2.772

Treré, E., & Mattoni, A. (2015). Media ecologies and protest movements: Main perspectives and key lessons. *Information Communication and Society, 19*(2), 290–306.

Treré, E., & Mattoni, A. (2021). De-westernising digital activism. *Global Media and Communication, 17*(1), 79–98.

Vlavo, A. (2017). Visual semiotics in digital activism: Memes, GIFs, and emojis. *Media Culture & Society, 39*(5), 789–804.

Vlavo, F. A. (2017). *Performing digital activism: New aesthetics and discourses of resistance* (1st ed.). Routledge. DOI: 10.4324/9781315692869

Waugh, E. (2014). Teaching pragmatics and intercultural communication online. *TESL Canada Journal, 30*(7), 98–107. DOI: 10.18806/tesl.v30i7.1154

Wolfson, T. (2014). *Digital rebellion: The birth of the cyber left.* University of Illinois Press. DOI: 10.5406/illinois/9780252038846.001.0001

Word Gate. (2025). *Understanding pragmatics in online communication.* Word Gate Linguistics Blog.

Xie, C., & Yus, F. (2018). Digital pragmatics: New theoretical frameworks. *Journal of Language and Digital Communication, 5*(1), 1–20.

Xie, C., & Yus, F. (2018). Introducing internet pragmatics. *Internet Pragmatics, 1*(1), 1–12. DOI: 10.1075/ip.00001.xie

Yang, G. (2016). Activism. In Peters, B. (Ed.), *Digital keywords: A vocabulary of information society and culture* (pp. 1–17). Princeton University Press.

Yang, G. (2016). *The Red Guard generation and political activism in China.* Columbia University Press.

Yus, F. (2019). An outline of some future research issues for internet pragmatics. *Internet Pragmatics, 2*(1), 1–33. DOI: 10.1075/ip.00018.yus

# Chapter 6
# Multimodal Representation of Herder–Farmer Conflicts in Selected Nigerian Online Cartoons

**Omolade Ilesanmi**
https://orcid.org/0009-0008-7742-4684
*McPherson University, Seriki Sotayo, Nigeria*

## ABSTRACT

*Cartoons reveal complex dimensions of clashes between nomadic herders and agrarian farmers in Nigeria. This study examines 13 cartoons published in e-publishing unit of The Punch, one of Nigeria's most widely read newspapers, to explore how multiple modes combine to depict herder-farmer conflicts (HFCs), in order to describe how semiotic resources contextualise HFCs and how digital resources function in humorising HFCs in online newspapers. Multimodal discourse exploration of HFCs is performed via Kress' (2010) social semiotic approach to multimodal discourse. Findings reveal that The Punch deploys diverse modes of representation – image, writing, caricature. Interaction among semiotic resources, shared situation and linguistic forms reveals dimensions of insecurity, ethnoreligious bigotry, human rights violation, hypocrisy. Cartoonists are critical of Nigerian government's level of involvement in HFCs, revealing state actors as cohorts in herders' attacks; and sedentary farmers as victims. HCFs are framed as complex sociopolitical crises, intensifying ethnic tensions and divisions.*

DOI: 10.4018/979-8-3373-5297-8.ch006

## INTRODUCTION

In recent times, Herder-Farmer Conflicts (HFCs) in Nigeria have become a long-lasting issue posing security challenges to Nigerians, particularly in the northern and Middle Belt regions of the country. These conflicts commonly involve rattles between sedentary farmers who depend on agrarian lands for cultivating crops and Fulani herdsmen who engage in nomadic livestock grazing (Gürsoy, 2019). Scholars have offered refreshing debates as to the underlying factors contributing to the conflicts. For instance, Nassef et al. (2023) and Efobi et al. (2025) submit that ecological pressure and climate change have informed the movement of northern herders southward in quest of water and grazing land, causing increased rivalry with farmers. However, others (Oghuvbu & Oghuvbu, 2020) have attributed these conflicts to diversities in their land-use practices including their ethnic-based outlook on land ownership. The disputes are increasingly growing into religious and tribal clashes and remain a threat to state integration. Drawing on the aforementioned views, one could safely assert that HFCs in these regions are often intensified by religious and ethnic divisions. A complex dimension of HFCs is also presented by scholars who remark on the complications posed by the disputes in attempts to reach a resolution (Ajayi & Sennuga, 2022). In the arguments, government's negligence, absence of security forces as well as economic and political interests of the ruling class, particularly in rural areas, exacerbate the clashes, leaving agrarian communities vulnerable to violent attacks from farmers or armed herders (Oli et al., 2018). Ultimately, armed groups often hijack the disputes, leading to casualties, insecurity and displacement (Bello & Abdullahi, 2021). In Osisanwo's (2024) corpus-based study on gunmen, bandits and ransom demanders in the Nigerian context, the root of insecurity has been moored on power struggle, corrupt practices, bad governance and government's lapses as regards unemployment.

HFCs offer chances for online media to express vantage points about teeming dilemmas of insecurity as well as series of land-use clashes between herders and farmers across North Central Nigeria. Online newspapers are deployed as powerful tools to project this contextual issue and often provide platforms for columnists and editorial cartoonists to project their contextual goals and to shape the views of the public. Indeed, online entry of most Nigerian newspapers have made the perspectives (opinions created in graphical forms) of cartoon strip artists more accessible. Nigerian editorial cartoons produced online are presumed to function as communicative tools for unveiling sociopolitical trends indexing serious subjects by means of humour. Editorial cartoons are understood as multimodal texts as they represent a number of semiotic components (Amore & Atoloye, 2016). While unearthing critical thoughts from readers constitute the specific goal of cartoonists in the pictorial representation of HFCs, they are engrossed with eliciting mirth in a bid to convey sociopolitical and ethnoreligious matters through a less offensive strategy. Each multimodal representation by cartoonists deploys contextual properties involving reference, shared situation, implicature, inference and metaphor to realise specific goals. In Nigerian context, sociopolitical, religious and ethnic comic strips are measured as ways of parodying political failures and exhuming unseen agencies sponsoring terrorism, armed banditry, and militancy among other vices within the Nigerian ambience.

## Statement of the Problem

Although studies (Gürsoy, 2019; Oghuvbu & Oghuvbu, 2020) demonstrate that herder-farmer disputes emanated from succession of heated clashes over tillable lands, there are religious and ethnic dimensions to such clashes. Genyi (2017) have noted that ethnoreligious dimensions play greater role in the struggles as both parties needed strong bonds to guard themselves and their communities against opposition parties. Olaniyan and Yahaya (2016) have also established that armed groups, usually pastoral herders blatantly discharge gruesome acts devoid of charges and penalties, with quite a few security officers as cahoots. As serious as this issue between rural farmers and itinerant Fulani herders are, they are expressed in humorous forms using two or more modes of representations (cartoon images and written language) to generate meaning (Kress, 2010). Some other studies (Ohaja & Momoh, 2023; Chukwuokoro et al., 2024) have noted that visual composition constructs and possesses obscure meanings which could simply be teased out with ample understanding of its interactive, compositional and representational aspects.

However, this study argues that multimodal representations of HFCs in online cartoons transcend the use of multimodal choices to amuse or tease out covert intentions of humorists. Multimodal texts equally express complex dimensions of herdsmen attacks in order to sway readers' perceptions about specific social actors in the caricatures. Some of the ways of representing HFCs are the use of shared semiotic elements such as gaze, colour, layout, gesture, and language as an ancillary mode. To Kress and Leeuwen (2001), multimodality describes the grammar of visual and non-visual communication by expressing what are difficult to describe with semiotic resources through linguistic choices. Kress (2010) notes that communication with the exclusive influence of language produces complexities. Such complexities, he notes, obscure intended messages which could be better communicated in their widest metaphorical and analogical sense with cartoon strips. The researcher's interest in the multimodality of HFCs is premised on the fact that online humour features extreme ethnoreligious conflicts, and representation of such conflicts are laden with relevant semiotic resources which express multifaceted dimensions of herder-farmer feuds. Though cartoons have exaggerating and simplifying effects, they are mostly politically motivated and are disposed to fulfilling censuring functions.

## LITERATURE REVIEW

Herder-Farmer Conflict in Africa remains a dynamic discourse of insecurity which has attracted attention of academics, policy makers, national and international mainstream and online media. There have also been fascinating discussions on related unease about rising intensities of clashes between opposition groups. Studies (Flintan et al., 2021; Nassef et al., 2023) have confirmed that HFCs are generally devoid of direct involvement of security agencies and governments, as conflicts are commonly sporadic and aboriginal, yet demand urgency. While discourses label pastoralist herders as aliens and unlawful immigrants, they are often associated with terrorist groups (Nassef et al., 2023). A number of studies (Genyi, 2017; Gürsoy, 2019; Oghuvbu & Oghuvbu, 2020) on herder-farmer disputes in Nigeria have branded ethnic and religious dynamics as liable for escalating conflicts. These studies argue that one of the groups involved in the clash is gruesome and dreaded (Olaniyan & Yahaya, 2016) with ample support of security agents.

Besides the conflicted parties involved in the ongoing violence, the Nigerian Federal and State Governments, the Nigerian Army and the Nigerian Police are identified as secondary actors involved in the conflict (Gürsoy, 2019). Oghuvbu and Oghuvbu's (2020) submission is premised on the fact that the displacement of farmers, loss of lives, farm crops and animals are among the most grievous effects of this situation. In their research, the scholars note that the struggle between herders and farmers has the propensity to aggravate food crisis and living costs. This occurs when cattle hooves compact the farm's soil, plummeting its productivity for farmers (Adisa & Adekunle, 2010). Studies (Olomojobi & Ajilore, 2018; Chiluwa & Chiluwa, 2020) have attested to the subjective and objective portrayal of HFCs in the Nigerian media. The studies claim that media framing of conflicts between the opposing parties has either led to escalation or de-escalation. Abdulbaqi and Ariemu (2017) argue that herdsmen have been ranked as the fourth deadliest group, worldwide, based on global terrorism index. Chiluwa and Chiluwa (2020) hold that the representation of the conflicts between southern and north-central herders and agrarian farmers in the Nigerian media is extremely divisive and sensational. Such representation, they note, complicates the issue rather than resulting in peace building.

However, Chukwuma (2020) contends that interest groups and state officials have made significant efforts to represent the conflict as either producing insecurity or disputing such assertions of insecurity (Nwankwo et al., 2020). Olomojobi and Ajilore's (2018) argument is based on the premise that Nigerian newspapers primarily rely on security operatives, eye-witnesses, government officials and victims of attacks as key sources in their reports on HFCs. Aside the use of subjective means to obtain data, the newspapers often identify herdsmen as the main perpetrators of violence while framing HFCs as criminal attacks on agrarian communities rather than land-use clashes between opposing parties (Osisanwo, 2024). These representations reveal herders and farmers as villains and victims, stressing the account of a religious rivalry against Christian ranchers. The abovementioned studies essentially argue that Nigerian media constructs such conflicts as deliberate attempts to sedentarise the nomadic communities and to islamise Nigeria (Chukwuma, 2020; Nwankwo, 2024).

A plethora of studies (Olomojobi, 2018; Nwankwo et al., 2020) on media discourse in Nigeria have identified the level of involvement of the Nigerian government in the HFCs. Such studies portray the government as cohorts in herders' attacks based on *ThePunch* and *Sun* newspapers' articulation of government's response to the clash. While Olomojobi (2018) surmises that *ThePunch, The Guardian* and *Vanguard* were mostly critical of government's level of intervention, Nwankwo et al. (2020) argues that *Daily Trust* is on the defensive side, articulating the Nigerian government's response to the conflict as passable and non-supportive of nomadic herders.

From the foregoing, several researches have advanced stimulating debates on the clashes between herdsmen and farmers in Nigeria, especially in north-central and southern regions. While these studies are revealing in their description of such conflicts, they have not been articulate in how semiotic features are deployed to attain contextual effects in multimodal representations. Albeit research in Nigerian context (Chiluwa & Chiluwa, 2020) have interrogated verbal discourses on terrorist groups especially in North Central region of Nigeria, the present research maintains that nonverbal cues in cartoons express complex dimensions of herdsmen attacks by capturing imitable contexts. While extant studies (Nwankwo, 2020; Nwankwo, 2021) have examined the discourse representation of farmer-pastoralist clashes in the Nigerian context from the discourse analytical standpoint, studies have paid less attention to the theory of multimodality in evaluating how HFCs are portrayed in Nigerian e-newspapers. The current study maintains that relevant multimodal resources in online cartoons help to uncover the contextual goals of cartoonists. The study also holds that the use of more than one mode in the representation of HFCs reveals how specific multimodal resources unveil dimensions of ethnic, religious, social and political reinforcements in the visual texts.

## Theoretical Orientation

The present study is anchored on Gunther Kress' (2010) social semiotic approach to contemporary multimodal discourse. Textual and visual communication are considered as crucial aspects of critical discourse analysis as they are well-suited for carrying out various kinds of semiotic analysis. Visual elements, such as images, colour and layouts have meaning-making potentials different from textual representation. Traditionally, visual analysis has paid attention to connotative and denotative as well as context-based meanings (Kress & Leeuwen, 2021). Kress and

Leeuwen's work on multimodal discourse contributed significantly to the growth of critical discourse analysis as an interdisciplinary approach within the wider fields of communication studies, linguistics and social sciences.

To Kress and Leeuwen, the overarching social semiotic theory involves all instances of meaning-making at every level, integrating the study of images into the general study of meaning. In his book, "Multimodality: a social semiotic approach to contemporary communication", published in 2010, Kress maintains that written texts, images and colour are disposed to doing diverse forms of semiotic works as each owns its distinct meaning-making capacities. It is, therefore, presumed that social semiotics sees to "meaning in all its forms" and "cultural sites" (Kress, 2010, p.2). Kress labels what guides multimodal communication and representation as modes – image, gesture, layout, writing, 3D objects and so forth. Such modes, according to him, are culturally fixed and socially shaped semiotic resources for creating meaning. He further notes that each semiotic resource draws from the happenings in the social world (*ideational function*), detailing the social activities, relations and interactions of supposed community members (*interpersonal function*) and forming socially coherent semiotic entities (*textual function*) to function as a mode (Kress & Leeuwen, 2021). Each of the aforementioned modes is limited in semiotic capacity while attempting to meet the demands of the ideational, interpersonal and textual functions. Hence, an interaction among different modes, fashioned by multimodality, overcomes the limitations of each of the modes in seclusion. To this end, multimodality can be interpreted as a matter of adequacy and extensiveness of meanings rather than of choice.

This study upholds that multimodal discourse approach is appropriate in probing how multimodal resources function in representing these several dimensions of HFCs. The contributions of this study to multimodal communication and representation are guided by the aforementioned modes – image, gesture, layout and writing. Since meaning making is a significant aspect of multimodal discourse, tracking the goals of cartoonists requires connecting the different modes and implicatures in each representation via social semiotic theory. The social semiotic approach is adopted in this study to investigate how HFCs are represented in online newspapers in order to describe the dimensions of HFCs and the implications of such representations. The study argues that implicit meanings are much more inherent in visual communication. A multimodal discourse investigation of HFCs in online newspapers would exhume the roles of reference, shared situational knowledge (SSK), exaggeration, irony, metaphor, inference and analogy in communicating specific goals in HFCs. This elucidates why a multimodal discourse exploration of HFCs in e-newspapers, through social semiotic approach to contemporary multimodal discourse, is required to tease out how multimodal resources contextualise HFCs and how digital resources function in humorising HFCs in online newspapers. To achieve this, contextual features (SSK, reference and inferences) in the selected cartoon strips are connected, to describe the implicatures and intentions inherent in each representation.

## SIGNIFICANCE OF THE STUDY

Discourse of HFCs has been laudably approached from wide-ranging perspectives. Studies have engaged HFCs realised as part of social media discourse, newspaper feature, television documentaries and so forth, through linguistic and non-linguistic enquiries. While these studies have advanced stimulating arguments on the ethnoreligious dimensions of HFCs and insecurity in Africa, typically southern and North Central Nigeria, they have paid less attention to how multimodal resources function in reflecting multifarious scopes of HFCs in Nigeria. Inattention to multimodal reading of these clashes in online newspapers has inhibited an exposition of how caricatures unearth invisible agencies sponsoring terrorism and banditry within the Nigerian environment. This study argues that interaction between contextual features and humour strategies used in cartoons teases out cartoonists' opinions about dimensions of herdsmen attacks through imitable contexts.

### Aim and Objectives

The study aims to explore how multiple modes combine to depict HFCs in Nigerian online cartoons. The specific objectives are:

i. To identify the specific multimodal features in representing HFCs in online cartoons
ii. To investigate how multimodal resources contextualise HFCs in online cartoons
iii. To examine how digital resources function in humorising HFCs in online cartoons

### Research Questions

The current study examines the following questions.

i. What are the specific multimodal features in representing HFCs?
ii. How do multimodal resources contextualise HFCs?
iii. How do digital resources function in humorising HFCs?

## METHOD

In the analysis of multimodal choices signifying HFCs in online newspapers, qualitative research design is employed. Relevant semiotic resources such as image, gesture, colour, gaze, space alignment and linguistic forms in cartoons signaling HFCs provide data requisite for the qualitative research. The interaction between such semiotic elements, shared situation and surrounding linguistic forms syndicate to express messages of insecurity, ethnic and religious bigotry, violation of human rights and hypocrisy in Nigerian context. Specifically, cartoon strips were obtained from *Punch Digital*, the online publishing unit of *ThePunch*. These comic-based texts were accessed and retrieved through advanced search with key phrases as "Nigerian editorial cartoons", "herdsmen attacks", "comic strips on middle-belt conflicts", "online humour on herder-farmer clashes", among other operational words. Thirty (30) multimodal texts got from the online publishing version of *ThePunch* constitute the population of the study. Nonetheless, thirteen (13) cartoon strips which offer sufficient data for the present study were purposively selected. This selection is anchored on intense deployment of semiotic media and linguistic forms used in representing HFCs in the cartoon strips. Data were accessed and labelled as Figures 1-13. The choice of *The Punch* is informed by the multimodal relevance (Akanni & Ibuot, 2023) of the cartoons, including their integration of textual, visual and symbolic resources which align with multimodal discourse analysis. Also, *The Punch* is widely recognised for its critical posture on sociopolitical issues, making it a significant repository for exploring representations and bias. *The Punch* has a strong digital presence and the cartoons are published in such extensively accessible newspaper, rendering them a piece of the public domain for critical analysis (Chiedozie et al., 2023).

The multimodal texts deploy contextual features such as shared knowledge about places and persons. The relation between multimodal elements and contextual features creates inferences from the representations and reflects the cartoonists' vantage point of current realities. Colour, image, gesture, gaze and caricature in the multimodal texts constitute the visual codes which are binding elements in generic structure of editorial cartoons. To provide responses to the specific multimodal features in representing HFCs in online newspapers, aspects of Kress' (2010) social semiotic approach to multimodal discourse were employed to account for the multimodal resources deployed in meaning-making. How the aforementioned multimodal resources contextualise HFCs in online newspapers were revealed in the interrelation between visual codes, reference, metaphor, inference, implicature and shared situation. Finally, humour strategies such as satire and irony reveal how digital resources function in humorising dimensions of HFCs in online newspapers.

## RESULTS

Analysis of data shows that cartoonists deploy semiotic resources (image, gesture, colour, space frame, and gaze), contextual features (shared situation, reference, inference) and linguistic forms to communicate extents of violent conflicts involving nomadic herders and sedentary farmers. The relations among the semiotic resources, contextual features and surrounding linguistic forms reveal dimensions of insecurity, ethnoreligious bigotry, human rights violation and government hypocrisy. Cartoon strips as digital resources comically portray HFCs through humour strategies, such as, satire, exaggeration, juxtaposition, irony and analogy, to emphasise its absurdities. While diffusing the pressure surrounding the subject, digital resources present conflicts between both parties in a humorous way to rouse public thought and criticism. Analysis also reveals that images, visual elements and written texts in e-newspapers contextualise HFCs by offering the viewers with several layers of meaning. Four social actors are portrayed in the analysis - nomadic pastoralists/herders, sedentary farmers, security operatives and government authorities. Multimodal representation of HFCs is explored under two main captions: blame attribution and victim role ascription. These bifurcate into activation of nomadic herders as dynamic forces in HFCs, criminalisation of nomadic herders as murderers, genericisation of Nigerian security operatives as cohorts in herders' attacks, identification of Nigerian authorities as passive allies of nomadic herders, representation of sedentary farmers as victims of security operatives' ferocity and depiction of sedentary farmers as victims of herders' attacks. Cartoonists are found to be mostly critical of the Nigerian government's level of involvement in the conflicts, revealing political leaders and security operatives as allies in herders' attacks against sedentary farmers.

### Blame Attribution

Blame attribution, in HFCs, in online *Punch* newspapers determines the social perception of the root causes of conflicts between farmers and herders and those perceived as the principal assailants or victims. Social actors – itinerant herders, security operatives and Nigerian authorities, are held accountable for the sources, escalation and effects of the clashes between two opposing parties (sedentary farmers and herders) notably in the southern and north-central regions of Nigeria. The idea of blame attribution indicates the perceived roles of actors in the strife and casualties. Blame attribution and responsibility diverges into four themes which are: activation of nomadic herders as dynamic forces in HFCs, criminalisation of nomadic herders as murderers, genericisation of Nigerian security operatives as cohorts in herders' attacks, identification of Nigerian authorities as passive allies of nomadic herders.

## Activation of Nomadic Herders as Dynamic Forces in HFCS

Several semiotic and linguistic resources mobilise nomadic and semi-nomadic herders as the active visual participants in the clashes. Herders' activation as dynamic forces accentuates the motives of the conflicts and their participation in such conflicts. In Figures 1 and 2, multimodal representation endows a herder with an active role in the activity of assaulting a farmer, visually portrayed as one at the receiving end of an assault. In the representation of nomadic herders as active perpetrators in the violence against farmers, image, posture, colour, gesture and writing are modes deployed for meaning-making. Each of the modes offers diverse possibilities for meaning making.

*Figure 1. Herder assaulting farmer.*

*Figure 2. Dividends of central policing system.*

Kress' notion of multimodality highlights the interaction of image and text in the cartoon strips offers a narrative which evaluates the asymmetrical power relations between agrarian farmers and itinerant herders and the inactions of the governing authority. In Figure 1 the farmer is framed as an object caught between restrained authorities, portrayed as passive agents, and an armed herder, depicted as an active agent in the assault, revealing wider issues of insecurity and human rights violation in Nigeria. Images of four principal social actors – a herdsman, a farmer and two political actors including the ex-president of Nigeria, General Muhammadu Buhari, are displayed within a framed space. While all the visual elements in the representation are simultaneously presented, the arrangement of the aforementioned social actors and other essentials in the space remain a means for creating meaning. The interaction of the concurrently present visual elements in the edged space essentially supplies the key semiotic logic of the image. The layout of the visual representation illustrates local agrarian communities in Nigeria. In the context of their creation, images of "cows", "grass" and the "firearm" held by the herder, communicate meaning owing to their social making and the consistency of their usage in social life as well as in their cultural environments.

Though visual caption of written text is displayed spatially in the frame, it relies on the lucidity of sequence in time, attributable to speech. Writing, in this frame mimics time sequence feature by deploying "spatial sequence of elements" (Kress, 2010). Here, the understanding of written texts is controlled by directionality of line that is, left to right and the organisation of sentence structure. Verbal meaning is added to the pictorial representation through the text, "**AH! NO! NO! NO! DON'T GRAZE ON MY FARM!**" This signifies a resolute entreaty to thwart the herder's attempt to destroy his source of revenue. The response of the second state actor, "**BUT WHAT SHALL IT PROFIT A FARMER TO GAIN HIS FARM AND LOSE HIS LIFE**", alludes to Mark chapter 8 verse 36 and 37 of the Holy Bible which reads, "for what shall it profit a man, if he shall gain the whole world, and lose his own soul? Or what shall a man give in exchange for his soul?" Here, implicature helps in conveying his judgment more efficiently than by stating every word explicitly. This biblical reference infers a caution directed at the farmer to prioritise his life over protecting his farmland. This represents a mockery of sedentary planters' resistance even in the face of loss and highlights the vainness of their struggles. Instead of addressing the basis of insecurity, he places a responsibility on him to accept the status quo.

The visual frame in Figure 2, together with the visual text captions demonstrates the attacks launched by social actors involved in the conflicts against opposing parties. The visual and textual modes collaborate to communicate reflective meanings about conflicts, abuse and supremacy. Considering the distinct affordances of each mode of communication, they can be deployed to perform definite semiotic functions. The ideational aspect of meaning is evidently involved in the creation of meaning in Figure 2. Consequently, the assailing aspect of herder-farmer clashes is presented as what is already known. However, perceptions about government's response to violence between herdsmen and farmers remain divisive. The interactions between distinct semiotic resources in the visual representation have social implications. In view of what is "given" or known to the viewers about the clashes, a specific representation is implicitly ascribed to herders through posture and other semiotic elements – caps, attire and firearm.

Multiple layers of meaning are conveyed in the visual text. First, the maladroitness and complicity of Nigerian central policing system with respect to HFCs and violence are delivered through text caption and visual elements. The ascription of an active aggressor to herders is highlighted in the pastoralist posture and hand gesture. He is depicted as standing over an agrarian farmer, whose hands are tied, holding a large machete. The machete and the rifle slung across his left shoulder symbolise violence while his positioning signifies dominance. The police officer's (identified with his uniform and weapon) hesitation to intervene in the situation suggests his dependence on higher powers in the country capital as evinced in the text "**ARREST WHO? ALLOW ME TO DO MY JOB THOROUGHLY: I'M CALLING MY BOSS IN ABUJA**! His role as a passive agent in the herdsman's attack against the agrarian farmer is emphasised through his wide-eyed expression and his arm upstretched in an explanatory motion. The dishonesty and ineffectiveness of law enforcement in handling local conflicts are sarcastically highlighted in the text caption "**DIVIDENDS OF CENTRAL POLICING SYSTEM**." The police officer's detachment from the violent scene and the fact that he is armed but fails to take no action portray him as an active ally in the attack. More so, the governor's portfolio labelled "**GOVERNOR**" performs semiotic work of physical identification. The exclamation mark as well as his stance, with his fingers under his chin, reveals his seeming concern about the bureaucratic actions of the law enforcement. Yet, he is depicted as an active observer whose political power is weary of protecting citizens. This satirises the failure of the state actors to secure the rights of vulnerable farmers. By implication, both caricatures satirise political inaction about HFCs and finally reveals the severe realities of oppression, survival and the asymmetrical power relation between Fulani herdsmen and agrarian farmers.

## Criminalisation of Nomadic Herders as Murderers

Criminalisation of nomadic herders as murderers highlights aspects of narratives where itinerant herdsmen are progressively depicted as intrinsically vicious and culpable of criminal acts and murder crimes against sedentary agrarian farmers, over arable land disputes. Media framing of HFCs has contributed largely to the criminalisation of this group, concentrating on violent hostilities against farmers (Olomojobi, 2018; Chiluwa & Chiluwa, 2020) without details of herders' grievances and the complexities of the conflicts. The generalisation of farmers, mostly Christians, as victims of herders' criminal acts often depicts herders, mostly Fulanis by tribe and Muslims by religion, as executioners in public discourse, reinforcing negative perceptions and ethnoreligious intolerance among both parties. The semiotic properties (image, colour and text) deployed in the visual participation in Figures 3 and 4 lend themselves to carrying out distinct types of semiotic work.

*Figure 3. Attacks against sedentary farmers.*

*Figure 4. Gruesome attacks.*

To maximum effect, the above images show gruesome attacks against sedentary farmers in their communities and farmlands by herders; colour highlights gory sights and frames the extent of the acts and writing names political actors and contexts of the crimes. Figure 3 draws on shared situation and reference as contextual features together with exaggeration, satire and irony as humour strategies to depict the violent attacks involving Fulani herders in the Nigerian context.

Multiple communication modes integrated in the visual representations – semiotic resources, spatial frame and visual text offer ample annotation on violence involving farmers and herders, rising insecurity, chaos, helplessness and political failure. The dominant political figure in the representation is General Muhammadu Buhari, the former president of the Federal Republic of Nigeria, identified through exaggerated body features and pictured in white agbada attire. The white attire ironically frames his concocted innocence and goodwill. His knee and head posture, his eye expression and his hands raised in the direction of the heavens and his words "**OVER TO YOU, OH GOD ALMIGHTY**!" communicate a state of resignation, signifying that the federal government has relinquished responsibility for addressing the chaos and beseeching a higher authority to intervene in the crisis. His positioning in the centre of the image frames him as a prominent yet detached figure from the crisis. To the right and left of the dominant figure are men armed with rifles and machetes slaying several defenseless victims in their rustic communities indicated through huts, one of which is set on fire. The hats worn by some of the executioners and the cattle in the frame identify them as herders, mostly Fulanis, given what is known about nomadic herders. Postures assumed by the herders reveal them as perpetrators of the crisis while their weapons as semiotic elements convey conflicts and violence. On the other hand, traditional apparels are deployed in signifying local farmers, some of whom are seeking escapes, being injured and shot. Opposite movements in the representation represent chaos and escalation of the violence. Skulls and blood in both texts symbolise death, danger and the severe effects of the conflicts. The presence of the cattle enhances the context of the symbolic representation of littered skulls by directly pinning the violent killings to HFCs. The framing context is reinforced by writing mode as evinced in the phrase, "**RISING INSECURITY IN NIGERIA**", featured at the top left angle of the image.

Like 3, Figure 4 deploys writing mode to identify the former president of Nigeria by depicting him with the acronym "FG" – Federal Government. Other representational choices – gesture and image are significant in creating meaning. Kress (2010) surmises that, across diverse cultures and societies, the reach of modes differ such that areas of the cultural domain consisted in a mode in a particular society do not exist in the same mode in a different culture. Gesture, as a mode of communication and representation differs in the way it communicates meaning across societies. The political figure's shoulder gesture, in this case, becomes significant in interpreting his position about HFCs in conflict-ridden areas in Nigeria. While writing plays a crucial role in the identification of the social actor, the image counts more on modes distant from writing. His raised shoulders and the fact that his back is turned to the violent scene help to draw inferences about his indifferent attitude towards the massacre. Image as a mode reveals that he is far removed from the scene through space frame. The context conveys, significantly, messages of chaos, fear, appeal and fierceness through semiotic resources, including the herder's weapon, wide-eyed facial expression of one of the farmers, and the raised hand motion of each of the victims. By means of space frame, the herder is positioned in an intimidating posture while the farmer is pictured as being under enemy control. The cartoons are both dominated by human skulls, blood (Figure 3), fear, destruction and undaunted political leaders, accentuating chaos, suffering, government's hypocrisy and the exigent need for public intervention.

## Genericisation of Nigerian Security Operatives as Cohorts in Herders' Attacks

Genericisation of security operatives in Nigeria highlights the tendency to depict Nigerian security operatives, specifically the Nigerian Police and the Nigerian Army as complicit in attacks involving herders and farmers. While such genericisation arises from presumed alliance and the perceived patterns of the inaction of security personnel in crisis resolution, it may perhaps overlook the drives of specific operatives, the complexities of the conflicts and their encounters while trying to address the conflicts. Visual elements arrayed in this representation deploy multiple modes, such as, written text – to provide the context of the frame, image – to instantiate meaning through spatial ordering of visual elements, and colour as an ideational reserve – to indicate danger.

*Figure 5. Despite curfew, suspected herdsmen kill 27.*

*Figure 6. Power imbalance.*

Images deployed in the representation of Nigerian security operatives as cohorts in herders' attacks adopt similar visual and textual elements, including image, writing, gesture and colour to communicate messages of collusions and complicities in herders' attacks against farmers in the discourse of HFCs. The degree of power possessed by nomadic pastoralists in the visual representations in Figure 5 and Figure 6 is gestured by a coherent use of suitable signifiers in the headline to communicate complex signs of power relations. For example, the headlines "**DESPITE CURFEW, SUSPECTED HERDSMEN KILL 27 IN FRESH PLATEAU ATTACK- NEWS**", "**DOMAIN OF POWER**…", "**HERDSMEN**…" and "**POLICE**…", provide a contextual ground that signifies power imbalance between herders and farmers, and Nigerian security operatives and Nigerian citizens. Contextual features and humour strategies like shared situational knowledge, inference, reference, irony and satire highlight aspects of realities in thought provoking ways. The gun as a semiotic resource in both images denotes a reference to power and authority wielded by both law enforcement agencies and herdsmen against local farmers and citizens. In the images, the choice of red tints and a mound of skulls in the visual representation is a horrific reference, leaning on ideational meaning and inducing notions of ruthlessness, brutality and massacre carried out by herdsmen. Uniforms of security operatives are used in signifying their roles as security forces. Paradoxically, they are portrayed as passive agents in the attack through their postures and complacent gestures. In Figure 5, the soldier's sleeping posture symbolises negligence and suggests a mockery of Nigerian security forces and the absence of security actions in conflict-ridden regions. Foregrounding the soldier in the visual representation suggests his agency; yet, his inaction and ineptness even with the curfew are highlighted in the headline, which anchors the context of the image. The ideational function of meaning is deployed as the text caption and semiotic resources allude to the horrible killings in Plateau region of Nigeria and the Military's inability to control the massacre even under restricted conditions.

Figure 6 describes two supposed domains of power labelled in the visual text as: herdsmen and police, reflecting an annotation on forces of power in the Nigeria context. Guns serve as semiotic resources for depicting power imbalance between herders and farmers in the first image. Positioning of the herders behind the farmers running over a pile of human skulls and a man in his own pool of blood, in the first image signifies viciousness linked with herders over land-use clashes. The farmers' wide-eyed expressions, legs and hand gesture while they flee from the herders communicate messages of fear and terror. Depicting the police in an intimidating position with stern expressions on their faces and facing a motorcyclist who holds a fifty naira note projects some sort of monetary demand from local citizens. The two "domains of power", that is, state actors (Nigerian police) and non-state actors (nomadic herders) are visually represented as oppressors through gaze, facial expression, posture and gesture. The two scenes depict a juxtaposition of two domains where power is wielded in oppressive ways. In both Figures, the blood stain on the grass as well as the blood-stained machete held by the armed group (in Figure 5) has quite a few significances. First, the blood stain serves as a powerful semiotic element that highlights extreme violence, revealing the clash as fierce and deadly and intensifying the brutality of such attacks as well as the anguish of victims. In addition, these symbols are expected to arouse emotional reactions as they reveal universal signs of loss. They underpin the urgency required by the conflict, representing a call for immediate action. The machete signifies a primitive or uncontrolled hostility.

## Identification of Nigerian Authorities as Passive Allies of Nomadic Herders

Identification of political actors as allies in herders' attacks suggests specific allegations against state actors premised on perceived inactions and failure to act decisively when conflicts break out between herdsmen and farmers. More so, HFCs have been profoundly debated, with diverse regional groups critical of government's position about the conflict. This situation adds to the complexities of the conflict by reflecting political, religious and ethnic identity. Figures 7 and 8 deploy shared situation, reference and exaggeration to communicate messages of nepotism by the Federal government of Nigeria against agrarian farmers in the Middle Belt region of Nigeria. Gunther Kress' approach to contemporary multimodal discourse pays specific attention to meaning creation through diverse modes, including gesture, image, space, text and posture within specific cultural and social contexts. Consequently, the images revealed in Figures 7 and 8 draw resources from each of these modes to convey aspects of realities in Nigeria, specifically in conflict-ridden zones.

*Figure 7. Conflict-ridden zones*

*Figure 8. Nepotism*

*Figure 9. A strong message on the inadvertent implications of political actions and Nigerian leaders' empowerment*

In the three representations, the cartoonists physically represent state and non-state actors through (exaggerated) body features which inimitably identify them. The visual representation demarcates two ethnic and cultural groups by specific semiotic resources. While the semiotic resource, hoe is used in the representation of some actors as agrarian farmers, gun and cows are deployed to represent the other party as herdsmen. The spatial arrangement in both visual representations conveys strong messages about the displacement of farmers and violence in Benue, a state in Nigeria. In Figure 7, the exaggerated physical features and attire of the political actor labelled "FG" contribute to his identification as the former president of Nigeria, General Buhari. Complex signs in the gesture, proximity and gaze of herders, farmers and the political actor indicate power imbalance. The folded arm gesture and calm composure of the political figure symbolise disinterest in the plight of farmers who are depicted as falling off the cliff based on posture and spatial positioning. Depicting his posterior against the violent scene signifies his indifference and negligence. The foregrounded text "**BENUE STATE**", the text caption at the top left of the image and the forward-moving active postures of herders contribute to the image's description of violence and overall context of the frame. Writing as a mode significantly conveys the cartoonist's vantage point on real life events, by alluding to Samuel Ioraer Ortom's (former governor of Benue State) caveats about the jeopardies of constant violence in the state with the headline "**BENUE KILLINGS: WE RISK ANNIHILATION, Ortom raise alarm**." The use of capitialisation to foreground the first five lexical choices projects the cartoonist's key focus.

The everyday clothing worn by some of the figures and the colour of the vegetation appeal to the world of realities about farming communities. The modes of writing, image, gesture and gaze, thus, depict local farmers in Benue region of Nigeria as victims of the violence executed by herders and government's inattention. The arrangement of visual elements in the image (left to right) echoes a description that progresses from Federal Government's (FG's) passiveness to herders' activeness in continuous criminality. The cartoon strip metaphorises state and non-state actors' involvement in the conflicts through the deployment of the cliff, representing a visual metaphor, to incriminate and connect them to Benue's imminent collapse. Figure 8, like 7 uses semiotic resources like hoes, sandals, green vegetation, wide hats, cattle and firearm linked to farming and rustic activities as symbolic elements representing farmers' and herders' means of livelihood. The spatial positioning of herders dominating a larger sitting space and their disengaged body language connote an attempt to eradicate the farmer even from the tiny space available to him. Semiotic resources such as a patch on the farmer's shirt and his barefooted appearance signifies him as indigent. Lastly, a profound message of rustic communities' disintegration from national discourse is conveyed through a lack of attention from the state actor despite his gross engagement with the media, signified by the massive news board.

As allies in the HFCs, multimodal elements like text captions, visual contrasts and semiotic resources like books, farming tools and weapons in Figure 9 convey a strong message on the inadvertent implications of political actions and Nigerian leaders' empowerment. A wide range of semiotic resources (stack of papers handed to wards and hoes, cutlasses, shovels and wheelbarrows offered to farmers) imply favouritism in the top and bottom left panels of the image. A juxtaposition of two diverse types of empowerments reveals the way political dynasties are preserved and the paradox of youths' empowerment and violent attacks launched by oppositions over land use. The farmer's posture and semiotic elements – cutlass and hoe depict him as an object of a herdsman's attack; whereas the herdsman is represented as a plunderer on account of his posture in the space frame. The detachment of leadership from grassroots struggles is depicted through the newspaper (signifying media influence and the spread of subjective narratives by the media) and the political figure's sunglasses (demonstrating feigned unawareness of public issues). Overall, Figures 7, 8 and 9 critiques the constant conflicts between Fulani herdsmen and local communities, manipulation by the media and political inaction.

## Victim Role Ascription

Ascription of victimhood in the representations is contingent upon the frames deployed by cartoonists and the relations between the active force and beneficiary of actions enacted in the frames. An analysis of social actors' portrayal as victims in the visual representations involves exploring how different modes of communication and representation – visual texts (headlines), images, gestures, colour, spatial configuration and posture help to advance understanding of the context of conflicts between herdsmen and farmers. Consequently, modes of representation collaborate with one another to attribute blame and responsibility to social actors (herdsmen and security operatives) in the conflicts based on how victimhood is conveyed in the contextual frame.

### Representation of Sedentary Farmers as Victims of Security Operatives' Ferocity

This representation in HFCs highlights aspects of subjection of agrarian farmers to state violence, in the context of security agents' involvements in land clashes. Semiotic resources are deployed to portray farmers as not only susceptible to herdsmen's invasion, but also as victims of careless policing which further intensifies their victimhood. Media magnify this representation with the portrayal of farmers in vulnerable situations in relation to police and military interventions in herdsmen's attack. Sedentary farmers' perception as jointly mistreated by state actors and Fulani herdsmen are enhanced by the pictorial portrayal of bruised farmers and confrontations involving gun threats by armed officers. While such representation questions the roles and responsibilities of law enforcement agencies, it often frames farmers' quandaries in conflict-ridden regions of Nigeria as disregarded by the government, signifying the ineffectiveness and biasness of the Military and Police arms in dealing with the conflicts and forming the wider narrative of prejudice around HFCs.

*Figure 10. Deploys semiotic elements*

*Figure 11. Tensions involving governance and ethnic bigotry in HFCs*

A multimodal approach to the representations in Figures 10 and 11 delivers a choice of modes – image, writing, gesture, colour, gaze and posture. Visual elements in the representations show herdsmen as assailants of vulnerable local citizens and farmers; whereas Nigerian Police and Army are portrayed in an even more vicious light, reflecting the brute force used against local farmers under Buhari's administration. Essentially, satire, shared situation, exaggeration, symbolism, reference and inference are deployed to reveal a broader narrative of sociopolitical realities in Nigeria. Through exaggerated caricatured and symbolic representations, the images signal a satirical tone to draw focus on grave sociopolitical issues. Relying heavily on images, Figure 10 deploys semiotic elements (weapons, traditional wear, and military uniform), colour and posture for interpretation. A semiotic reading of the visual representation reveals the passiveness and active participation of state authorities in violent attacks involving herders and farmers. Images in the frame depict a shift in posture and facial expression in the left and right panels. In the left panel, the positioning of the farmer (identified with traditional attire) with hands stretched out in submission to the armed Fulani herdsman (identified with a wide-brimmed hat) and the security agent's passive posture, convey a message of connivance. With context change in the right panel, the military and police officers are portrayed as belligerent with energetic postures and wide-mouth expressions, intimidating the unarmed farmer with weapons in his attempt to requite.

In Figure 11, visual representation is reinforced by the text "**BUHARI REGIME ENCOURAGING HERDSMEN TO SUBJUGATE OTHERS – President, middle-belt forum**", revealing tensions involving governance and ethnic bigotry in HFCs. The police's active complicity through gesture and posture reveals how herders' interests are served contrary to the marginalisation met by other groups in conflicts involving herdsmen in the middle-belt region of Nigeria. The involvement of law enforcement in HFCs is represented multimodally to critique the power wielded by these state actors on agrarian farmers in the service of herders. Semiotic resources, such as, guns, army and police uniform as well as colour, spatial positioning, gesture and posture index the power and supremacy of security operatives and the herdsman depicted in the image. Multimodal choices such as gesture, posture, gaze, proximity and text are means of communicating power relations between farmers and security operatives in the cartoons. In both representations, the chronologically organised sequence of events within the framed space imitates the semiotic logic of image as a mode, where elements are presented to viewers simultaneously.

The images are supplied with gesture mode coupled with semiotic resources – (guns and whip as tools of violence), signifying elements of control, subjugation and attack. By means of exaggerated body features and semiotic resources, the images identify the former president of the Federal Republic of Nigeria, General Muhammadu Buhari and Nigerian security operatives. The use of analogy in Figure 11 to depict Buhari, strapping a Fulani herder to his back within the space frame, is significant in conveying messages of religious and ethnic bigotry within the Nigeria context. The left top and left bottom panels of Figure 11 reveal two different representations involving gaze. The former portrays a police officer's direct gaze at the visual participant reporting the gruesome action of a herdsman by pointing towards a certain direction; whereas the latter reveals an indirect gaze at the political actor coupled with anger and disappointment, signified by the streaks positioned above the officer's head. By implication, both Figures expose systemic prejudice against farmers and scorn selective justice by law enforcement agencies. State-authorised repression and the hypocrisy in handling HFCs in Nigeria are critiqued by means of visual irony.

## Depiction of Sedentary Farmers as Victims of Herders' Attacks

Victimhood is communicated across multiple modes of representation as revealed in the analysis which supplies acumens into the power dynamics and contextual frames that impact an understanding of the clash. Space frame, posture, visual and textual elements tease out the complexities of victim role assignment and the implication on stereotyping an opposing group as violent attackers. Key elements of multimodal analysis – texts (headlines), visuals and social contexts describe violent attacks on farmers through representational choices and semiotic resources that reveal farmers as innocent victims and herdsmen as violent aggressors. Visual elements in Figures 12 and 13 portray violent scenes of attacks perpetrated against local farmers by herdsmen, strengthening victim narratives. As composite as HFCs are, they are simplified by caricature of herdsmen, farmers and state actors in the representations, leading to a distortion of realities, reinforcement of stereotypes and an emphasis on the dilemma of local farmers.

*Figure 12. Distortion of realities*

*Figure 13. Message regarding the management of HFCs in Nigeria is delivered*

With symbolic representation and irony, a strong message of misdirected focus of governance is conveyed in Figures 12 and 13, highlighting the costs of political actions. Cow symbolism and the protest sign bearing the inscription, "**COWS LIVES MATTER**" reveal the context of tensions between farmers and Fulani herdsmen. The text denotes an intertextual allusion to the movement, "Black Lives Matter", which signifies a way to accentuate the alleged ranking of cows over humans. This satirical reference lampoons the Nigerian Senate's protection of cattle at the expense of human lives. The size and the depiction of the cow at the halfway point of the frame signal its perceived significance in Nigeria's sociopolitical context. The left to right progression of the visual elements reveals a juxtaposition of two events: the bureaucratic act to shield cows in contrast to vicious loss of lives. The state actors' identities are signified by their traditional attire and reinforced by the text caption, "**SENATE MOVES TO CREATE DATABASE FOR COWS**", portraying them as members of Senate. The text mode represents an irony and satire against Nigerian government's attention to livestock's protection amidst fierce conflicts between Fulani herdsmen and farmers. The proportions of the frame occupied by the cow and the violent scene convey a critical message about the value placed on herders' livestock over violence against farmers.

In Figure 13, a strong message regarding the management of HFCs in Nigeria is delivered through writing mode, visual mode, symbolism and reference. A number of semiotic elements (incarcerated farmers, smoke, burning hut, fire, skulls) are deployed to indicate the violence produced by herders' crisis. The representation is reinforced by a portrayal of sedentary farmers as victims of herders' attacks through resources such as prison bars, piles of skulls, posture, text and gesture. Gesture of the state actor shows urgency to save the trapped sedentary farmers from the hut labelled "**HERDSMEN KILLINGS**", whereas Nigerian farmers (signified by green and white flag) are metaphorically the victims of both herdsmen's killings and RUGA policy decision. Symbolically, the flag held behind bars is a semiotic sign alluding to the entrapment of the country within the issue of herders' attacks.

The misguided approach used by Buhari's government is highlighted by a combination of visual resources (burning shed) and linguistic signals (**RUGA SOLUTION**; **CAUTION**; **HIGHY INFLAMMABLE**). Concentrating the label on the can at the midpoint of the space frame and tinting the text, "**CAUTION**" with red, symbolise the hazardous nature of RUGA. Contextually, while RUGA (rural grazing area and Fulani word for settlement) solution as presented by the Buhari regime is intended to resolve HFCs in Nigeria to prevent encroachment of farmlands, it is perceived as a policy designed for the advantage of Fulani herders, particularly in the north central and southern regions of Nigeria. An intertextual reference to the presidency's push for the RUGA programme regardless of its potential to degenerate the existing state as indicated by the inflammable solution is specified by the text mode (**FG SUSPENDS RUGA- News**). The juxtaposition between the RUGA solution and the burning hut filled with victims of herdsmen's attack suggests the presidency's ineffective solution while disregarding the actual crisis which has claimed lives. The cartoons communicate messages of misplaced priorities and failed policies by political actors, uncovering government's permissiveness and censuring delayed responses including the deteriorating crisis of HFCs-associated violence in Nigeria as portrayed by the skulls and blood stains.

## DISCUSSION OF FINDINGS

This study has examined the multimodal representation of HFCs in selected Nigerian online cartoons. It explored the violent conflicts involving nomadic herders and sedentary farmers in online humour, using 13 cartoon strips selected from the digital version of *ThePunch*, in order to study how multimodal resources function in representing these conflicts. While extant critical debates (Chiluwa & Chiluwa, 2020; Nwankwo et al., 2020) have identified the divisive and polarity tendencies of online representations of HFCs, this study argues that cartoonists deploy digital and multimodal resources to contextualise and humourise HFCs in order to unearth complex dimensions of the conflicts. Also, it argues that cartoons reflecting HFCs are shaped by diverse contextual influences which are articulated through specific contextual resources. From multimodal discourse perspective, the study remarks that cartoonists negotiate contextual issues like insecurity, ethnic bigotry, human rights violation and government insincerity and ascribe representations to herders, farmers and state actors by relying on multimodal resources to achieve specific goals. With respect to methodology, the current research provides a nuanced understanding of how visual and textual elements function to ascribe representations through semiotic elements (image, gaze, colour), humour strategies (satire, exaggeration, analogy) and contextual features (reference, symbolism, implicature). While this study shares specific similarity with existing studies in terms of scope (Chukwuma, 2020; Nwankwo, 2021; Nassef et al., 2023; Nwankwo, 2024) most extant studies frame HCFs as either creating insecurity or as attempts to Islamise Nigeria.

However, this study is premised on the position that linguistic and semiotic elements in cartoons function as powerful tools for reflecting power dynamics, social tensions and wider sociopolitical realities. Also, dimensions of the conflict are revealed through the identified recurring patterns – victimisation, blame attribution, genericisation, criminalisation and activation of social actors, which frame the conflicts. The representation of herders and farmers in the cartoons highlight the irregularity of the conflict, reflecting a group (herders) as aggressors and the other (farmers) as the defenseless. This supports studies that position farmers as the oppressed and herders as agents of attack against farming communities (Nwankwo et al., 2020; Osisanwo, 2024). The use of a social semiotic approach to contemporary multimodal discourse communicates crucial messages about the representational affordances such that the interaction between multimodal and contextual features creates inferences which reflect the cartoonists' vantage point of current realities.

## CONCLUSION

The analysis reveals six representations conveyed with multiple modes (image, gesture, colour, gaze and space), contextual features (shared situation, reference, inference, implicature), linguistic forms (text captions) and humour strategies (satire, irony, exaggeration, analogy, juxtaposition). Image, writing, gesture, colour, gaze and spatial configuration are deployed to represent state and non-state actors involved in the conflicts including farmers and herders. Such representations describe the roles and activities of each social actor within two key themes: Blame attribution and victim role ascription. Blame attribution reveals several dimensions of ethnic and religious bigotry, human rights violation, brutality and hypocrisy ascribed to herdsmen and state actors, including Nigerian police and military officers through four representations: nomadic herders as dynamic forces in HFCs and as murderers, Nigerian security operatives as cohorts in herders' attacks and Nigerian political actors as passive allies of nomadic herders. Victim role ascription bifurcates into two themes, namely, sedentary farmers as victims of security operatives' ferocity and as victims of herders' attacks. While visual elements offer the first means of engagement and representation, meaning-making is contingent upon contextual features.

## Limitations of the Study and Recommendations for Further Studies

This study has quite a few limitations. First, the deployment and analysis of thirteen cartoons from *The Punch* alone may not account for the diversity of representations of HFCs across diverse virtual newspapers, creating a bias. Also, it is limited by its inability to determine the interpretations given to the comic strips by the viewers. However, the representative data offer insights into tropes and recurring patterns of Nigerian online cartoons addressing HFCs. The dataset could be expanded by future studies to include more comic strips from diverse online newspapers. While the analysis is effective in revealing meaning potentials, future studies might examine other modes, including sound and animation, in other online media platforms. Finally, future research could deploy interview techniques or surveys to explore audience reception and interpretation of cartoons. This would provide perceptions on the effects of cartoon narratives.

## REFERENCES


Abdulbaqi, S. S., & Ariemu, O. (2017). Newspaper framing of herdsmen-farmers' conflicts in Nigeria and its implication on peace-oriented journalism. *The Creative Artists, 11*(2), 77–105.

Adisa, R. S., & Adekunle, O. A. (2010). Farmer-herdsmen conflicts: A factor analysis of socio-economic conflict variables among arable crop farmers in North Central Nigeria. *Journal of Human Ecology (Delhi, India), 30*(1), 1–9. DOI: 10.1080/09709274.2010.11906266

Ajayi, A. H., & Sennuga, S. O. (2022). Perceived factors responsible for herders-farmers' communal conflict in Plateau State, Nigeria. *International Journal of Agricultural Extension and Rural Development Studies, 9*(2), 32–46. DOI: 10.37745/ijaerds.15vol9n23246

Akanni, T., & Ibuot, U.P. (2023). Visual compositions and layout designs of the front pages of nigerian newspapers: a study of *Vanguard, Punch, Daily Sun* and *Leadership. The International Journal of Humanities & Social Studies,* 11 (7), 213-223. DOI No.: DOI: 10.24940/theijhss/2023/v11/i7/HS2307-025

Amore, K. P., & Atoloye, L. (2016). A systematic functional-multimodal discourse analysis of some cartoons connected with Nigeria's 2015 general elections. *The Nigerian Journal of Communication, 13*(1), 23–46.

Bello, B., & Abdullahi, M. M. (2021). Farmers-herdsmen conflict, cattle rustling, and banditry: The dialectics of insecurity in Anka and Maradun Local Government Area of Zamfara State, Nigeria. *SAGE Open, 11*(4), 21582440211040117. Advance online publication. DOI: 10.1177/21582440211040117

Chiedozie, P. A., Okpala, N. V., & Alaku, M. E. (2023). A comparative analysis of the headlines of *The Punch* newspaper and *Instablog* in Nigeria. *International Journal of African Research and Sustainability Studies, 2*(2), 22–35.

Chiluwa, I., & Chiluwa, I. M. (2020). 'Deadlier than Boko Haram': Representations of the Nigerian herder-farmer conflict in the local and foreign press. *Media, War & Conflict, 15*(1), 3–24. Advance online publication. DOI: 10.1177/1750635220902490

Chukwuma, K. H. (2020). Constructing the herder–farmer conflict as (in)security in Nigeria. *African Security, 13*(1), 54–76. DOI: 10.1080/19392206.2020.1732703

Chukwuokoro, I., Ononye, C., & Ngene, E. (2024). Multimodal discourse analysis of editorial cartoons on insecurity in Nigeria's 2023 general elections. *EBSU Journal of Social Sciences and Humanities, 14*(2), 334–343.

Efobi, U., Adejumo, O., & Kim, J. (2025). Climate change and the farmer-pastoralist's violent conflict: Experimental evidence from Nigeria. *Ecological Economics*, *228*, 1–14. DOI: 10.1016/j.ecolecon.2024.108449

Flintan, F., Robinson, L., & Bello, M.A. (2021). *A review of tenure and governance in the pastoral lands of East and West Africa.* Supporting pastoralism and agriculture in recurrent and protracted crisis (SPARC).

Genyi, G. A. (2017). Ethnic and religious identities shaping contestation for land based resources: The Tiv-farmers and pastoralists conflicts in central Nigeria until 2014. *Journal of Living Together*, *4-5*(1), 136–151.

Gürsoy, G. (2019). *Farmers-herders conflict in Nigeria: an analysis of the root causes and the effects of the conflict.* [Masters dissertation, Philipps-Universität Marburg]. Research Gate. https://www.researchgate.net/publication/347948827

Kress, G. (2010). *Multimodality: A social semiotic approach to contemporary communication*. Routledge.

Kress, G., & van Leeuwen, T. (2001). *Multimodal discourse: The modes and media of contemporary communication.* Arnold.

Kress, G., & van Leeuwen, T. (2021). *Reading images: The grammar of visual design* (3rd ed.). Routledge.

Nassef, M., Eba, B., Islam, K., Djohy, G., & Flintan, F. (2023). *Causes of farmer-herder conflicts in Africa: A systematic scoping review*. SPARC.

Nwankwo, C. F. (2021). Discursive construction of the farmer-pastoralist conflict in Nigeria. *Open Political Science*, *4*(1), 136–146. DOI: 10.1515/openps-2021-0014

Nwankwo, C. F. (2024). Constructing farmer-pastoralist conflict as Islamization: Transformation and adaptation of resource competition discourse in the Nigerian Benue Valley. *Geoforum*, *148*, 1–9.

Nwankwo, C. F., Ayadiuno, R. U., Ali, A. N., & Madu, I. A. (2020). Farmer-herder conflict: The politics of media discourse in Nigeria. *International Journal of Scientific Research*, *76*(1), 191–221. DOI: 10.21506/j.ponte.2020.1.13

Oghuvbu, E. A., & Oghuvbu, O. B. (2020). Farmers-herdsmen conflict in Africa: The case of Nigeria. *Vestnik RUDN.International Relations*, *20*(4), 698–706. DOI: 10.22363/2313-0660-2020-20-4-698-706

Ohaja, E. U., & Momoh, T. N. (2023). Multimodal analysis of the aesthetic appeals of cartoons in selected Nigerian dailies. *GVU Journal of Management and Social Sciences*, *8*(2), 119–130.

Olaniyan, A., & Yahaya, A. (2016). Cows, bandits, and violent conflicts: Understanding cattle rustling in northern Nigeria. *Africa Spectrum*, *51*(3), 93–105. DOI: 10.1177/000203971605100305

Oli, N. P., Ibekwe, C. C., & Nwankwo, I. U. (2018). Prevalence of herdsmen and farmers conflict in Nigeria. *International Journal of Innovative Studies in Sociology and Humanities*, *3*(1), 30–39.

Olomojobi, O., & Ajilore, K. (2018). Press coverage of herders-farmers conflict in selected Nigerian newspaper. *Journal of Communication and Media Research*, *10*(1), 38–51.

Osisanwo, A. (2024). Gunmen, bandits and ransom demanders: A corpus-assisted critical discourse study of the construction of abduction in the Nigerian press. *Corpus-based Studies across. Humanities (Washington)*, *2*(1), 1–22. DOI: 10.1515/csh-2024-0003

## ADDITIONAL READING

Ajakaye, D. O., & Dubamo, T. (2022). Ideological representation of the e-images on herders-farmers conflict. In Ibileye, G. (Ed.), *Studies in media and ideological representation of herders/farmers conflict in Nigeria* (pp. 91–108). Malthouse Press.

Brottem, L. (2021, July 12). *The growing complexity of farmer-herder conflict in West and Central Africa.* https://africacenter.org/publication/growing-complexity-farmer-herder-conflict-west-central-africa/

Chiluwa, I., & Chiluwa, I. M. (2020). 'Deadlier than Boko Haram': Representations of the Nigerian herder-farmer conflict in the local and foreign press. *Media, War & Conflict*, *15*(1), 3–24. Advance online publication. DOI: 10.1177/1750635220902490

Lulu, A. L., Racman, S. M. H. A., & Habeeb, L. S. (2022). A multimodal analysis of political cartoons and the discourse of Palestinians' displacement: Sheikh Jarrah case. *Reflections: The SoL Journal*, *29*(3), 700–717. DOI: 10.61508/refl.v29i3.262809

Nwankwo, C. F. (2022). Grammar of geopolitics: Geographical imaginations of farmer-herder conflicts in Nigeria. *Cografya Dergisi*, *44*, 1–18. DOI: 10.26650/JGEOG2022-888146

## KEY TERMS AND DEFINITIONS

**Agbada:** A flowing regalia with broad sleeves, typically worn by males in some parts of West Africa

**Cartoon Strips:** Illustrations conveying humour and commentary by means of images and text captions

**Herder:** One who raises or manages livestock

**Multimodal Representation:** An integration of multiple modes to communicate meaning

**Nigerian E-Newspapers:** Digital forms of newspapers available for information and news online

**Political Actors:** Individuals influencing government policies and decisions

**Sedentary Agrarian Farmers:** Groups who are permanently settled in one community, typically cultivating lands

**State Actors:** Government officials acting on national interests

# Chapter 7
# Multimodality In the Representation of the Nigerian Police Identity on Social Media

**Moses Olusanya Ayoola**
https://orcid.org/0000-0003-1291-2675
*Bamidele Olumilua University of Education, Science, and Technology, Ikere-Ekiti, Nigeria*

**Mercy Adenike Bankole**
https://orcid.org/0009-0001-3980-4239
*Bamidele Olumilua University of Education, Science, and Technology, Ikere-Ekiti, Nigeria*

## ABSTRACT

*This chapter presents a multimodal analysis of social media memes that represent and construct the identity of the Nigerian Police, using Kress and Van Leeuwen's (2001) framework. The study examines ten memes from Facebook, TikTok, and Instagram, selected between 2020 and 2024 using hashtags like #NigerianPolice, #EndSARS, and #PoliceBrutality. Through analysis of multimodal elements, text, images, and speech, the memes critique police practices while also reflecting attempts at positive identity construction by the police. The memes are categorized based on themes such as inefficiency, corruption, and abuse of power. Findings reveal that although the Nigerian Police use memes to portray themselves positively, public sentiment, expressed through humour in the memes, consistently highlights their institutional failures. These representations, rooted in Nigeria's sociopolitical landscape, underscore social media's role in shaping and reinforcing public distrust of the police*

DOI: 10.4018/979-8-3373-5297-8.ch007

*as an institution of government.*

## INTRODUCTION

The Nigerian Police is a social institution that evokes both negative and positive perceptions among Nigerian citizens regarding its role and effectiveness. It is widely perceived to have failed in its original responsibility due to persistent issues of inefficiency, corruption, human rights abuses, and lack of accountability (Tiwa, 2024; Hills, 2012). It is often perceived to have outgrown its original design, despite undergoing numerous reforms and transformational periods marked by reports, media commentaries, protests, and legislative scrutiny over the years (Hills, 2008, 2012). It now turns to exert power on the very citizens it is designed to protect (Nwoke, 2022). This perception was reinforced by the persistent abuse of power that characterised the activities of members of the Nigerian Police. Tiwa (2024) has rightly observed that "at the same time, police officers resort to informal processes that further undermine public trust in the criminal justice system and create a self-defeating cycle that allows many to justify support for or active participation in illegal forms of crime control, including lynching by mobs and extra-legal killing by security forces". This has also led to many court litigations and several protests by the citizens against the brutality and abuses by the members of the Nigerian police such as the ENDSARS protest of 2020 (Ekoh & George, 2021). Police identity in Nigeria has been demystified, with the public expressing their frustrations with the way it operates through several public demonstrations and social media platforms. Thus, Social media is an ecosystem where the Police are visibly abused, ridiculed, and lampooned. Police identity attribution in Nigeria is reflected in social media's multimodal and discursive influences. Some previous studies (Oluremi & Olaniyan, 2023; Okesola & Oyebode, 2023) have shown that several Nigerian memes depict in comic mode how police perform their various roles in frontstage and backstage settings. Such identity attributions have also led the Nigerian police to embark on reputation management to shape, maintain or improve the public image of the police force through television programmes, press releases, and documentaries in various media channels. While many citizens criticize the police for inefficiency and abuse, others still acknowledge the constraints of inadequate funding, poor working conditions, and political interference, which hinder optimal performance (Akinlabi, 2020).

The public's relationship with the Nigerian Police is therefore a complex one, characterized by both negative and positive perceptions regarding trust, legitimacy, effectiveness, and accountability. On the one hand, widespread allegations of police brutality, corruption, and inefficiency have fuelled protests, social media outcries, and public distrust (Akinlabi, 2020; Amnesty International, 2020). Movements such as EndSARS have highlighted systemic issues, including extrajudicial killings, harassment, and abuse of power (Ojebode et al., 2021). On the other hand, the police force is also recognized for its efforts in maintaining law and order, combating crime, and responding to security threats despite institutional challenges (Alemika, 2021). Positive representations of the Nigerian Police in the media often emphasize acts of bravery, community engagement, and crime prevention initiatives (Olowojolu, 2022). The representation of the Nigerian Police on social media is, therefore, a multifaceted phenomenon that reflects the public's diverse and sometimes contradictory perceptions of the institution's identity. In recent years, social media platforms such as Twitter, TikTok, Facebook, and Instagram have become crucial spaces where the public engages in discourse on issues of public concern such as security and law enforcement. Memes are also a popular form of social media expression, that expresses ideas through a combination of text, images, speech, and humor, making them a powerful tool for public opinion (Knobel & Lankshear,2007; Davison, 2012; Shifman, 2013, 2014). Oluremi and Olaniyan (2023) describe memes as "cyber weapons now integrated into our digital social life and discourse structure". Okesola and Oyebode (2023) also describe memes as "communicative tools and discursive weapons conceived and created for humour, digital activism, socio-political dissent or protest in different areas of human society". They went further to explain that "the nature of internet communication, vis-a-vis its ability to interact instantaneously, remove social boundaries, and make contents flow faster from one person to another, and from one medium to another, has helped in making memes to be a popular means of communication among Internet users". However, how these multimodal representations contribute to constructing the Nigerian Police's identity and influence public perception remains underexplored. Hence, this study intends to investigate how the Nigerian Police is perceived and how these perceptions are constructed and propagated on social media This research aims to fill the gap in existing literature by focusing on the intersection of identity construction, public perception, and social media representation. This study, therefore, focuses on how the identity of Nigerian Police is constructed by the citizens and the police reputation management strategies on social media. By analyzing these multimodal representations, the research seeks to provide insights into the public's attitudes toward the Nigerian Police, identify common themes and tropes, and explore the impact of these representations on public discourse and sentiment.

## OBJECTIVES OF THE STUDY

This research has the sole objective of examining the multimodal representation of the Nigerian Police on social media, specifically focusing on memes sourced from TikTok, and Instagram. The study delves into how the Nigerian Police is perceived, constructed, and represented on social media platforms, with a focus on understanding the intersection between identity construction, public perception, and social media representation. The specific objectives are to:

i. Identifies the multimodal elements (text, images, symbols) used in these memes, and how they contribute to the overall message of the memes
ii. Examine the identity of the Nigerian police represented and constructed in social media memes.
iii. Examine how the representations reflect and influence public perception of the Nigerian police and discuss the role of humour in the construction of police practices and authority in these memes within the Nigerian context.

## LITERATURE REVIEW

The representation of police forces on social media has been a subject of significant scholarly interest from diverse fields of study. Some studies have explored how police departments utilize social media to engage with the public, enhance transparency, and manage their public image (Schneider, 2016; Crump, 2011; Ajayi, 2016). For instance, Ajayi (2016) discusses how the Nigerian Police use social media to combat crime and interact with citizens, noting the potential for both positive engagement and negative backlash. The study provides a comparative framework for understanding how the Nigerian Police, within its local sociopolitical context, utilizes social media to shape its public perception. The present study extends Ajayi's work by examining how multimodal resources are used in online representations—both by the police institution itself and by social media users—to construct, contest, and negotiate police identity.

Several studies within and outside Nigeria (Aboh, 2024; Adetiba, 2021; Chiluwa & Ifukor, 2015; Denisova, 2019) have examined the role of social media in organising protests against Nigeria Police activities and the government. Aboh (2024) studies the discursive strategies used by EndSARS protesters in their tweets and Facebook comments to construct SARS officers; hold the Nigerian government accountable, and demand social change. The study revealed three strategies: constructing SARS as oppressors, representing the Nigerian government as insensitive, and issuing a clarion call for action. The analysis shows that these strategies enabled the protesters to construct the victim-aggressor categorisation, thereby legitimizing their resistance to police brutality and demand for change. Adetiba (2021) discusses the role of Twitter, Facebook, and WhatsApp in facilitating #EndSARS protests, arguing that social media served as both an organizational tool and a digital archive for police brutality incidents. These studies demonstrate that social media enhances modern protest movements, including those against Nigerian police misconduct. The present study extends this discourse by investigating how digital memes function as tools of resistance, satire, and advocacy for police reform.

Akerele-Popoola, Azeez, and Adeniyi (2022) examined how Twitter was used to organize the #EndSARS protest in Nigeria. They also investigated the extent to which Twitter has promoted or degraded democracy in Nigeria through its support for enhancing freedom of expression and being a driver of social protests. The study adopted a qualitative approach using in-depth interviews. Twenty Nigerian youths were purposely selected across the Southwestern states of Nigeria through the snowballing technique. The study found that Twitter is effective for social protests, as witnessed in the #EndSARS protest, because it is a magnificent and functional tool that is powerful in creating a strong tie and thick engagement during and after the protest. However, the effect of Twitter is temporal as the ties it can create get weaker by the day. The study concluded that Twitter can either enhance or degrade democracy depending on how its users, who are the core drivers of change, use it in the democratic process. Their study confirms that social media provides a space for the public to construct and contest police identity, aligning with our study's interest in how the police are perceived and represented.

Ahaotu and Oshamo (2023) carried out a Multimodal Discourse Analysis of Selected Social Media Posts on the #BlackLivesMatter Protest. The research goal was to explore the socio-semiotic meaning exposed in participants' posts on the #BlackLivesMatter protests through social media #hashtag (Twitter, Facebook, Instagram, and online articles), using Kress and van Leeuwen's theory of Visual Grammar to unravel visual-verbal synchrony in selected posts used in the Black Lives Matter protest. The study identified evidence of multimodality, such as verbal-visual synchrony expressed through text, font, images, colours, and framing, and found, among others, that these features of the posts enhanced the overall theme of the #BlackLivesMatter protest. The study concluded that the themes that emerged from the analysis were projected in the posts with the aid of multimodality. The application of multimodal Discourse Analysis by Ahaotu and Oshamo (2023) is directly connected to our present study, as we aim to analyse how similar multi-modal strategies are used in social media memes and digital content to construct the Nigerian Police identity—whether as corrupt, inefficient, oppressive, or, in some cases, as reformative agents.

In a related study, Awopetu and Aseniserare's (2021) presented social media as a feasible medium and instrument for activism and protest movements using the case of the #EndSARS protests in Nigeria. The study adopted Kress and van Leeuwen's (2006) theory of visual grammar to examine how visual images could be deployed in activism and protest movements in the analysis of some images of the 2020 #EndSARS protests in Nigeria. The study demonstrates that the depiction of visual elements, such as objects, people, and events, in these images suggests a preponderant involvement of youth in the events as well as a depiction of law enforcement officials, the police, as opponents to the protesters' activities, which provides insights into the protests. The study concludes that the effectiveness of visuals, such as protest photos can serve as a narrative and record of the protest activities in addition to conveying the anger, demands, and concerns of the demonstrators. Awopetu and Aseniserare's (2021) research underscores the power of multimodal discourse in shaping law enforcement narratives on social media. Their findings validate our approach in examining digital memes as a medium for public discourse on the Nigerian Police. By extending their focus on protest images to memes and other social media representations, our study will offer a broader understanding of how social media-driven narratives influence the identity construction and perception of the Nigerian Police in contemporary Nigeria.

These existing studies provide insights into the use of social media by both the public and the security agents. Some of the studies suggest that social media allows police to present a controlled narrative, often focusing on community engagement, crime prevention, and positive interactions with the public while others imply that social media is a means explored by the public to protest against police anti-public activities and approaches. However, the representation of the Nigerian Police identity through multimodal texts on social media is a relatively underexplored area. Hence, the gap this study intends to fill; is to provide a comprehensive understanding of the multimodal representation of the Nigerian Police on social media. By focusing on memes, the study seeks to explore how various modes of communication are employed to convey complex messages that influence public opinion and reflect societal attitudes toward law enforcement in Nigeria.

## THEORETICAL FRAMEWORK

The analysis in this study draws on Kress & van Leeuwen's (2001) multimodal analysis framework, which involves examining the various modes of communication used in the memes. It has to do with the use of more than one semiotic resource to inform. Multimodality involves the integration of various modes such as text, image, video, and audio to convey messages. Kress and van Leeuwen (2001) define multimodality as the use of several semiotic modes in a single communicative act or text. “As an interdisciplinary study, multimodality examines the semiotic resources people use to communicate and interact in social settings. Multimodality can thus be seen as a broader definition of the study of language, since it studies language, which traditionally is understood as writing and speech, as an act of meaning-making that also involves non-linguistic semiotic resources, e.g. typography, color, sound, gesture” (Poulsen,2015; O’Halloran, 2011). Kress and Van Leeuwen's approach to multimodality is chosen as the theoretical framework for this study because it provides a valuable framework for analyzing how meaning is made across different modes of communication. Their work has contributed to a broader understanding of communication as a multimodal process, with applications in media studies, education, and digital communication. By focusing on the affordances of modes, the role of design, and the importance of social context, their approach offers tools for analyzing the complex ways in which meaning is constructed in contemporary texts

Kress and Van Leeuwen’s approach to multimodality is grounded in social semiotics, which focuses on how meaning is socially constructed through signs and symbols. Social semiotics considers all forms of communication as inherently influenced by the social, cultural, and historical contexts in which they occur. Meaning is never fixed; it is negotiated between individuals and groups shaped by shared conventions and social norms (Hodge & Kress, 1988; van Leeuwen, 2005). Kress and Van Leeuwen developed a “grammar” of visual design that is parallel to the grammar of verbal language. Just as sentences are structured using syntactic rules, visual elements like colour, composition, and framing also have structures that guide how they are interpreted. This visual grammar is essential for understanding how meaning is represented through images and other visual modes. In Kress and Van Leeuwen’s framework, a mode is a socially shaped resource for meaning-making. Modes include language, images, gestures, sound, and even layout and typography (Jewitt 2009, 2014; van Leeuwen, 2005; Kress, 2010). Each mode has specific affordances or potentials for meaning-making that are determined by its physical, social, and cultural properties. Modes are shaped by cultural conventions and practices. Communication rarely relies on a single mode. Instead, different modes work together to create meaning. Each mode has its affordances, meaning that it provides different possibilities for expressing meaning. The concept of affordances refers to the potential uses and constraints of each mode. Kress and van Leeuwen emphasize that different modes offer different affordances based on their material and cultural properties.

Kress and van Leeuwen’s (2006) concept of Visual Grammar adapts Halliday’s three metafunctions of language to multimodal communication, emphasizing how images contribute to meaning-making. These three metafunctions are representational (experiential) meaning, interactive (interpersonal) meaning, and compositional (textual) meaning. (Jewitt & Oyama, 2001). Representational meaning explains how images depict people, objects, and actions, distinguishing between narrative images, which show action and movement (through action processes, reactional processes, speech/mental processes, and conversion processes), and conceptual images, which focus on classification, analysis, or symbolism. Interactive meaning examines the relationship between the image and the viewer through three key aspects: contact (where direct gaze creates engagement, while indirect gaze allows observation), social distance (intimate, social, or impersonal relations suggested by image proximity), and attitude (viewer involvement, detachment, or alignment with the subject's perspective)(Machin & Mayr, 2012). Lastly, compositional meaning analyzes how elements are arranged to guide interpretation, considering factors such as information value (left-right, top-bottom positioning of elements), salience (use of size, color, and contrast to highlight key elements), and framing (how boundaries within the image create connections or separations between elements).(Kress & van Leeuwen, 2006; Bateman, 2014). These metafunctions provide a systematic approach to how images function grammatically in meaning-making processes.

Thus, in Kress and Van Leeuwen's multimodality framework, representation is inherently multimodal. They posit that "Meaning is not confined to words (language) alone but extends to images, gestures, sounds, and other semiotic resources". Representation is influenced by the social, historical, and cultural environment in which it occurs. Different societies or communities may have different conventions for representing the same objects or actions and often involve interplay between modes i.e. the interaction of different modes.

Therefore, relations among modes are key to understanding every instance of communication. Social media platforms like Facebook, Twitter, and Instagram are inherently multimodal, offering users the ability to combine text, images, videos, and other interactive elements in communication. So, the main issue that forms the apex of this study is to look at how the identity of the Nigerian police force is represented on social media by the public and how the Nigerian police for also construct identity on social media.

## METHODOLOGY

The study focuses on Nigerian memes of Nigerian police sourced from TikTok and Instagram. These platforms are chosen due to their high user engagement and the prevalence of meme culture. Ten (10) memes purposively selected between 2020 and 2024, ensuring representation across both platforms were identified using specific hashtags and keywords related to the Nigerian Police, such as #NigerianPolice, #EndSARS, and #PoliceBrutality. Five memes were randomly selected from each of the platforms. The selection process was purposive, focusing on memes that had significant engagement (likes, shares, comments) and relevance to police representation. A number of the memes are video memes which combine short moving images (video) with overlaid text that conveys a socially relevant or humorous message. The screenshots of such video memes containing their overlaid text are presented in the form of image-based memes because the motion and sound cannot be captured on paper but the analysis takes full cognizance of the audio-visual modes. The time frame is selected to capture a range of representations and reactions to significant events involving the Nigerian Police, including the EndSARS movement and other notable instances of police activity, and the hashtags and keywords are chosen because they are commonly associated with discussions and representations of the Nigerian Police on social media. The analysis employs Kress & van Leeuwen (2001) multimodal analysis framework to examine the different modes of communication used in the memes. The memes were categorized according to themes, modes of communication and discursive strategy. The results were interpreted in the context of Nigeria's sociopolitical landscape and social media's role in shaping public perceptions of the Nigerian Police.

## ANALYSIS AND DISCUSSION

The memes are analysed and discussed based on the type of identity they either represent or construct. The two broad categories are: the public's perception of the Nigerian Police (negative identity representation) and the Nigerian Police's construction of their own identity (positive identity). The following themes are discussed under the first category as represented by the memes: The Nigerian Police as inefficient and unresponsive; The Nigerian police as abusive and oppressive; The Nigerian police as corrupt; The Nigerian police as incompetent, while the second category captures the following themes; The Nigerian police as defenders of citizens' right and the Nigerian police as Agents of reform. Each category now captures how memes shape police identity in social media discourse.

a. Public's Negative perception/representation of Nigerian police:
   i. The Nigerian Police as Inefficient and Unresponsive: A Social Critique through Memes

The memes in this category represent the the Nigerian police force's perceived lack of responsiveness and effectiveness which is a negative identity for the Nigerian Police. All the modes of the memes in this category combine to communicate this identity as found in the analysis of Figure 1 below:

*Figure 1. Police and public perception of unresponsiveness*

This meme has a textual mode and a visual mode. The meme adheres to widely recognized internet conventions for meme formatting: text at the top, and image at the bottom. This layout leads the viewer to first read the humorous critique before looking at the image of the police officers, creating a punchline effect. The text, "Hours after Robbery have ended, #9japolice be like 'Oga where did they pass?" is in Nigerian Pidgin English, which is widely understood across Nigeria; that immediately connects with a Nigerian audience. The hashtag #9japolice refers to the Nigerian police force, drawing attention to issues of police response times and inefficiency. The phrase "be like" is a common informal phrase used to imitate or parody someone's speech, highlighting how the police are portrayed as always arriving late after incidents have occurred. Pidgin English is used not only for ease of understanding but also for humour. The informal tone ("Oga where did they pass?") mimics real-life casual conversations, making the meme relatable. It portrays the police as clueless, creating a humorous and critical social commentary on their efficiency.

The image shows a group of police officers walking casually with no visible urgency. Their body language (holding weapons loosely, walking in a line) suggests nonchalance and a lack of readiness for action. The officers are in uniform, signalling their authority, but their casual demeanour contradicts their role of enforcing the law, furthering the humorous critique. This contrasts sharply with the context of "robbery" in the text, reinforcing the stereotype that Nigerian police are often late to emergencies or crises.

Culturally, the meme is situated within the widespread public frustration with the Nigerian police force's perceived lack of responsiveness and effectiveness. The humour comes from the fact that the situation is an exaggerated but familiar scenario, where police arrive after a robbery is long over and ask irrelevant questions. The hashtag "#9japolice" also makes the meme part of a larger online discourse surrounding police performance and public dissatisfaction. Though the image is static, the body language of the police officers walking leisurely implies inaction. The lack of urgency in their gait reinforces the critique of their delayed response, contributing to the overall humour and irony of the meme. The interplay between the image of the officers and the sarcastic text in Pidgin English produces a humorous critique of the police's delayed response to emergencies.

ii. The Nigerian Police as Abusive and Oppressive: A Public Representation in Memes

The analysis here focuses on how the public uses social media memes to portray the Nigerian Police as abusive, irrational, and oppressive. The multimodal elements (text, visuals, symbols, gestures) of the memes in this category reinforce themes of harassment, extrajudicial practices, and misuse of power by the Nigeria police as found in figures 2, 3 and 4 here.

*Figure 2. Nigerian police's superficial profiling of citizens*

This meme involves both textual and visual modes. The meme's text, "*You wear red shirt inside a black car, how many cult you dey?*", accompanied by the hashtag #9jaPolice, provides insight into the representation of the police-citizen interaction and the underlying cultural and societal discourses in Nigeria. The image on the other hand, depicts two police officers interacting with a man (presumably a civilian) wearing a red cap and a white shirt, under a pedestrian bridge in a public space, likely a street in Nigeria.

In the linguistic mode, the phrase "how many cult you dey?" is in Nigerian Pidgin English, which signifies a less formal form of communication typical of the Nigerian police. The phrase "*You wear red shirt inside a black car*" implies superficial profiling by the police based on appearance, associating colours and attire with cultism. This illustrates how clothing choices are linked to perceptions of crime and cultism, which is a significant issue in Nigeria, especially concerning young men and police surveillance. However, the hashtag further highlights the context, alluding to widespread issues with the Nigerian Police Force, including profiling, harassment, and misuse of power. It suggests that this scenario is part of broader patterns of misconduct associated with the police.

In the visual mode, there is a portrayer of power dynamics. In the image, the police officers are shown standing over the civilian, who is in a subdued position. This visual framing underscores the power imbalance between police and citizens in Nigeria. The civilian appears to be physically restrained indicating potential coercion or intimidation. The interaction takes place in a public area, likely a busy road, which signifies the normalcy or routine nature of such police-civilian encounters in Nigeria. It suggests that such interactions are not hidden or unusual but occur in full view of the public.

Exploring the interplay among text, image, language, gesture and layout, the meme highlights the absurdity of the situation: being interrogated or suspected of cult membership simply because of clothing colours (red and black). The police's action seems exaggerated or irrational, adding a layer of critique about how individuals are often unjustly profiled and maltreated by the police in Nigeria. This connection between colour and criminality points to the broader discourse around youth profiling, gang culture, and law enforcement in Nigeria, especially how young men are targeted based on arbitrary factors like clothing.

The meme, therefore, serves as a critique of Nigerian policing, particularly the arbitrary nature of stop-and-search operations that often rely on stereotypes and prejudice. The casual tone of the caption amplifies the everyday reality of such situations, turning what is likely a serious and potentially dangerous interaction into a piece of satirical commentary. There is irony in how the seemingly random combination of wearing a red shirt and being inside a black car leads to an interrogation about cultism; a practice commonly associated with violence or secret societies in Nigeria. The meme, by capturing this moment, uses humour to expose the irrationality of the police's logic in the Nigerian context.

*Figure 3. Nigerian police's irrationality*

Just like figure 2 above, this meme represents the abuse of power by the Nigerian police and their irrationality in profiling people as criminals. The two modes involved here are textual mode and visual mode. The linguistic element of the meme is a statement credited to #9jaPolice(Nigerian police) and it reads*:" the picture in your license is carrying afro, but you're on lowcut, abeg follow us to the station.*" The image also shows two police officers engaging with a civilian in a public space, under a pedestrian bridge, with cars and passersby around. The analysis of this meme focuses on the interaction among the text, image, and gesture, as well as the cultural and social messages conveyed through both.

The linguistic element uses a blend of Pidgin English and Nigerian English. The phrase "carrying afro" refers to the civilian's hairstyle in the picture used in his licence, while "on lowcut" refers to his current hairstyle. The humorous tone, particularly the use of "abeg" (a Nigerian pidgin term meaning "please"), adds a layer of irony to the situation. The police are portrayed here as focusing on a superficial, almost trivial detail - the discrepancy between the civilian's current hairstyle and the one in his license photograph. This suggests an absurd justification for bringing someone to the station, which, in reality, should not be a serious matter. The hashtag again points to this being a critique of police behaviour in Nigeria, using humour to highlight the irrationality of certain police actions.

The images in the visual mode enhance the message of the text. The civilian is in close physical contact with one of the officers, implying that he is being restrained or led, while the other officer looks on. The police officers' stances and uniforms convey authority, and the civilian appears to be at a disadvantage.

The public setting emphasizes the routine nature of this type of police stop and check, suggesting that such interactions are a common occurrence in everyday Nigerian life. The setting, which includes a pedestrian bridge and busy road, reinforces the idea of public surveillance and the visibility of police power.

The civilian is wearing casual clothing and a red cap. The red cap might also play into cultural associations or stereotypes, similar to the first meme, where clothing/attire choices are linked to suspicion.

The text and the image work together to emphasize the ridiculousness of the situation. The police are shown interrogating someone about his hairstyle, which, in real life, is unlikely to be a valid reason for arrest or interrogation. The visual depiction of a man being stopped by the police for such a trivial reason adds humour, making a critical point about the misuse of power. This multimodal pairing exposes the inefficiency and arbitrariness of some police actions in Nigeria. The text reveals how citizens may be unfairly harassed for inconsequential reasons, such as a hairstyle change, pointing to larger issues of profiling and arbitrary policing. The meme critiques how the Nigerian police are often perceived to prioritize unimportant details over real criminal behaviour. The use of language (Pidgin English, informal phrasing) adds to the humour while remaining grounded in the local context, making the critique both culturally specific and accessible to a Nigerian audience.

By focusing on trivial details like hairstyles, the meme reflects the larger societal issues of profiling and the disconnect between police actions and actual crime prevention. The meme taps into the discourse around police harassment and abuse of power in Nigeria. This meme is another effective piece of social commentary, leveraging humour, text, and imagery to critique the arbitrary nature of Nigerian policing. The meme highlights the absurdity of Nigerian police focusing on trivial details like hairstyle changes, exposing a broader pattern of profiling and harassment. The visual and textual modes work together to create a humorous and satirical, yet poignant representation of power abuse by the Nigerian police.

*Figure 4. Nigerian police and stereotypes of young men with cars*

This meme, like Figure 3 above, represents the police irrationality and arbitrariness in profiling the young men as criminals in Nigeria. We can break down the components of this meme into visual and textual modes. In the visual mode, the meme features two side-by-side images of an older man (likely a police officer) with an intense or suspicious facial expression. The man's facial expression is key to the meme, as it conveys suspicion and judgment. The officer's slightly tilted head and narrowed eyes further reinforce the idea of suspicion or scrutiny. His facial expression could be interpreted as a questioning look, as though he doubts the legitimacy of the person he is observing. The facial expressions in both images are the key gestures. The furrowed brow and scrutinizing gaze communicate suspicion without any words, drawing on a stereotype of how police officers in Nigeria often view young men. These gestures are non-verbal cues that indicate an assumption of guilt or mistrust. The two images are juxtaposed side by side, showing the progression or slight change in the officer's expression. This creates a sense of continuity in the gesture, as though his suspicion deepens or remains constant. The close-up nature of the photos brings the viewer into the officer's personal space, intensifying the interaction

The linguistic elements, "*The way a Nigerian policeman looks at you if you're a young guy with beards and you drive a nice car*" sets the stage for the image by describing a common stereotype in Nigeria where police officers often target young men with beards who drive expensive cars, suspecting them of *yahoo yahoo* and other criminal activities. The statement creates a humorous expectation for the audience by connecting the description with the image of a stern, judgmental officer. The hashtag, #9japolice further situates the meme within a specific socio-cultural context. It emphasizes the focus on the Nigerian police. There is a shared cultural understanding of the phrase "*young guy with beards and you drive a nice car,*" which reflects a stereotype of someone involved in "*Yahoo Yahoo*" (internet fraud). The meme taps into this phenomenon, making it instantly recognizable and humorous to a Nigerian audience familiar with police attitudes. Thus, making it a social critique of Nigerian police

This meme plays on the common stereotype in Nigeria that young men who drive flashy cars and have beards are often profiled by police officers as internet fraudsters or criminals. It critiques a societal issue where profiling based on appearance and material possessions is frequent. This meme uses multimodal elements--text (caption), visuals (images of the officer), and gestures (facial expressions)--to convey a satirical comment on police profiling in Nigeria. The stern expressions of the police officer in the images, combined with the linguistic element, create a humorous but critical narrative about how young men are often judged based on their appearance and the type of car they drive. The meme relies heavily on the visual mode to enhance the sarcastic tone of the text. It draws upon a shared societal experience to make a statement about the profiling habits of Nigerian police officers, while the juxtaposition of the two images emphasizes the depth of the officer's suspicion. The meme critiques societal norms around policing, appearance, and assumed criminality in Nigeria.

iii. The Nigerian police as Corrupt: A public representation

The third identity that the memes try to represent for the Nigerian police is that of their penchant for bribery and corruption. The analysis of Figure 5 below portrays the Nigerian Police as corrupt.

*Figure 5. Nigerian police and the culture of roadside extortion*

The components of this meme can be broken down into visual and textual modes. In the visual mode, a uniformed police officer wearing a helmet and protective gear is stretching his hand toward a vehicle. His attire represents authority. The officer's

gesture appears to be a request or expectation for something, which is typically understood in Nigerian contexts as a subtle demand for a bribe. The background, a road with a clear sky, suggests a highway or road checkpoint, a common site where these interactions occur. The textual mode has the linguistic element "*Anything for the boys?":* This phrase is crucial in shaping the meme's meaning. It's an informal expression often used in Nigeria, where "the boys" refers to police officers, and "anything" suggests a bribe or "settlement." The tone is non-confrontational but with an underlying expectation. The simple font conveys an everyday situation, emphasizing that this is a common occurrence. The police officer's outstretched hand is a key gesture that supports the meaning of the text. The body language reinforces the expectation for an exchange, making the non-verbal demand clear even without the accompanying text. In Nigeria, interactions like this between police and citizens at checkpoints are often associated with bribery, which is an unspoken social reality. The meme taps into a shared understanding of this social practice. The phrase "*Anything for the boys*?" is culturally charged. It represents a euphemism for corruption, implying the normalization of such encounters between police and law-abiding citizens.

The meme uses multimodal elements--visual (image of the police officer), textual ("Anything for the boys?"), and gestural (hand gesture) --to communicate a familiar socio-cultural situation (bribery and corruption). The combination of these modes reinforces the interaction's meaning: a subtle demand for a bribe from a police officer. This meme relies heavily on shared cultural knowledge and social practices to convey its humour and critique of the bribery and corruption culture in Nigeria. The juxtaposition of text and image creates a powerful critique of the Nigerian Police as corrupt.

iv. The Nigerian Police as incompetent: A public representation

The fourth identity of Nigerian Police that is represented in our data set that of incompetence and unprofessionalism. The video meme in Figure 6, below, effectively combines different modes—text, visual imagery, sound, and social context to create a humorous critique of the Nigerian police force as incompetent in the use of the English Language and unprofessionalism in making arrests.

*Figure 6. Nigerian police and stereotypes of Incompetence*

The analysis of this video meme was done by paying attention to how each mode (language, visuals, gestures, etc.) conveys meaning. This meme effectively combines different modes—text, visual imagery, and social context to mock police incompetence and lack of professionalism.

In the video mode, the young man in the meme mimics the Nigerian police by repeating a typical legal phrase common to Nigerian Police: "*It is better you remain silent because anything you say shall be used against you in the court of law.*" This phrase is emblematic of formal, legal language, but the humorous tone and the loud laughter and sound that follows the statement "*that is the only English Nigerian police can speak fluently*" in the meme highlight the inadequacy of the police force, suggesting that this may be the only English phrase they can recite fluently. Through his mimicry, the young man exposes an underlying societal belief that the Nigerian police are limited in their mastery of English, making this common legal phrase a crutch for them. The humour derives from the mismatch between the authority the police represent and their supposed linguistic competence. However, the humour suggests that this is a superficial authority, rooted more in the rote memorization of phrases than in genuine linguistic or legal competence. This raises questions about the professionalism and linguistic competence of the officers of the Nigerian police.

Analysing the visual Mode, the young man does not wear a police Uniform but rather appears casual to carry out the mimicry of police. This itself adds to the humour. In Kress's terms, even the decision not to use uniforms or props is a form of representation, suggesting that the language alone is enough to evoke the police stereotype.

In the gestural mode (body language and facial expressions) of the meme, the young man's body language, tone, and facial expressions serve to amplify the mockery of the police. His exaggerated imitation of the police's common statements and the affirmative conclusion that "*that is the only English Nigerian police can speak fluently" accompanied by a giggling reinforces the public*'s perception of the police as inept or overly reliant on formality to assert power. These gestures underscore the social critique of police professionalism. The video meme, intended to engage with an online audience familiar with the Nigerian Police force, relies on shared knowledge of the police's image in popular culture. The humour works because of the collective social experiences of the audience with the police's interaction style, especially their use of legal language to assert authority. Considering the linguistic mode of the meme, the phrase is a signifier of police authority. However, its repetitive usage across encounters with the police renders it a symbol of incompetence in the meme's narrative.

Through the combination of verbal mimicry and gestural exaggeration, the young man critiques the police's identity, portraying them as figures who over-rely on formal language to mask deeper inefficiencies. Following Kress's Multimodality theory, this analysis highlights how these modes—language, gesture, and humour—interact to construct a critical representation of the police in this meme as incompetent and unprofessional.

b. Positive Identity Construction by the Police Through Memes
   i. The Nigerian Police as Defenders of Citizens' Rights: Institutional Identity Construction through Memes

This section examines how the Nigerian Police use social media memes to construct a positive identity as protectors of law and human rights. Figures 7, and 8 in our data set are memes used by the Nigerian police to construct their identity as being proactive, ethical, lawful, and professional.

*Figure 7. Nigerian police and their strategic approach to crime prevention*

The meaning being communicated by this meme can be explicated by examining the combination of text and image. The image shows a group of police officers, with at least one leading officer in the foreground, walking alongside a line of marked police vehicles. This setup emphasizes a show of order and preparedness. The officers walking calmly, without rushing or engaging in any action, supports the text's claim that their focus is on maintaining order and preventing crime rather than reacting to it through arrests. The body language of the officers conveys readiness and vigilance, as they walk in a composed, organized manner. The uniform the face masks (suggesting a pandemic-era context), and vehicles symbolize the state's power and capacity for enforcing the law. The use of masks could also signify the officers' awareness of public safety concerns beyond crime prevention, such as health, subtly indicating a multi-faceted approach to policing. The palm trees and well-maintained environment suggest a location within an urban setting, potentially portraying a peaceful environment, which aligns with the discourse of crime prevention. The textual mode has a headline: *"We Are Not Interested in Arrest But Crime Prevention – Cross River CP":* This headline is crucial in shaping the meaning portrayed by the meme. It suggests a shift in focus from punitive law enforcement (arrests) to a more proactive approach (crime prevention). The text is positioned above the image, indicating that it provides the interpretive frame through which the image is viewed. The placement helps readers prioritize the textual message over the visual elements, even though both work together to form the overall message. The choice of words "not interested in arrest" contrasts with the typical association of police forces with punitive action, thus communicating a potentially more progressive or strategic form of policing. The text includes the source of the information. The mention of "Cross River CP" in the text (Commissioner of Police) situates the statement within a specific context--Cross River State in Nigeria--further giving it a socio-political and local meaning. It suggests that this is a real statement made by an official of the police force which serves as reputation management to improve the public image of the police force and it adds a level of seriousness or authority to the meme.

Looking at the socio-cultural mode of the meme, it taps into the broader discourse on the role of the police in society. In Nigeria, where there is often public criticism of police for being reactive or overly punitive, this statement ("not interested in arrest but crime prevention") challenges those criticisms by suggesting a proactive and preventive approach. There is also an implied critique or satire here, depending on the audience's interpretation. While the statement seems to be from a police official, the meme format could suggest that viewers may question the sincerity or effectiveness of this claim, especially if they perceive the police as primarily focusing on arrests in practice. The text's claim, "We are not interested in arrest but crime prevention," could be seen as a form of public relations or rhetoric that may not always align with public perceptions of police actions. However, the multimodal interaction of image and text ultimately represents an attempt by the police to reshape their public image against the widespread negative perception by the Nigerian citizens.

*Figure 8. Nigerian police and protection of citizens' rights*

Just like figure 7 above, this video meme taken from Tiktok effectively combines visual, textual, and audio modes to communicate a piece of important information from the police to the public. In the textual mode, the text, *"Police can't Harass or Arrest you for nothing*" serves as the primary verbal message in the meme. It conveys a sense of assurance to the viewer, highlighting the legal boundaries of police authority. The foregrounding of "Harass" and "Arrest" by capitalization emphasizes the key actions, drawing attention to them as significant concerns of the public. The negation in the sentence ("can't") strengthens the reassurance by indicating a limitation on police powers, which could be comforting to the citizens.

In the audio-visual mode, the police officer (who is a Police Public Relations officer (PPRO)) is the central figure and he is dressed in full police uniform, which represents authority. His posture and the serious look on his face suggest formality and credibility. The police car behind him adds to the scene's official nature. The background shows a formal building, possibly a police station, reinforcing the institutional context. The officer (PPRO) in the video stands to address the audience (Public) on the theme of the textual mode. The meme places the text at the top in bold, ensuring it's the first element seen before the viewer's attention shifts to the officer. The direct gaze of the police officer at the camera creates a connection with the viewer, which can either be interpreted as an attempt to build trust or to project authority. The direct eye contact encourages the audience to take the message seriously. The tone of the meme is authoritative but reassuring, positioning the officer as a figure who upholds the law without overstepping boundaries. The image appears highly realistic due to the sharp focus, recognizable uniform, and real-world setting, which adds to the authenticity of the message.

From the perspective of the socio-cultural context of the meme, this is one of the memes that the Nigerian police use in addressing concerns around police misconduct. The text responds to a widespread fear of unjust harassment by the police likely aiming to inform or reassure citizens of their rights.

The use of an audio-visual mode having a police officer in uniform lends authority to the statement, which could resonate with viewers in regions where issues of police abuse are prevalent. The speech mode allows for a more detailed explanation compared to the succinctness of the text, helping to reinforce the broader context of the meme's content. The target audience likely consists of everyday citizens who may have encountered or are worried about unjust treatment by police. The meme represents the police's attempt to reconstruct their identity and change the public perceptions of police as oppressive and abusive.

ii. The Nigerian Police as Agents of Reform: Countering Negative Narratives in Digital Spaces

The memes in Figures 9 and 10 below are samples of how the police attempt to reshape their public image by engaging with memes that depict reforms, accountability measures, and justice enforcement.

*Figure 9. Nigerian police and their stance for justice*

This TikTok video meme was made by the Nigerian Police to educate and reassure the Nigerian youth of their right. The meme has an audio-visual mode and a textual mode. Analysing the audio-visual mode, a police officer is standing before the camera to address the public on a topic of concern for the public. The officer is verbally affirming the youths' rights, which subverts the typical expectations of police interactions in Nigeria. Historically, Nigerian police interactions with citizens, especially youths, have often been perceived as aggressive or invasive. In this case, the officer acts as an advocate for legal rights, reinforcing the message of empowerment. The officer appears to be speaking with an open body posture, possibly indicating a non-confrontational or informative stance. This gesture suggests an effort to engage or educate the audience rather than to intimidate them. The image shows a typical police station, further reinforcing the institutional context. The location is visually plain, with no distractions, which keeps the focus on the officer and the message conveyed. The textual mode is an overlay text. The text presents an assertive instruction directed to the youth, reinforcing the officer's spoken message. It directly addresses the audience by saying *"All Nigerian youths must have this video on"*, encouraging them to actively save and use the video as evidence if they encounter police abuse. The text makes a clear declaration: *"Police has no right to check your phone"*. This statement directly challenges perceived police overreach and frames the youth as empowered legal subjects. It also shifts the discourse from passive compliance to active resistance against unlawful searches. The statement *"Let it go around"* indicates the meme's viral nature, urging viewers to share the video widely. This transforms the meme into a tool for social change; advocating the protection of civil rights. The message implies that the Nigerian Police as an institution is supportive of protecting citizens' rights, at least in this context. This could also be an attempt at rebuilding public trust through digital memes. The choice to disseminate this video on TikTok suggests that the message is designed to appeal to younger, digitally savvy audiences who are already active in discussing and mobilizing around police reform.

The textual, visual, and verbal elements work together to highlight how Police use social media memes to construct a positive identity as protectors of law and human rights.The meme recontextualizes the Nigerian Police Force within a framework of legal reform and civic rights. It presents an image of law enforcement that is willing to inform citizens about their rights, thus attempting to challenge the dominant discourse of police as oppressors. By making this shift, the meme contributes to a discourse of police reform in Nigeria. It is a multimodal strategy aimed at reshaping public perception of the police while encouraging the youth to assert their legal rights. This integration of modes turns the meme into a tool of digital activism, advancing the discourse on police reform and civil liberties in Nigeria.

*Figure 10. Nigerian police and their intolerance for bribery and corruption*

Here is an exploration of how various modes (image, text, and context) in this meme combine to create and communicate a specific identity about the Nigerian Police. The image in the meme has two officers who appear in police uniform, indicating their official capacity as members of the Nigerian Police Force. However, in this context, the representation of the officers shifts due to the text, as they are implicated in corrupt practices. The facial expressions and Posture of the officers seem neutral or disengaged, not actively participating in any dialogue which might symbolize their loss of authority or control in the situation due to the accusation of bribery. The setting (likely a rural roadside or highway) suggests a typical scenario where such acts might occur, further contextualizing the incident.

The textual element has an overlay text. The text is bold and clear, stating: *"Bribe seeking Police officers dismissed from the Police force"*. This presents a straightforward accusation of corruption, which frames the officers as guilty of misconduct. The text also informs viewers of the consequence—dismissal from the force—which implies a form of justice or corrective action taken by the institution. The use of terms like *"Bribe seeking"* invokes a moral judgment, placing the blame squarely on the officers. This suggests a larger discourse on police corruption in Nigeria, a systemic issue that has often undermined the credibility of Nigerian police. The text communicates a punitive action taken to uphold justice.

The image engages with the widely held perception of police corruption in Nigeria, where officers are often accused of soliciting bribes, particularly at roadblocks. This scenario is familiar to many Nigerians, making the image resonate with the public's frustrations. However, the dismissal of the officers suggests that the police institution is responding to public outcry by taking disciplinary action. This could be interpreted as an attempt to rebuild public trust or as part of broader efforts toward reform by addressing corruption in the force. In the context of social media, this meme serves as a message that corrupt practices are no longer tolerated in the Nigerian police force.

## DISCUSSION

This section discusses the multimodal analysis of ten social media memes focusing on the representation and identity construction of the Nigerian Police using Kress and Van Leeuwen's (2001) approach. The analysis has revealed how the public uses social media memes to portray the Nigerian Police as corrupt, abusive, and untrustworthy and how the Nigerian Police engage in institutional branding in countering digital negative narratives, use social media memes to construct a positive identity as protectors of law and human rights.

The analysis shows that the perception of the public about the identity of the Nigerian Police is predominantly negative in the memes. Themes of inefficiency, delayed response, and irrationality dominate the representations in the memes, with police officers often depicted as clueless, incompetent, corrupt, or abusing their authority. In the theme of bribery and corruption, memes use direct visual metaphors—such as officers requesting and accepting bribes in broad daylight—to depict an institution deeply entrenched in unethical practices. Linguistic and legal incompetence is also a recurrent theme, where police are shown making basic legal errors or communicating in poor English, reinforcing the public perception of inadequacy in their training and professionalism. Memes depicting police harassment and misuse of power tend to show officers engaging in aggressive behaviour, such as threatening civilians or extorting money at checkpoints. These visual and textual cues align with the real-life experiences of Nigerians, contributing to the notion that the police often act as predators rather than protectors.

Despite the overwhelming negative perception, there are instances where the Nigerian Police attempt to reconstruct their identity as proactive, vigilant, and community-oriented. In these memes, officers who were dismissed for requesting bribes were shown to imply that corrupt practices are no longer tolerated in the Nigerian police force. The analysis considers how official police statements, responses to viral memes, and dismissal of corrupt officers contribute to a new digital identity. In other instances, Police officers were shown engaging the public in a broader narrative of reform and the right of the public against police harassment. These video memes shift the traditional narrative of police as enforcers of power, instead presenting them as advocates for the law and citizens' rights.

However, these positive memes often seem out of sync with the broader narrative of corruption and inefficiency. In many cases, users repurpose these positive images to create new memes that highlight contradictions between the portrayed identity and lived realities, thus reasserting the negative perceptions.

## Public Perception and Influence of Representations

The multimodal representations in these memes reflect and reinforce public perceptions of the Nigerian Police as an institution mired in inefficiency and corruption. The widespread use of humor, sarcasm, and satire in these memes adds a layer of critique that resonates deeply with the Nigerian public. The negative portrayals are not merely fictional or exaggerated but echo genuine frustrations with the police's failures in delivering justice and security, for example, are not abstract concerns but part of the lived experience of many Nigerians, who often have to pay bribes to avoid harassment. The memes thus serve a dual purpose: they entertain while also acting as a form of social commentary and activism. Memes have become a powerful tool for identity construction and identity management, both for the police and the public. While the Nigerian Police may use memes to project a more positive image, the overwhelming public sentiment, reflected in the memes still points to deep-seated distrust and dissatisfaction. In this way, social media becomes not just a platform for entertainment but also a battleground for shaping and contesting institutional identities.

## The Role of Humour in Police Identity Construction

Humour is an essential element in these memes, particularly in how it is used to critique the ineptitude and delinquencies of the Nigerian police. This affirms the assertion that social media memes use humour and satire as effective tools to critique institutions of authority, such as the Nigerian police. (Adetunji, 2013, Obadare, 2009). The humorous representation of police incompetence allows individuals to voice their frustrations in ways that are culturally and socially acceptable. By mocking the police's failures, these memes provide a form of catharsis and solidarity among the public, highlighting a collective critique of the institution. For instance, the use of Pidgin English and exaggerated facial expressions as well as background laughter in some of the video memes convey not just the ineptitude of the police but also the absurdity of the system that allows such incompetence to persist. Through humour, the memes mitigate the seriousness of the issues being addressed, making them more familiar and easier to share in digital spaces.

## CONCLUSION

The analysis of these memes using Kress and Van Leeuwen's (2001) multimodal approach reveals the intricate ways in which public perception of the Nigerian Police is constructed and communicated. Through text, images, and symbols, the memes highlight the institutional failures and abuses associated with the police, while also exploring attempts at positive identity construction. However, the power of humor, satire, and social media interaction keeps the negative narratives alive, reflecting a broader sociopolitical landscape in Nigeria where public trust in law enforcement remains low. Social media thus plays a critical role in shaping and reflecting the ongoing discourse around the Nigerian Police, contributing to both their public representation and their contested identity.

This study expands the understanding of how police identity is constructed in digital spaces by incorporating a multimodal framework. This approach provides a richer analysis of how various semiotic resources interact to create meaning and shape public perceptions. Overall, social media serves as a platform where traditional notions of authority can be questioned, critiqued, and reshaped. The multimodal analysis of the representation of the Nigerian police on social media reveals that the image of the police is largely negative, shaped by public critique and ridicule. Social media users leverage a combination of language, gestures, satire, and visual cues to construct an image of the police as corrupt, linguistically limited, ineffective, and reliant on rote legal phrases to assert authority.

## REFERENCES


Aboh, S. C. (2024). 'It will never be well with SARS': A discourse analytic study of the #EndSARS protests on social media. *Discourse & Society, 35*(2), 153–173. DOI: 10.1177/09579265231200994

Adetiba, T. (2021). Social media activism and police reform: The #EndSARS movement in Nigeria. *African Journal of Political Communication*, *8*(2), 56–78.

Adetunji, A. (2013). The interactional context of humour in Nigerian stand-up comedy. *Pragmatics*, *23*(1), 1–22. DOI: 10.1075/prag.23.1.01ade

Ahaotu, J. O., & Oshamo, O. A. (2023). A Multimodal Discourse Analysis of Selected Social Media Posts on the #BlackLivesMatter Protest. *Journal of Pragmatics and Discourse Analysis*, *2*(1), 25–35. DOI: 10.32996/jpda.2023.2.1.4

Ajayi, A. I. (2016). Social Media and Crime Prevention: Perceptions of the Nigerian Police Force. *Social Media + Society*, *2*(3), 1–12. DOI: 10.1177/2056305116662666

Akerele-Popoola, O. E., Azeez, A. L., & Adeniyi, A. (2022). Twitter, civil activisms and EndSARS protest in Nigeria as a developing democracy. *Cogent Social Sciences*, *8*(1), 2095744. Advance online publication. DOI: 10.1080/23311886.2022.2095744

Akinlabi, O. (2020). Police legitimacy in Nigeria: Understanding the influence of procedural justice and performance. *International Journal of Law, Crime and Justice*, *63*, 100420.

Alemika, E. E. (2021). Policing, public perception, and security sector reforms in Nigeria. *Journal of African Security Studies*, *6*(2), 45–61.

Amnesty International. (2020). *Nigeria: End SARS protests and police brutality.* Retrieved from www.amnesty.org

Awopetu, I., & Aseniserare, A. (2021). Visual communication for activism: The case of the EndSARS protests in Nigeria. In 4th International Academic Conference on Research in Social Science. 78-87. www.iacrss.org/ 42-5091.pdf (dpublication.com)

Bateman, J. A. (2014). *Text and image: A critical introduction to the visual/verbal divide*. Routledge. DOI: 10.4324/9781315773971

Chiluwa, I., & Ifukor, P. (2015). 'War against our children': Stance and evaluation in *#BringBackOurGirls* campaign discourse on *Twitter* and *Facebook.Discourse & Society*, *26*(3), 267–296. DOI: 10.1177/0957926514564735

Crump, J. (2011). What Are the Police Doing on Twitter? Social Media, the Police and the Public. *Policy and Internet, 3*(4), 1–27. DOI: 10.2202/1944-2866.1130

Davison, P. (2012). *The language of Internet memes.* New York University Press., DOI: 10.18574/nyu/9780814764077.003.0013

Denisova, A. (2019). *Internet memes and society: Social, cultural, and political contexts.* Routledge. DOI: 10.4324/9780429469404

Ekoh, P. C., & George, E. O. (2021). *The Role of Digital Technology in the End-SARS Protest in Nigeria During COVID-19 Pandemic. Journal of Human Rights and Social Work, Hodge, R., & Kress, G. (1988). Social semiotics.* Polity Press.

Hills, A. (2008). The dialectic of police reform in Nigeria. *The Journal of Modern African Studies, 46*(2), 215–234. DOI: 10.1017/S0022278X08003200

Hills, A., (2012). Lost in translation: why Nigeria's police don't implement democratic reforms. International affairs (Royal Institute of International Affairs 1944-), 88 (4), 739–755

Jewitt, C. (Ed.). (2009). *The Routledge Handbook of Multimodal Analysis.* Routledge.

Jewitt, C. (2014). An Introduction to Multimodality. In Jewitt, C. (Ed.), *The Routledge Handbook of Multimodal Analysis* (2nd ed.). Routledge.

Jewitt, C., & Oyama, R. (2001). Visual meaning: A social semiotic approach. In van Leeuwen, T., & Jewitt, C. (Eds.), *Handbook of visual analysis* (pp. 134–156). SAGE Publications.

Knobel, M., & Lankshear, C. (2007). Online Memes, Affinities, and Cultural Production. In Knobel, M., & Lankshear, C. (Eds.), *A New Literacies Sampler.* Peter Lang.

Kress, G. (2010). *Multimodality. A Social Semiotic Approach to Contemporary Communication.* Routledge.

Kress, G., & van Leeuwen, T. (2001). *Multimodal Discourse: The Modes and Media of Contemporary Communication.* Arnold.

Kress, G., & van Leeuwen, T. (2006). *Reading images: The grammar of visual design* (2nd ed.). Routledge. DOI: 10.4324/9780203619728

Machin, D., & Mayr, A. (2012). *How to do critical discourse analysis: A multimodal introduction.* SAGE Publications.

Nwoke, C. (2022). Representations of the Nigerian Police and Policing in Stand-up Comedy: Tracking Embedded Meanings and Implications. *Nokoko 10.*

O'Halloran, K. (2011). 'Multimodal Discourse Analysis'. In K. Hyland and B. Paltridge (eds.) Companion to Discourse (London: Continuum): 120–137. O'Halloran, K. and Smith, B.A. (2011). 'Multimodal Studies'. In K. O'Halloran and B.A. Smith (eds.)

Obadare, E. (2009). *Humor, Silence, and Civil Society in Nigeria*. Cambridge University Press.

Ojebode, A., Adedayo, A., & Adedeji, W. (2021). Social media activism and police accountability in Nigeria: The #EndSARS movement. *African Journal of Criminology and Justice Studies, 14*(1), 1–19.

Okesola, S., & Oyebode, O. (2023). "The *soro-soke* [speak up] generation": Multimodality and appraisal choices in selected #EndSars civil protest-related memes in Nigeria. *Language and Semiotic Studies, 9*(2), 290–312. DOI: 10.1515/lass-2022-0016

Olowojolu, O. (2022). Positive media portrayal of the Nigerian Police: A discourse analysis of institutional rebranding strategies. *Medicine and Society, 10*(1), 78–92.

Oluremi, T. A., & Olaniyan, O. R. (2023). Nigeria Policemen's Abuse of Power Memes as Reformative Indices. Anaphora. *Journal of Language, Literary, and Cultural Studies, 06*(02). Advance online publication. DOI: 10.30996/anaphora.v6i2.9651

Poulsen, S. V. (2015). "Multimodality." In Key Terms in Multimodality: Definitions, Issues, Discussions, edited by Nina Nørgaard. https://multimodalkeyterms.wordpress.com/

Schneider, C. J. (2016). *Policing and Social Media: Social Control in an Era of New Media*. Lexington Books. DOI: 10.5040/9781978725768

Shifman, L. (2013). Memes in a digital world: Reconciling with a conceptual troublemaker. *Journal of Computer-Mediated Communication, 18*(3), 362–377. DOI: 10.1111/jcc4.12013

Shifman, L. (2014). *Memes in digital culture*. The MIT Press.

Tiwa, D. F. (2024). Institutional distrust trap: An analysis of the effect of public distrust in the Nigeria Police Force. *Policing and Society, 34*(8), 846–860. DOI: 10.1080/10439463.2024.2341121

Van Leeuwen, T. (2005). *Introducing Social Semiotics*. Routledge.

# Chapter 8
# Culture and Arts in Pandemic Times:
## COVID-19, Strategic Communication, and the Case With SALT Initiative

**Sahika Dogan**
https://orcid.org/0000-0001-6248-7289
*Istanbul Bilgi University, Istanbul, Turkey*

## ABSTRACT

*As the COVID-19 outbreak took over the world population, artists and institutions who contributed to the production and dissemination of arts and cultures had to give a break to their professional activities. It was March 2020, when Turkish government decided to stop arts and culture related activities, in order to prevent the spreading of the disease. Actors of arts and culture scene quickly adopted themselves to the "stay at home" days, and continued their productions while in self-isolation. As a result of this unexpected incident, many domestic and international arts and culture institutions have opened their archives on digital media platforms. As the epidemic broke out in the beginning of March 2020 in Turkey, SALT quickly reconstructed and updated their online historical archives and art collections by making 1.840.000 documents accessible to individuals via the Internet. The current study aims to analyze communication strategy of SALT initiative during the COVID-19 outbreak.*

DOI: 10.4018/979-8-3373-5297-8.ch008

## INTRODUCTION

On December 31, 2019, China Office of World Health Organization (WHO) was informed about the first report regarding an unknown virus (later identified as the Coronavirus disease caused by the SARS-CoV-2 virus), that caused a number of pneumonia cases in Wuhan, located in Eastern China, whose population is approximately 11 million (Reynolds and Weiss, 2020). What was then unknown, turned out to be a global epidemic in a short period of time. By August 2, 2020, the confirmed cases were known to be approximately 18 million in the world, while the death cases were around 670.000 in total (World-o-meter, 2020). Despite there were more than 10 million cases that were closed due to recovery, COVID-19 created anxiety global level with high death rates and challenges in the recovery processes. As a consequence, the majority of world cities, with high number of COVID-19 cases had to take restrictive measures to prevent further spread of the disease to the rest of the populations.

Turkiye announced its first case of novel coronavirus on March 11, 2020, as the Turkish Health Minister Fahrettin Koca stated the infected person contracted the disease while returning from a trip to Europe (Zorlu, 2020). As a result, schools and universities immediately shut down and online education activities started. The majority of companies encouraged their employees to work from their homes. Nightclubs and playgrounds were closed down, while social events were postponed to later dates to prevent large number of individuals from meeting in social spaces.

The COVID-19 cases and the death rates have reached its peak in late April 2020 in Turkiye, while the number of daily cases started to decrease gradually until late July the same year. The restrictive measures taken to limit everyday life practices positively impacted on combatting the virus during this period. As a consequence, the government enacted its normalization plan, starting from May 11, 2020, by opening shopping malls and beauty centers such as hairdressers (Anonymous reporter, 2020).

As the opening of arts and cultural organizations and events were positioned at a later stage of normalization, the majority of arts and culture initiatives transferred their activities into online platforms in Turkiye. One of these initiatives was Zorlu Performing Arts center, which started online concerts via Instagram Live broadcasts. The artists included recognized local and international musicians such as Mark Eliyahu, Alexis French and Erdem Tunalı (Zorlu, 2020). Another online project, titled *Drama after 6* was initiated by Kumbaracı 50, which is a contemporary performing arts and dance venue in Beyoğlu district of İstanbul. The artists associated with the initiative announced that actors would perform live via YouTube after 6 pm every day throughout the self-isolation days (İçözü, 2020).

A similar trend was observed with the international arts and culture organizations. For instance, The Metropolitan Opera, based in Manhattan New York, the United States, started broadcasting opera performances online by offering tickets for 20$ in July 2020 (Fox, 2020). A similar attempt was made by the Berlin Philharmonic Orchestra, which hosted an online free concert in March 2020. The initiative also launched its 2020-2021 online concert season with several paid options (Rowat, 2020).

Although the online practices of Zorlu and Kumbaracı 50 initiatives seemed inspiring, they offered short-term, tactical and motivational solutions for the on-going epidemic. SALT was one of the rare arts and culture initiatives, that treated the COVID-19 outbreak as a long-term crisis, and created a strategic communication plan to continue its regular operation.

The SALT initiative, launched in 2011 by Garanti Bank, a Turkish financial services company, unified its contemporary art center, the Ottoman Bank Museum, and its gallery under a single institution. The initiative established three cultural centers, two in Istanbul's Beyoğlu district and one in Ankara, Turkiye's capital city. Collectively, these centers attract an average of 508,000 visitors annually (Garanti BBVA, 2020). 86% of Garanti Bank's stakes were acquired by Banco Bilbao Vizcaya Argentaria (BBVA) in late 2010s. Following this financial transaction, the name of the bank was updated to Garanti BBVA, emphasizing the partnership between the Spanish company, BBVA, and the investors based in Turkiye.

While SALT has been widely recognized for its contributions to cultural engagement and artistic expression, there is a limited understanding of how similar institutions strategically navigate crises, particularly in the context of the COVID-19 pandemic. Unlike many cultural organizations that primarily focused on motivation and performance-based responses during the pandemic, SALT adopted a multifaceted approach encompassing research, archiving, interaction, conceptual thinking, and continuous stakeholder communication.

Despite the increasing interest in crisis communication within cultural institutions, existing studies have not sufficiently examined how interdisciplinary strategies—such as SALT's integration of digital engagement, historical archiving, and artistic discourse—contribute to institutional resilience and audience connectivity in times of crisis. This chapter addresses this gap by exploring SALT as a unique case study, analyzing how its strategic communication methods shaped its response to the COVID-19 outbreak. By doing so, this discussion contributes to broader conversations on the role of cultural organizations in crisis adaptation and long-term sustainability.

## LITERATURE REVIEW

### Strategic Communication Management

Strategy is defined as a well-coordinated approach to reach designed goals by an organization (Wilson & Ogden, 2008, s. 5). According to theorists, communication can be strategic, when it is designated as a process that fosters seamless and coordinated interactions to fulfill envisioned goals among relevant departments and stakeholders (Wilson & Ogden, 2008, s. 6).

Strategic management is characterized by two main stages: Strategy formation and strategy application (Porter, 2008). Porter explains that communication is a key component in both stages, since communication is not solely about applying communicative practices during the strategy application process. Communication is also essential for consideration during strategy formation, in order to curate a planned approach in the application and communication of the designated strategy (Porter, 2008, s. 96). In line, strategic communication can be defined as a concern behind communicative attempts of organizations in order to actualize and advance their organizational goals (Hallahan et al., 2007). Hallahan et al. (2007) perceive strategic communication as a necessity for both for-profit and non-profit organizations due to the rising complexity of the digitized global society (p. 29). The theorists also emphasize the interdisciplinary nature of the concept, as strategic communication is both related with organizational management discipline and communication studies (p. 30).

Due to the concept's interdisciplinary nature, approaches towards understanding of the concept also show differentiations. For instance, while Zerfass and Huck (2007) associate strategic communication with innovation and leadership practices, Stern (2003) positions strategic communication management within the context of organizational communication, by emphasizing the necessity of building stronger bonds with stakeholders. According to Stern (2003), an organization should focus on "what" content should be communicated to its stakeholders "in which" ways (s. 171). In this study, Stern's conceptual approach is embraced, as strategic communication will be considered within the context and as part of the organizational management process.

In their 2000 study, Steyn and Puth underline the importance of symmetrical communication for strategic communication management. Symmetrical communication concept was developed by Grunig et al. in 1992, and defined as a strategic action in which the organization applies a two-way communication model, conducts environmental scanning, assesses potential risks and receives feedback from its stakeholders. In other words, the organization prioritizes the dynamics of the industry and the opinions of stakeholders in order to minimize or eliminate organizational risks.

When expectations of stakeholders are known by the organization, both parties can build a mutual dialogue and understanding over issues of concern. Building such relationships can especially enable organizations with social goals such as arts and culture institutions to actualize their critical social roles, serving their community.

## Crisis Management as Part of the Strategic Communication

One should take crisis management into consideration, while considering the COVID-19 outbreak and organizational communication practices at the height of the pandemic. Crisis is defined as a specific and non-routine incident that fosters high levels of uncertainty and pose threat against actualization of organizational goals (Coombs, 2007, p. 56). Ulmer et al. (2017) point out various types of crises under two categories: Intentional and unintentional. Intentional crises occur as a consequence of an intended harmful action, such as terrorism, sabotage, workplace violence and poor risk management, while unintentional crises take place as a result of unforeseeable events such as natural disasters and disease outbreaks (Ulmer et al., 2017, p. 98).

Disease outbreaks are inevitable, some of which take place for natural reasons (Ulmer et al., 2017). One of the most recent incidents has been experienced with the spread of H1N1 (also referred as the bird flu) virus in 2009, which caused thousands of deaths around the world. A similar case was experienced when a Chinese physician, later identified to be a super-carrier, was diagnosed with a novel virus called SARS (Severe Respiratory Acute Syndrome) in 2003, which turned into a global health threat, mainly effecting China, Hong Kong, Taiwan, Canada and Singapore (McKie, 2017). Another major disease outbreak was experienced with Western Africa Ebola Virus (also shortly referred as Ebola) that mainly effected Guinea, Liberia and Sierra Leone between 2013 and 2016 (WHO, 2015).

The COVID-19 outbreak has turned into the one of the biggest pandemics at the global level, since its impact has not been limited with a particular geography. Besides the scientific studies to develop a vaccine or treatment ritual for the disease, various scholars have pointed out the need to manage the process strategically in order to abstain from the emergence of a global anxiety. For instance, Wu et al. (2020) recommended three strategic principles for health care organizations while dealing with the COVID-19 pandemic, which are centered around resilience, empowerment and staff support. Researchers state effective crisis management paves the way for a clear and frequent communication pattern, which can result with the spread of right sets of information that would potentially empower individuals. They also emphasize the essentiality of staff support within the organization, as researchers anticipate long working hours and the psychological intensity of the outbreak may result with mental health problems among health care professionals (Wu et al., 2020).

Previous literature explored COVID-19 from the perspectives of risk communication and community management in the context of disability, country and community-based responses to the incident, and the creative arts. For example, Ndzinisa and Govender (2024), who study the pandemic response in Estawini, explore how cultural interpretations of the incident, assisted by the government policies and news media, impact on the positionality of the individuals towards the COVID-19 vaccines. Similar to the stigmatization of the vaccines, certain cases reveal that the virus itself can turn into a stigma in certain societies. The study of Naugle et al. (2024) aims to shed some light on this situation, by analyzing how fear, efficacy and stigma can shape behaviors of individuals within the context of a pandemic. In terms of efficacy, the research of Gumede and Govender (2024) argues that the perceptions of risk and self-efficacy are impacted by the individuals' cultural and physical environments. Similar to the studies of Griffiths and Naugle et al., Gumede and Govender (2024) emphasize the importance of community level engagement and participatory communication in times of pandemic such as the COVID-19, in order to create effective culture-specific responses towards the incident.

The companies and the employers have also been financially impacted by the outbreak. An April 2020 research, conducted by the Business for Goals Platform (B4G) in coordination with the TÜRKONFED (Turkish Business Confederation), TÜSİAD (Turkish Industry & Business Association) and UNDP (United Nations Development Program) reveal 36% of micro and small-scale companies have suspended their activities, while only 3% were not impacted at all (UNDP, 2020). Even though the outbreak has been financially advantageous for several industries such as e-commerce and transportation services, entertainment and arts and culture industries have been negatively affected by the situation. Thus, COVID-19 outbreak presented a new challenge for arts and culture organizations, which forced them to look for ways to develop novel strategies in order to reduce the negative outcomes of the pandemic.

## RESEARCH METHODOLOGY

This study aims to analyze the strategic communication patterns of arts and cultural institutions during crises situations, with a particular focus on the COVID-19 pandemic. The outbreak posed unprecedented challenges, disrupting operations, disengaging audiences, and causing financial instability. While the existing research has examined crisis communication in corporate and governmental settings, there is limited understanding of how cultural institutions, which depend on public engagement and experiential interaction, adapted their communication strategies during such crises.

The primary objectives of this study are:

1. To examine the communication strategies employed by arts and cultural institutions during the COVID-19 crisis.
2. To assess the effectiveness of these strategies in maintaining audience engagement and institutional resilience.
3. To identify key lessons and best practices that can guide future crisis communication in the cultural sector.

The COVID-19 experience provides a critical case study for evaluating the resilience and adaptability of these institutions. The findings of this study will contribute to the broader discourse on crisis communication in the arts and cultural sector, offering insights into how institutions can ensure their long-term sustainability in the face of future crises.

The current study employs the case study method, by focusing on the SALT initiative of Garanti BBVA, which was founded in 2011 and based in İstanbul, Turkiye. SALT is a non-profit cultural institution serving the public. Its exhibitions, as well as its public and research programs, are made possible through individual and institutional support. The study utilizes from the secondary resources, including SALT initiative's press bulletins, online publications and the contents on social media.

As Crowe et al. (2011) explain, "the case study approach allows in-depth, multi-faceted explorations of complex issues in the real-life settings" (p. 100). Stake (1995) has previously categorized different approaches while conducting case study under three categories: *intrinsic*, *instrumental* and *collective*. In intrinsic case studies, researchers define and explain the unique features of a particular phenomenon, while in instrumental case studies, researchers focus on a particular case to reveal the broader perspective. Lastly, in collective case studies, multiple cases are involved to provide an overall appreciation of a particular phenomenon (Stake, 1995).

In this study, the instrumental case study approach is employed, where a single case is selected to understand the broader perspective evolving around the COVID-19 phenomenon. The study aims to provide insights for future arts and cultural institutions in terms of conducting strategic communication in times of anxiety, fear and crisis. The sample materials were mainly selected from the publications between March and July 2020, since it represents the time period when the impact of the COVID-19 outbreak was at its peak, not only in Turkiye, but also around the world.

## FINDINGS

### SALT Initiative

SALT is a cultural institution that was launched in 2011. Focusing on research, exhibition, publication, web and digitization projects, the initiative organizes mainly free-of-charge public programs such as talks, conferences, screenings and workshops and provide a platform for mutual learning and discussion with its stakeholders (SALT Blog, 2020). The majority of the initiative's activities take place in Istanbul in two different locations based in the same district (SALT Beyoğlu and SALT Galata – both in Beyoğlu), while it also organizes various gatherings and art exhibitions in Ankara (SALT Ankara). The building of SALT Galata, which was designed by Alexandre Vallauri, used to be the headquarters of the Ottoman Bank between 1892 and 1999 (SALT Blog, 2020). The building also hosts the Ottoman Bank Museum, which visualizes the 145-year history of Turkiye's first private banking company. Besides the Ottoman Bank Museum, SALT Galata also hosts a bookstore (Robinson 389), SALT Research and Coffee Shop, while SALT Beyoğlu includes a large forum space for performing artists. The initiative is the only Turkish member of L'Internationale Confederation of European Museums.

Garanti BBVA, the founder and the financial sponsor of SALT initiative, was established in Ankara in 1946 as a joint stock company with the participation of 103 partners (Garanti BBVA, 2020). Garanti opened its first branch in Ankara on Anafartalar Avenue in 1946, and its second branch in Bankalar Avenue in Istanbul, increasing its number of branches to 22 in 7 years. By the end of the 1970s, a significant part of Garanti's shares were gathered in the hands of Koç Group and Sabancı Group, during a time when the holding banking speeded up in Turkiye. In the early 1980s, Koç Group and later Sabancı Group sold their shares in Garanti to Doğuş Group. Doğuş Group completely owned Garanti in 1983 (Garanti BBVA, 2020).

In 2011, upon the decision of General Electric to leave the financial sector in the USA and Europe with the effect of the global crisis, the Spanish banking giant BBVA became a strategic partner with the Doğuş Group under the management of Garanti Bank. The customer-oriented business approach, reinforced by "BBVA's strong technology and innovation", is claimed to overlap with Garanti's business model, providing positive contributions to both parties in terms of experience sharing and cooperation opportunities (Garanti BBVA, 2020).

When the relationship between Garanti BBVA and SALT initiative is analyzed, it can be seen that the arts and culture initiative serve to reflect the company's sustainability-based goals and future vision. By raising awareness about Turkiye's cultural heritage and collective memory, the initiative serves as a symbolic bridge between the past experiences of the republic and its future vision. It can be stated that the sustainability has had been a main concern for both Garanti BBVA and SALT prior to the emergence of COVID-19 pandemic as well. For example, in December 2019, SALT commemorated its fifth anniversary with an emphasis on sustainability by screening the *Is This Our Last Chance?* documentary to raise awareness about the climate change, right before the COVID-19 pandemic that took over the world (Garanti BBVA Arts and Culture, 2019).

## Precautions Taken Against the COVID-19 Pandemic

Despite there were no limits regarding the number of visitors to SALT buildings, the COVID-19 outbreak brought along several precautions to preserve the public health. Following the emergence of the outbreak, the maximum number of visitors to SALT Beyoğlu remained limited to 40, while to 50 in SALT Galata. The research team of the initiative was made accessible only via appointments, which were to be held on Tuesdays and Saturdays every week. Additionally, each visitor was required to wear a mask and should not have had indications of the COVID-19 illness such as high fever, coughing and breathing problems. Elevators in SALT buildings were closed down to preserve public health, while collections in the SALT Research collection were being disinfected with ultraviolet (UV) rays after each use. The air conditioning mechanisms of the initiative's buildings were renovated to provide %100 fresh air inside spaces open for visitors (Salt Blog, 2020).

Similar to the SALT initiative, its founders and financial sponsor, Garanti BBVA[1] treated COVID-19 pandemic in a cautious manner. In order to fight against the COVID-19 experience, Garanti BBVA mainly took financial measures and supported the National Financial Solidarity Campaign, launched by the Turkish government. The support included 200 respiratory devices worth 30 million Turkish Liras at that time, which were delivered to Turkish Ministry of Health to be provided to quarantine hospitals. The company aimed to provide a financial support of 10 million Turkish Liras at the eve of the outbreak, however extended the amount due to the seriousness of the pandemic (Garanti BBVA, 2020).

In June 2020, Ebru Dildar Edin, the Deputy Director General of Garanti BBVA published an article, where she stated that the company put sustainability at the center of their future vision and strategy (Edin, 2020). Edin (2020) explained any step taken in the short term by prioritizing profit would result with the emergence of new crisis situations in the long term that would challenge global social development and environmental sustainability. The statement was inspired by the World Bank report, titled *Proposed Sustainability Checklist for Assessing Economic Recovery Interventions*, that aimed to provide a guideline for companies in the period of uncertainty (World Bank, 2020).

## Online Arts and Culture Practices of SALT Initiative During Self-Isolation Days

### Free Movie Screenings and Online Blogging

During the "stay-at-home" period mandated by the Turkish government, SALT provided free access to nine films through its website, saltonline.org. Notably, five of these films were directed by artists known for their environmental and political activism.

One of the featured films, *The Salt of the Earth*, directed by Sebastião Salgado, captured the director's firsthand experiences with international conflicts, famine, and mass migrations. Another documentary, *The Wolfpack*, directed by Crystal Moselle, explored the true story of a family that homeschooled and raised seven children in isolation within their New York City apartment. The film originally premiered at the 2015 Sundance Film Festival, where Moselle was awarded the U.S. Documentary Grand Jury Prize (SALT Online, 2020b). The promotional content announcing these free online screenings amassed 496,982 impressions, while nine films received a total of 95,847 views (SALT Online, 2020a).

During the pandemic, the online blog of SALT initiative was expanded on a variety of issues. One expansion was associated with the İstanbul Encyclopedia of Reşad Ekrem Koç, in which the curator explored and analyzed İstanbul's streets, architecture and social life. Another content that was made available was an in-depth interview conducted with Sadık Karamustafa, a respected graphic designer based in Turkiye. In the interview, Karamustafa explored the visual culture of leftist groups, by analyzing how leftist activists utilized from visual symbols and tools in order to reflect and impose their political beliefs in the country.

*Figure 1. Blog homepage*

Another collection that was made public was associated with the architectural transformation of the Turkish Grand National Assembly. The collection included notes and commentaries from respected architectures and interior designers in the country. The initiative also started a series of articles that pointed out the importance of attitude and care in cultural institutions. The series was launched in order to celebrate the 9th anniversary of SALT museum in 2020 (SALT Blog, 2020).

## Online Consultancy and Photo Albums

Another attempt that was made right after the emergence of COVID-19 outbreak has been regarding the online photo albums made available via Flickr platform. One of the photo series was called "Streets: From 1850s to 1990s", which reflected scenes from everyday life in various cities of Turkiye. The collection included works of Turkish artists such as Kayıhan Türköz and Gaston Mizrahi, as well as anonymous contributors. The photos portrayed mobile barbers, dining benches, coffee shops, fairground squares, busy streets and venues, as well as repair stations. Another photo album that was launched via Flickr was titled *Library Photography Archives*, which included stills from *Architecture and Design* and City, *Society and Economy* collections of the initiative.

*Figure 2. Stills from Architecture and Design and City, Society and Economy*

Starting with the quarantine days, SALT initiative also collaborated with a group of volunteer researchers, instructors and experts to respond to the visitors on time, who wanted to raise questions regarding any document that was made available online on SALT initiative web platforms. The available collections included architectural drawings, historical maps and photographs. This attempt was to increase the interaction between the initiative and its stakeholders at the height of the pandemic.

SALT representatives additionally started emailing academics and students to inform them about the opening of online SALT Architecture and Design and Turkey Art Archives. In total, 2213 academics, specialized in architecture/design and 947 academics, specialized in fine arts, were reached via e-mail and asked to share the news with their students. In total, academics from 52 cities of Turkey were reached, including Diyarbakır, Niğde, Pamukkale, Yozgat, Tekirdağ, Sivas, Siirt and Van (Salt Online, 2020a).

## Online Projects and Call for Production

European Confederation of Museums L'Internationale, in collaboration with SALT initiative, called for fifteen artists to develop content from their living and working spaces to address the on-going global conditions. The program, which was curated as a consequence of the online call, included the works of artists Babi Badalov, Osman Bozkurt, Simnikiwe Buhlungu, Ola Hassanain, Sanja Iveković, Siniša Labrović, Rogelio López Cuenca, Elo Vega, Kate Newby, Daniela Ortiz, Zeyno Pekünlü, Maja Smrekar, Isidoro Valcárcel Medina, Guy Woueté, Akram Zaatari and Paweł Zukowski. The collective theme of the online exhibition focused on new propositions regarding the public and private spaces (SALT Online 2020a). Art works created were also shared from member institutions' websites and social media accounts.

*Figure 3. Transferring to online platforms.*

As individuals started self-isolating due to the COVID-19 outbreak, SALT initiative also transferred the majority of its projects to online platforms. One of these projects was *Ev-Kesit* (Home-Section in English) project, which was curated as part of the initiative's *Tek ve Çok* (One and Many in English) exhibition. The project included objects and materials, which represented the daily life of 1980s in Turkiye (SALT Online, 2020e).

*Figure 4. SALT online*

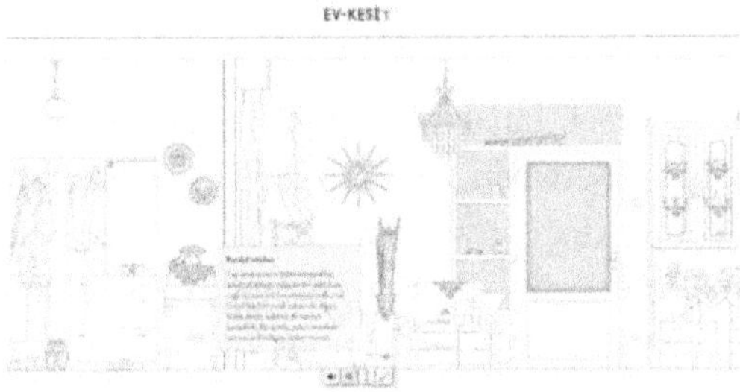

Another project transferred to the SALT online platform was *Osmanlı İstanbul'unda Kadın Bani Yapıları Haritası* (The Bani Structure Map of Ottoman Istanbul, Curated by Women in English). The project aimed to exemplify the role women in the urbanization of Istanbul between 15th and 20th centuries, while exploring the role of gender in economy and politics (SALT Online, 2020f). The project was initiated via a Google Map installation, that was accompanied with historical photos and drawings from the SALT archives.

## Google Arts & Culture Presentations and Ad Strategy

Throughout the self-isolation days, SALT initiative also utilized from Google Arts & Culture services. One of the primary presentations that was shared with the audience was a compilation regarding the works of Turkiye's first female illustrator painter Sabiha Rüştü Bozcalı (1904-1998). An additional compilation presented was *Saloon*, which was a conceptual work that questioned the relationship between space and object (SALT Online, 2020c).

*Figure 5. Culture presentations.*

Another presentation was related to the painting department of Gazi Educational Institute, which was active between 1932-1973. The presentation solely focused on Gazi Educational Institute, since it was marked for being a symbolic representation of national identity and modernization in Turkiye (SALT Online, 2020d).

While various arts and culture institutions tactically opened their archives to the audience in digital environments during the days of quarantine, the advertising communication of SALT initiative was rapidly reconstructed to highlight the content and archive collections already presented in the digital sphere of the institution, in a strategic and long-term approach. The institution emphasized that the majority of its operations would be transferred to the online platforms. A continuous communication flow was sustained via the digital media networks and alternative news platforms, where the world of arts and culture were (and are still) represented extensively.

*Figure 6. Expanding to wider audiences.*

The primary aim of curating such an advertising strategy was to increase the visibility of the institution in the digital sphere, as well as reaching wider audiences and spending quality time with the online community. In line to fulfill this aim, the SALT communication team curated e-newsletters, Google Academic publications, online blog posts, special day celebrations and Garanti BBVA Intranet-specific contents. The ad communication was mainly conducted via Facebook, Instagram,

YouTube ads and programmatic advertising alternatives. Similarly, the ad contents were regularly published in alternative arts and culture networks such as Sanat Atak, The Magger and Bant Mag to reach specific audiences.

## CONCLUSION

COVID-19 pandemic emerged as one of the major health-related challenges at the global scale (Saka, 2022). Primarily emerged in Wuhan, China at the eve of 2020, the virus spread to the various geographies of the world as a consequence of the intense mass mobility (Gorgulu, 2020). One of the major industries that was negatively affected by the pandemic remained tourism. March 2020 trends of the online flight ticket sales and hotel bookings revealed that there was a 43 percent decrease in desktop travel spending, in comparison with the data from March 2019.

In contrast, the impact of COVID-19 disease remained positive over the e-commerce industry. For example, the founder and CEO of Amazon e-commerce web site, Jeff Bezos, who was already recognized as the wealthiest person in the world, added £10 billion to his fortune, thanks to the increase in e-commerce sales as a consequence of the global self-isolation (Neate, 2020). Culture and arts industry, however, has not been that lucky, since the majority of the culture and arts events were cancelled or postponed due to the ongoing social restrictions of the time. Several governments took responsibility to financially assist the depriving arts and culture institutions. One of them was the government of the Britain, which announced £1.57 billion support to protect Britain's cultural, arts and heritage institutions (Gov.uk, 2020). Similarly, German government announced a £896 million support to preserve the arts and offer grants for freelance artists and researchers (Hill, 2020).

The COVID-19 experience revealed that a certain group of culture and arts activities could actually be also conducted online. Several art initiatives in the world, such as the Berlin Philharmonic Orchestra, the Museum of Modern Art and the Frida Kahlo Museum benefited from the opportunities provided by the Internet services. Similarly, SALT initiative in Turkiye, transferred the majority of its operations to the online and interactive platforms. As detailed in the findings section, these operations fostered the emergence of a symmetrical communication pattern, that encouraged visitors to engage with the initiative's contents, also with its representatives for consultancy.

The case of the SALT initiative proved that that it remains possible to create an engaging arts and culture sphere online in times of high risks - and even crises. The increasing number of online arts and culture activities during the pandemic was a reflection of this situation. SALT initiative of Turkiye stood out as an effective and outstanding example, which continued its institutional recognition despite the physical and social limitations imposed with the global pandemic.

## REFERENCES


Anonymous reporter. (2020, May 27). *Normalleşme takviminde tarihler belirleniyor (The dates on normalization to be determined)*. Hürriyet. https://www.hurriyet.com.tr/galeri-son-dakika-haberler-normallesme-takviminde-tarihler-belirleniyor-lokantalar-spor-salonlari-kafeler-ne-zaman-acilacak-41525226/1

Blog, S. A. L. T. (2020). *Resmi blog sitesi (Official blog page)*. https://saltonline.org/tr/blog

Comscore. (2020). *Consumer interest in travel categories remains significantly lower*. https://www.comscore.com/Insights/Press-Releases/2020/4/Consumer-Interest-in-Travel-Categories-Remains-Significantly-Lower

Coombs, W. T. (2007). *Ongoing crisis communication: Planning, managing and responding*. Sage Publications.

Crowe, S., Cresswell, K., Robertson, A., Huby, G., Avery, A., & Sheikh, A. (2011). The case study approach. *BMC Medical Research Methodology*, *11*(1), 100. DOI: 10.1186/1471-2288-11-100 PMID: 21707982

Edin, E. D. (2020). *Pandemiden sonra önemi daha da artan odağımız: Sürdürülebilirlik (The increasing importance of our focus after the pandemic: Sustainability)*. https://www.garantibbva.com.tr/tr/blog/yeni-normalde-surdurulebilirlik.page

Fox, A. (2020, July 15). *The Metropolitan Opera is staging live concerts around the World – and tickets are only 20$.* Travel + Leisure, https://www.travelandleisure.com/culture-design/music/met-opera-digital-concert-tickets

Garanti, B. B. V. A. (2020). *Kültür ve sanat (Arts and culture)*.https://www.garantibbvainvestorrelations.com/tr/surdurulebilirlik/detay/Kultur-Sanat/957/3817/0

Garanti BBVA Arts and Culture. (2019). *SALT commemorates fifth anniversary with emphasis on sustainability*.https://www.bbva.com/en/tr/salt-commemorates-fifth-anniversary-with-emphasis-on-sustainability/

Garanti BBVA Communications. (2020). *Garanti BBVA responds to the coronavirus pandemic*. https://www.bbva.com/en/tr/garanti-bbva-responds-to-the-coronavirus-pandemic/

Gorgulu, V. (2020). Fearing coronavirus: The role of digital health news consumption and competence. *Internet Applications and Management*, *11*(2), 101–112. DOI: 10.34231/iuyd.777356

Gov.uk. (2020). *£1.57 billion investment to protect Britain's world-class cultural, arts and heritage institutions.* https://www.gov.uk/government/news/157-billion-investment-to-protect-britains-world-class-cultural-arts-and-heritage-institutions

Grunig, J. E., & White, J. (1992). The effect of worldviews on public relations theory and practice. In Grunig, J. E., Dozier, D. M., Ehling, W. P., Grunig, L. A., Rpper, F. C., & White, J. (Eds.), *Excellence in Public Relations and Communication* (pp. 31–64). Erlbaum.

Gumede, T., & Govender, K. (2024). Risk perception and self-efficacy: The influence of cultural and physical environments during COVID-19. *International Journal of Environmental Research and Public Health, 21*(4), 198–215.

Hallahan, K., Holtzhausen, D., van Ruler, B., Vercic, D., & Sriramesh, K. (2007). Defining strategic communication. *International Journal of Strategic Communication, 1*(1), 3–35. DOI: 10.1080/15531180701285244

Hill, J. (2020, July 11). *Coronavirus: Germany takes on debt to rescue arts.* BBC. https://www.bbc.com/news/world-europe-53361962

İçözü, T. (2020, Mart 26). *Dijital olarak takip edebileceğiniz 17 konser, tiyatro ve sanatsal etkinlik platformu (17 platforms that you can digitally follow to watch concerts, plays and arts events).* Webrazzi, https://webrazzi.com/2020/03/26/dijital-olarak-takip-edebileceginiz-17-konser-tiyatro-ve-sanatsal-etkinlik-platformu/

McKie, R. (2017, December 10). *Scientists trace 2002 SARS virus to colony of cave-dwelling bats in China.* The Guardian, https://www.theguardian.com/world/2017/dec/10/sars-virus-bats-china-severe-acute-respiratory-syndrome

Naugle, D. A., Smith, J. P., & Lee, R. T. (2024). Fear, efficacy, and stigma: Behavioral responses during the COVID-19 pandemic. *Health Psychology Review, 18*(1), 112–130.

Ndzinisa, N., & Govender, E. (2024). Cultural interpretations and government policies: Impact on individuals' positionality towards COVID-19 vaccines in Eswatini. *Journal of Health Communication, 29*(3), 245–260.

Neate, R. (2020, July 21). *Jeff Bezos, the world's richest man, added £10bn to his fortune in just one day.* The Guardian, https://www.theguardian.com/technology/2020/jul/21/jeff-bezos-the-worlds-richest-man-added-10bn-to-his-fortune-in-just-one-day

Online, S. A. L. T. (2020a). *Resmi internet sitesi (Official web page).*http://www.saltonline.org

Online, S. A. L. T. (2020b). *Çevrimiçi gösterim: The Wolfpack (Online screening: The Wolfpack)*. https://saltonline.org/tr/2232/cevrimici-gosterim-the-wolfpack?tag=11

Online, S. A. L. T. (2020c). *Salon: Modern denemeler 4*. https://saltonline.org/tr/277/modern-denemeler-4?q=salon

Online, S. A. L. T. (2020d). *Çevrimiçi sunum: 1932'den 1973'e Gazi Eğitim Enstitüsü (Online presentation: The history of Gazi Eğitim Enstitüsü from 1932 to 1973)*. https://saltonline.org/tr/2244/cevrimici-sunum-1932den-1973e-gazi-resim-is?q=google

Online, S. A. L. T. (2020e). *Ev-kesit (Home-segment)*. https://saltonline.org/projects/evkesit/

Online, S. A. L. T. (2020f). *Osmanlı İstanbul'unda kadın bani yapıları*. https://saltonline.org/projects/kadinbaniyapilari/

Porter, M. E. (2008). On competition (Updated and expanded edition). *Harvard Business Review*.

Reynolds, M., & Weiss, S. (2020, May 27). *How coronavirus started and what happens next, explained*. Wired, https://www.wired.co.uk/article/china-coronavirus

Rowat, R. (2020, March, 13). *The Berlin Philharmonic made its digital concert hall free for everyone*. CBC, https://www.cbc.ca/music/the-berlin-philharmonic-has-made-its-digital-concert-hall-free-for-everyone-1.5497260

Saka, E. (2022). Researching political trolls as instruments of political conservatism in Turkey: A historical framework and methodological reflections on a discourse community. In Costa, E., Lange, P. G., Haynes, N., & Sinanan, J. (Eds.), *The Routledge Companion to Media Anthropology*. Routledge. DOI: 10.4324/9781003175605-44

Stake, R. E. (1995). *The art of case study research*. Sage Publications.

Steyn, B. (2003). From strategy to corporate communication strategy: A conceptualization. *Journal of Communication Management (London)*, *8*(2), 168–183. DOI: 10.1108/13632540410807637

Steyn, B., & Puth, G. (2000). *Corporate communication strategy*. Heinemann.

Ulmer, R. R., Sellnow, T. L., & Seeger, M. W. (2017). *Effective crisis communication: Moving from crisis to opportunity*. Sage Publications.

UNDP. (2020). *Four in every five SMEs substantially impacted by COVID-19 crisis*. https://www.tr.undp.org/content/turkey/en/home/presscenter/pressreleases/2020/04/B4G-anket.html

WHO. (2015). *Ebola situation report*. https://apps.who.int/ebola/current-situation/ebola-situation-report-22-july-2015

Wilson, J., & Ogden, J. (2008). *Strategic communication planning*. Kendal Hunt.

World Bank. (2020). *Proposed sustainability checklist for economic recovery interventions*. http://pubdocs.worldbank.org/en/223671586803837686/Sustainability-Checklist-for-Assessing-Economic-Recovery-Investments-April-2020.pdf

World-o-Meter. (2020). [*Coronavirus pandemic*. https://www.worldometers.info/coronavirus/]. *COVID*, *19*, •••.

Wu, A. W., Connors, C., & Everly, G. S.Jr. (2020). COVID-19: Peer support and crisis communication strategies to promote institutional resilience. *Annals of Internal Medicine*, *172*(12), 822–823. Advance online publication. DOI: 10.7326/M20-1236 PMID: 32251512

Zerfass, A., & Huck, S. (2007). Innovation, communication, and leadership: New developments in strategic communication. *International Journal of Strategic Communication*, *1*(2), 107–122. DOI: 10.1080/15531180701298908

Zorlu, F. (2020, March 11). *Turkey confirms first case of coronavirus*. Anadolu Agency, https://www.aa.com.tr/en/latest-on-coronavirus-outbreak/turkey-confirms-first-case-of-coronavirus/1761522

Zorlu. (2020). *Kurumsal*. https://www.zorlupsm.com/tr/kurumsal/basin-bultenleri/psmyle-kal-online-konserler

## ENDNOTES

1 Garanti BBVA also expanded its mobile services for its customers, to draw less individuals to its branches. While a limited number of staff continued daily operations at the banking branches starting from May 6, 2020, the majority of the bank's employees offered customer services from their homes. All customers visiting Garanti BBVA branches were required to use disinfectants and wear masks before entering buildings (Garanti BBVA Communications, 2020). The bank also expanded the daily cash limit on withdrawals to 5.000 Turkish Liras, while enabling consumers to withdraw money from ATM machines of other banks' free of charge (Garanti BBVA Communications, 2020). Additionally, the company updated their QR code service to make it more user-friendly and to enable customers withdraw money easier without touching the ATM machine. Money transfer fees were also made free of charge

via Garanti mobile services, while money transfer threshold was expanded to higher amounts, depending on the financial income of consumers (Garanti BBVA Communications, 2020).

# Compilation of References


Abdulbaqi, S. S., & Ariemu, O. (2017). Newspaper framing of herdsmen-farmers' conflicts in Nigeria and its implication on peace-oriented journalism. *The Creative Artists*, *11*(2), 77–105.

Aboh, S. C. (2024). 'It will never be well with SARS': A discourse analytic study of the# EndSARS protests on social media. *Discourse & Society*, *35*(2), 153–173. DOI: 10.1177/09579265231200994

Adeagbo, E. O., & Oyindamola, A. A. (2024). Multimodal Discourse Features in Selected Nigerian Political Cartoons. *Àgídìgbo. ABUAD Journal of the Humanities*, *12*(1), 141–160. DOI: 10.53982/agidigbo.2024.1201.10-j

Adebanwi, W. (2020). The affective infrastructures of digital activism in Nigeria. *African Studies Review*, *63*(4), 654–673. DOI: 10.1017/asr.2020.50

Adebomi, O. O. (2022). Language in a pandemic: A multimodal analysis of social media representation of COVID-19. *Journal of African Media Studies*, *14*(1), 7–28. DOI: 10.1386/jams_00062_1

Adegoju, A., & Oyebode, O. (2015). Humour as discursive practice in Nigeria's 2015 presidential election online campaign discourse. *Discourse Studies*, *17*(6), 643–662. DOI: 10.1177/1461445615602378

Adeiza, A. (2021). Social media, protest repertoires, and the evolving structure of political participation in Nigeria. *Media Culture & Society*, *43*(5), 921–938. DOI: 10.1177/0163443720957882

Ademilokun, M. (2016). A Multimodal Analysis of the Public Discourse of the 2013 University Lecturers' Strike in Nigeria. In Taiwo, R., & Opeibi, B. (Eds.), *The Discourse of Digital Civic Engagement: Perspectives from the Developing World* (pp. 57–74). Nova Science Publishers.

Adetiba, T. (2021). Social media activism and police reform: The #EndSARS movement in Nigeria. *African Journal of Political Communication*, *8*(2), 56–78.

Adetunji, A. (2013). The interactional context of humour in Nigerian stand-up comedy. *Pragmatics*, *23*(1), 1–22. DOI: 10.1075/prag.23.1.01ade

Adisa, R. S., & Adekunle, O. A. (2010). Farmer-herdsmen conflicts: A factor analysis of socio-economic conflict variables among arable crop farmers in North Central Nigeria. *Journal of Human Ecology (Delhi, India)*, *30*(1), 1–9. DOI: 10.1080/09709274.2010.11906266

Aguilar Forero, N., & Cifuentes Álvarez, G. A. (2019). Education, activism and digital technologies: A systematic review. *Education in the Knowledge Society*, *20*, 1–14. DOI: 10.14201/eks2019_20_a14

Ahaotu, J. O., & Oshamo, O. A. (2023). A Multimodal Discourse Analysis of Selected Social Media Posts on the #BlackLivesMatter Protest. *Journal of Pragmatics and Discourse Analysis*, *2*(1), 25–35. DOI: 10.32996/jpda.2023.2.1.4

Ahmed, I. L. (2021). The role of slogan in political mobilisation: A study on 'O To Ge'. *Journal of History and Social Sciences*, *12*(1), 36–44. DOI: 10.46422/jhss.v12i1.141

Ajayi, A. H., & Sennuga, S. O. (2022). Perceived factors responsible for herders-farmers' communal conflict in Plateau State, Nigeria. *International Journal of Agricultural Extension and Rural Development Studies*, *9*(2), 32–46. DOI: 10.37745/ijaerds.15vol9n23246

Ajayi, A. I. (2016). Social Media and Crime Prevention: Perceptions of the Nigerian Police Force. *Social Media + Society*, *2*(3), 1–12. DOI: 10.1177/2056305116662666

Akanni, T., & Ibuot, U.P. (2023). Visual compositions and layout designs of the front pages of nigerian newspapers: a study of *Vanguard, Punch, Daily Sun* and *Leadership*. *The International Journal of Humanities & Social Studies,* 11 (7), 213-223. DOI No.: DOI: 10.24940/theijhss/2023/v11/i7/HS2307-025

Akerele-Popoola, O. E., Azeez, A. L., & Adeniyi, A. (2022). Twitter, civil activisms and EndSARS protest in Nigeria as a developing democracy. *Cogent Social Sciences*, *8*(1), 2095744. Advance online publication. DOI: 10.1080/23311886.2022.2095744

Akinbobola, Y. (2021). Reframing African struggles: Transnational digital activism and the reimagining of political agency. *Information Communication and Society*, *24*(10), 1458–1473. DOI: 10.1080/1369118X.2020.1716035

Akingbe, N. (2012). Writing protest obliquely: Articulating the burden of a nation in Chinua Achebe's *Anthills of the Savannah. Transnational Literature, 5*(1), 1–17. https://doaj.org/article/7261bd85b69b4dc2b8ea6d5076d0e8e2

Akinlabi, O. (2020). Police legitimacy in Nigeria: Understanding the influence of procedural justice and performance. *International Journal of Law, Crime and Justice, 63*, 100420.

Al Zidjaly, N. (2017). Memes as reasonably hostile laments: A discourse analysis of political dissent in Oman. *Discourse & Society, 28*(6), 573–594. DOI: 10.1177/0957926517721083

Alemika, E. E. (2021). Policing, public perception, and security sector reforms in Nigeria. *Journal of African Security Studies, 6*(2), 45–61.

Alugbin, M., & Iyoha, O. (2024). Narratives of resistance: Discursive strategies in Nigeria's 2020 #EndSARS protest. *Àgídìgbo. ABUAD Journal of the Humanities, 12*(1), 105–121. DOI: 10.53982/agidigbo.2024.1201.07-j

Amnesty International. (2020). *Nigeria: End SARS protests and police brutality.* Retrieved from www.amnesty.org

Amore, K. P., & Atoloye, L. (2016). A systematic functional-multimodal discourse analysis of some cartoons connected with Nigeria's 2015 general elections. *The Nigerian Journal of Communication, 13*(1), 23–46.

Amore, K. P., & Atoloye, L. (2016). A Systemic Functional-Multimodal Discourse Analysis of Some Cartoons Connected with Nigeria's 2015 General Elections. *The Nigerian Journal of Communication, 13*(1), 23–46.

Androutsopoulos, J. (2011). Language change and digital media: A review of conceptions and evidence. In Kristiansen, T., & Coupland, N. (Eds.), *Standard Languages and Language Standards in a Changing Europe* (pp. 145–163). Novus Press.

Anonymous reporter. (2020, May 27). *Normalleşme takviminde tarihler belirleniyor (The dates on normalization to be determined).* Hürriyet. https://www.hurriyet.com.tr/galeri-son-dakika-haberler-normallesme-takviminde-tarihler-belirleniyor-lokantalar-spor-salonlari-kafeler-ne-zaman-acilacak-41525226/1

Ardèvol-Abreu, A. (2015). Framing theory in communication research. Origins, development and current situation in Spain. *Revista latina de comunicación social,* 70. 423-450.

Athira, V. S.Athira V S (2021). A study on Factors Influencing the adoption of Internet Banking - A gender wise analysis by Integrating TAM and TPB model in Kerala. *RESEARCH REVIEW International Journal of Multidisciplinary*, *6*(11), 19–27. DOI: 10.31305/rrijm.2021.v06.i11.004

Auliandri, T. A., & Arimbi, R. D. (2021). Pengaruh Technology Readiness Index Terhadap Keinginan Untuk Menggunakan Internet Banking Pada PT Bank Mandiri KCP Pondok Chandra Surabaya. *JAMIN : Jurnal Aplikasi Manajemen Dan Inovasi Bisnis*, *3*(2), 38. DOI: 10.47201/jamin.v3i2.79

Auvinen, J. (1996). IMF intervention and political protest in the Third World: A conventional wisdom refined. *Third World Quarterly*, *17*(3), 337–400. DOI: 10.1080/01436599615425

Awopetu, I., & Aseniserare, A. (2021). Visual communication for activism: The case of the EndSARS protests in Nigeria. In 4th International Academic Conference on Research in Social Science. 78-87. www.iacrss.org/ 42-5091.pdf (dpublication.com)

Ayodeji-Falade, M. B., & Osunkunle, O. O. (2021). Framing of FeeMustFall students' protest by Daily Dispatch Newspaper and the effect on readers' perceptions. *Heliyon*, *7*(8), e07782. Advance online publication. DOI: 10.1016/j.heliyon.2021.e07782 PMID: 34430751

Ayoola, K. (2021). Dimensions and applications of critical discourse analysis. In Ayoola, K., Arugbawa, O., & Oyebode, O. (Eds.), *Current Approaches to Discourse Analysis* (pp. 179–225). Obafemi Awolowo University Press.

Baker, S., & Green, S. (2014). The viral political cartoon: A case study. *Visual Communication*, *13*(2), 131–147. DOI: 10.1177/0957926511433478

Balasundaram, A., Sreedharan, N. V., Babu, D. D., & Gopinath, P. P. (2024). Social media use and impact on voters and candidates in Kerala. *Journal of Creative Communications*, 09732586231223841. Advance online publication. DOI: 10.1177/09732586231223841

Bamgbose, G. (2021). Multimodal analysis of post-election memes in the Edo State (Nigeria) 2020 Gubernatorial Election. *Argentinian Journal of Applied Linguistics*, *9*(2), 91–107.

Barnett, S., & Lee, S. (2022). Digital inclusion and co-operatives in the 21st century. *Journal of Co-operative Studies*, *40*(1), 45–59.

Barton, D., & Lee, C. (2013). *Language Online: Investigating Digital Texts and Practices*. Routledge. DOI: 10.4324/9780203552308

Bateman, J. A. (2014). *Text and image: A critical introduction to the visual/verbal divide*. Routledge. DOI: 10.4324/9781315773971

Bello, B., & Abdullahi, M. M. (2021). Farmers-herdsmen conflict, cattle rustling, and banditry: The dialectics of insecurity in Anka and Maradun Local Government Area of Zamfara State, Nigeria. *SAGE Open*, *11*(4), 21582440211040117. Advance online publication. DOI: 10.1177/21582440211040117

Benford, R. D., & Snow, D. A. (2000). Framing processes and social movements: An overview and assessment. *Annual Review of Sociology*, *26*(1), 611–639. DOI: 10.1146/annurev.soc.26.1.611

Bennett, W. L., & Segerberg, A. (2012). The logic of connective action. *Information Communication and Society*, *15*(5), 739–768. DOI: 10.1080/1369118X.2012.670661

Bezemer, J., & Jewitt, C. (2009). Social Semiotics. In Östman, J. O., Verschueren, J., & Versluys, E. (Eds.), *Handbook of Pragmatics: 2009 Installment*. John Benjamins. DOI: 10.1075/hop.13.soc5

Bhaskaran, A.ATHIRA BHASKARANDr. SWARUPA R. (2023). The influence of Social Media marketing on Impulsive Buying Behaviour of consumers in Kerala. *International Journal For Multidisciplinary Research*, *5*(4), 5729. Advance online publication. DOI: 10.36948/ijfmr.2023.v05i04.5729

Blog, S. A. L. T. (2020). *Resmi blog sitesi (Official blog page)*. https://saltonline .org/tr/blog

Bosancianu, C. M., Hilbig, H., & Humphreys, M. (2020). *Political protest in times of crisis: The role of digital media*. WZB Berlin Social Science Center. https://doi .org/DOI: 10.2139/ssrn.3582125

Bruns, A., & Burgess, J. (2011). The use of Twitter hashtags in the formation of ad hoc publics. In *Proceedings of the 6th European Consortium for Political Research General Conference* (pp. 1-9). University of Iceland.

Burgess, J., Mitchell, P., & Munch, F. (2018). Social media rituals: The uses of celebrity death in digital culture. In Papacharissi, Z. (Ed.), *A networked self: birth, life, death* (pp. 223–239). Routledge. DOI: 10.4324/9781315202129-14

Castells, M. (2012). *Networks of outrage and hope: Social movements in the Internet age*. Polity Press.

Chakraborty, D. (2019). Indian shoppers' attitude towards grocery shopping apps: A survey conducted on smartphone users. *Metamorphosis*, *18*(2), 83–91. DOI: 10.1177/0972622519885502

Chang, A.-M., & Kannan, P. K. (2006). Employee technology readiness and adoption of wireless technology and services. *Proceedings of the 39th Annual Hawaii International Conference on System Sciences (HICSS'06)*. DOI: 10.1109/HICSS.2006.148

Chatterjee, S. (2020). Internet of Things and social platforms: An empirical analysis from Indian consumer behavioural perspective. *Behaviour & Information Technology*, *39*(2), 133–149. DOI: 10.1080/0144929X.2019.1587001

Chatterjee, S. (2022). Why do people use IoT-enabled devices?: An empirical examination from Indian perspectives. *International Journal of Technology and Human Interaction*, *18*(3), 1–20. DOI: 10.4018/IJTHI.313626

Chiedozie, P. A., Okpala, N. V., & Alaku, M. E. (2023). A comparative analysis of the headlines of *The Punch* newspaper and *Instablog* in Nigeria. *International Journal of African Research and Sustainability Studies*, *2*(2), 22–35.

Chiluwa, I. (2018). A nation divided against itself: Biafra and the conflicting online protest discourses. *Discourse & Communication*, *12*(4), 357–381. DOI: 10.1177/1750481318757778

Chiluwa, I., & Chiluwa, I. M. (2020). 'Deadlier than Boko Haram': Representations of the Nigerian herder-farmer conflict in the local and foreign press. *Media, War & Conflict*, *15*(1), 3–24. Advance online publication. DOI: 10.1177/1750635220902490

Chiluwa, I., & Ifukor, P. (2015). 'War against our children': Stance and evaluation in *#BringBackOurGirls* campaign discourse on *Twitter* and *Facebook.Discourse & Society*, *26*(3), 267–296. DOI: 10.1177/0957926514564735

Chua, P. Y., Rezaei, S., Gu, M.-L., Oh, Y., & Jambulingam, M. (2018). Elucidating social networking apps decisions: Performance expectancy, effort expectancy and social influence. *Nankai Business Review International*, *9*(2), 118–142. DOI: 10.1108/NBRI-01-2017-0003

Chukwuma, K. H. (2020). Constructing the herder–farmer conflict as (in)security in Nigeria. *African Security*, *13*(1), 54–76. DOI: 10.1080/19392206.2020.1732703

Chukwuokoro, I., Ononye, C., & Ngene, E. (2024). Multimodal discourse analysis of editorial cartoons on insecurity in Nigeria's 2023 general elections. *EBSU Journal of Social Sciences and Humanities*, *14*(2), 334–343.

Comscore. (2020). *Consumer interest in travel categories remains significantly lower*. https://www.comscore.com/Insights/Press-Releases/2020/4/Consumer-Interest-in-Travel-Categories-Remains-Significantly-Lower

Coombs, W. T. (2007). *Ongoing crisis communication: Planning, managing and responding*. Sage Publications.

Crowe, S., Cresswell, K., Robertson, A., Huby, G., Avery, A., & Sheikh, A. (2011). The case study approach. *BMC Medical Research Methodology, 11*(1), 100. DOI: 10.1186/1471-2288-11-100 PMID: 21707982

Crump, J. (2011). What Are the Police Doing on Twitter? Social Media, the Police and the Public. *Policy and Internet, 3*(4), 1–27. DOI: 10.2202/1944-2866.1130

Crystal, D. (2006). *Language and the Internet*. Cambridge University Press. DOI: 10.1017/CBO9780511487002

Davison, P. (2012). *The language of Internet memes*. New York University Press., DOI: 10.18574/nyu/9780814764077.003.0013

Dawkins, R. (1993). Viruses of the mind. In Dahlbohm, B. (Ed.), *Dennett and his critics: Demystifying mind* (pp. 13–27). Blackwell.

Denisova, A. (2019). *Internet memes and society: Social, cultural, and political contexts*. Routledge. DOI: 10.4324/9780429469404

Ding, Z.-C., Yan, J., & Fu, J. (2021). Internet and mobile phone addiction self-control mediate physical exercise and subjective well-being in young adults using IoT. *Mobile Information Systems, 2021*, 1–6. DOI: 10.1155/2021/9923833

Divya, L. R., & Sudhier, K. G. (2019). Use of social networking tools and services among research scholars at the University of Kerala. *International Journal of Information Dissemination and Technology, 9*(1), 23. DOI: 10.5958/2249-5576.2019.00005.0

Dobrin, D. (2020). The hashtag in digital activism: A cultural revolution. *Journal of Cultural Analysis and Social Change, 5*(1), 3–14. DOI: 10.20897/jcasc/8298

Dobrin, S. (2020). Hashtag activism: Exploring digital discourse and social change. *Journal of Digital Activism, 12*(3), 122–135.

Dynel, M. (2021). COVID-19 memes going viral: On the multiple multimodal voices behind face masks. *Discourse & Society, 32*(2), 175–195. DOI: 10.1177/0957926520970385 PMID: 38603045

Edin, E. D. (2020). *Pandemiden sonra önemi daha da artan odağımız: Sürdürülebilirlik (The increasing importance of our focus after the pandemic: Sustainability)*. https://www.garantibbva.com.tr/tr/blog/yeni-normalde-surdurulebilirlik.page

Eesuola, S. O. (2013). Three dimensions of political protest: A theoretical analytical of Fela Anikulapo Kuti. *Redeemer's University Journal of Management and Social Sciences, 1*(1), 81–91.

Efobi, U., Adejumo, O., & Kim, J. (2025). Climate change and the farmer-pastoralist's violent conflict: Experimental evidence from Nigeria. *Ecological Economics, 228*, 1–14. DOI: 10.1016/j.ecolecon.2024.108449

Egbunike, N. (2018). Beyond hashtags and retweets: Twitter as a space of participation in Nigerian politics. In Dumova, T. (Ed.), *Social interaction and the Internet: A study of social media use in Nigeria* (pp. 75–92). IGI Global.

Ekoh, P. C., & George, E. O. (2021). *The Role of Digital Technology in the End-SARS Protest in Nigeria During COVID-19 Pandemic. Journal of Human Rights and Social Work, Hodge, R., & Kress, G. (1988). Social semiotics*. Polity Press.

Ellah, S. M. (2014). The language of industrial actions in Nigeria. *Research on Humanities and Social Sciences, 4*(26), 133–138.

Encyclopaedia Britannica. (2025). *Digital activism*. https://www.britannica.com

Eslami, Z. R. (2013). Online communication and students' pragmatic choices in English. *Lodz Papers in Pragmatics, 9*(1), 71–92. DOI: 10.1515/lpp-2013-0005

Eslami, Z. R. (2020). Pragmatic competence in online learning environments. *Intercultural Pragmatics, 17*(2), 245–264.

Fay, B. (1987). Critical social science: Liberation and its limits. *Polity*.

Feng, D., & O'Halloran, K. L. (2013). The visual representation of metaphor: A social semiotic approach. Review of Cognitive Linguistics. Published under the auspices of the Spanish *Cognitive Linguistics Association*, 11(2), 320-335.

Fifelola, D. A., & Unuabonah, F. O. (2025). "No work, No pay": A multimodal discourse analysis of selected online images on industrial actions by Nigerian public universities. *Discourse & Communication, 19*(2), 175–196. DOI: 10.1177/17504813241297205

Flintan, F., Robinson, L., & Bello, M.A. (2021). *A review of tenure and governance in the pastoral lands of East and West Africa*. Supporting pastoralism and agriculture in recurrent and protracted crisis (SPARC).

Folayan, B. J., Omojola, O., Egharevba, M., Oyesomi, K., Yartey, D., & Adeyeye, B. (2018). The use of ICT-rooted communication codes and slangs among Nigerian students. *The Journal of Social Sciences Research, 4*(12), 633–641.

Fox, A. (2020, July 15). *The Metropolitan Opera is staging live concerts around the World – and tickets are only 20$.* Travel + Leisure, https://www.travelandleisure.com/culture-design/music/met-opera-digital-concert-tickets

Freire, P. (1999). *Pedagogy of the oppressed.* Penguin Books.

Gao, L., & Bai, X. (2014). A unified perspective on the factors influencing consumer acceptance of internet of things technology. *Asia Pacific Journal of Marketing and Logistics, 26*(2), 211–231. DOI: 10.1108/APJML-06-2013-0061

Garanti BBVA Arts and Culture. (2019). *SALT commemorates fifth anniversary with emphasis on sustainability.*https://www.bbva.com/en/tr/salt-commemorates-fifth-anniversary-with-emphasis-on-sustainability/

Garanti BBVA Communications. (2020). *Garanti BBVA responds to the coronavirus pandemic.* https://www.bbva.com/en/tr/garanti-bbva-responds-to-the-coronavirus-pandemic/

Garanti, B. B. V. A. (2020). *Kültür ve sanat (Arts and culture).*https://www.garantibbvainvestorrelations.com/tr/surdurulebilirlik/detay/Kultur-Sanat/957/3817/0

Garrett, R. K. (2006). Protest in an information society: A review of literature on social movements and new ICTs. *Information Communication and Society, 9*(2), 202–224. DOI: 10.1080/13691180600630773

Gbadegesin, V. O. (2020). Gender ideology and identity in humorous social media memes. *Digital Scholarship in the Humanities, 35*(3), 529–546.

Genyi, G. A. (2017). Ethnic and religious identities shaping contestation for land based resources: The Tiv-farmers and pastoralists conflicts in central Nigeria until 2014. *Journal of Living Together, 4-5*(1), 136–151.

George, A., & Kumar, G. S. G. (2013). Antecedents of customer satisfaction in internet banking: Technology Acceptance Model (TAM) redefined. *Global Business Review, 14*(4), 627–638. DOI: 10.1177/0972150913501602

George, D., & Leidner, B. (2019). The algorithmic impact on digital activism: Visibility, virality, and influence. *Digital Media Studies, 15*(4), 98–110.

George, J. F., & Leidner, D. E. (2019). Digital activism and its effectiveness. *The Journal of Strategic Information Systems, 28*(4), 1–13.

George, J. J., & Leidner, D. E. (2019). From clicktivism to hacktivism: Understanding digital activism. [page numbers missing]. *Information and Organization, 29*(3), 100249. DOI: 10.1016/j.infoandorg.2019.04.001

Gerbaudo, P. (2012). *Tweets and the streets: Social media and contemporary activism*. Pluto Press.

Gerbaudo, P. (2017). From cyber-autonomism to cyber-populism: An ideological history of digital activism. *TripleC, 15*(2), 478–491. DOI: 10.31269/triplec.v15i2.773

Gerbaudo, P. (2018). *The digital party: Political organisation and online democracy*. Pluto Press. DOI: 10.2307/j.ctv86dg2g

Gillespie, T. (2018). *Custodians of the internet: Platforms, content moderation, and the hidden decisions that shape social media*. Yale University Press.

González-Bailón, S., Borge-Holthoefer, J., Rivero, A., & Moreno, Y. (2011). The dynamics of protest recruitment through an online network. *Scientific Reports, 1*(1), 197. DOI: 10.1038/srep00197 PMID: 22355712

Gorgulu, V. (2020). Fearing coronavirus: The role of digital health news consumption and competence. *Internet Applications and Management, 11*(2), 101–112. DOI: 10.34231/iuyd.777356

Gov.uk. (2020). *£1.57 billion investment to protect Britain's world-class cultural, arts and heritage institutions*. https://www.gov.uk/government/news/157-billion-investment-to-protect-britains-world-class-cultural-arts-and-heritage-institutions

Grunig, J. E., & White, J. (1992). The effect of worldviews on public relations theory and practice. In Grunig, J. E., Dozier, D. M., Ehling, W. P., Grunig, L. A., Rpper, F. C., & White, J. (Eds.), *Excellence in Public Relations and Communication* (pp. 31–64). Erlbaum.

Gumede, T., & Govender, K. (2024). Risk perception and self-efficacy: The influence of cultural and physical environments during COVID-19. *International Journal of Environmental Research and Public Health, 21*(4), 198–215.

Gupta, R., & Patel, M. (2021). Digital platforms for educational co-operatives: Opportunities and challenges. *Journal of Cooperative Education, 12*(3), 104–118.

Gupta, V., & Duggal, S. (2021). How the consumer's attitude and behavioural intentions are influenced: A case of online food delivery applications in India. *International Journal of Culture, Tourism and Hospitality Research, 15*(1), 77–93. DOI: 10.1108/IJCTHR-01-2020-0013

Gürsoy, G. (2019). *Farmers-herders conflict in Nigeria: an analysis of the root causes and the effects of the conflict*. [Masters dissertation, Philipps-Universität Marburg]. Research Gate. https://www.researchgate.net/publication/347948827

Hallahan, K., Holtzhausen, D., van Ruler, B., Vercic, D., & Sriramesh, K. (2007). Defining strategic communication. *International Journal of Strategic Communication, 1*(1), 3–35. DOI: 10.1080/15531180701285244

Halliday, M. A. K. (1978). *Language as Social Semiotic: The Social Interpretation of Language and Meaning*. Edward Arnold.

Hallinan, B., Kim, B., Mizoroki, S., Scharlach, R., Trillò, T., Thelwall, M., & Shifman, L. (2023). The value (s) of social media rituals: A cross-cultural analysis of New Year's resolutions. *Information Communication and Society*, *26*(4), 764–785. DOI: 10.1080/1369118X.2021.1983003 PMID: 39973900

Hansson, S., Page, R., & Fuoli, M. (2022). Discursive Strategies of Blaming: The Language of Judgment and Political Protest Online. *Social Media + Society*, *8*(4), 1–11. DOI: 10.1177/20563051221138753 PMID: 36447997

Hassan, A. O., Wang, L., Hasan, A. A., & Latif, S. (2022). Behaviour profile on social media: TikTok and QQ. In Lu, Y., & Cheng, C. (Eds.), *International Conference on Computer Application and Information Security (ICCAIS 2021)*. SPIE. DOI: 10.1117/12.2637412

Herring, S. C. (2013). Discourse in Web 2.0: Familiar, reconfigured, and emergent. In Tannen, D., & Trester, A. M. (Eds.), *Discourse 2.0: Language and New Media* (pp. 1–25). Georgetown University Press.

Highfield, T. (2016). *Social media and everyday politics*. Polity Press.

Hill, J. (2020, July 11). *Coronavirus: Germany takes on debt to rescue arts*. BBC. https://www.bbc.com/news/world-europe-53361962

Hills, A., (2012). Lost in translation: why Nigeria's police don't implement democratic reforms. International affairs (Royal Institute of International Affairs 1944-), 88 (4), 739–755

Hills, A. (2008). The dialectic of police reform in Nigeria. *The Journal of Modern African Studies*, *46*(2), 215–234. DOI: 10.1017/S0022278X08003200

Hossain, M., & Rahman, M. (2020). Entrepreneurial co-operatives in the digital era: A new paradigm for social enterprises. *Social Business*, *10*(2), 88–101.

İçözü, T. (2020, Mart 26). *Dijital olarak takip edebileceğiniz 17 konser, tiyatro ve sanatsal etkinlik platformu (17 platforms that you can digitally follow to watch concerts, plays and arts events)*. Webrazzi, https://webrazzi.com/2020/03/26/dijital-olarak-takip-edebileceginiz-17-konser-tiyatro-ve-sanatsal-etkinlik-platformu/

Idiagbon, A. (2014). A multimodal approach to the study of discourse of protest: An example of the Federal government of Nigeria and the Nigeria Labour Congress face off. *Zango, 31*, 81–98.

Ishihara, N., & Cohen, A. D. (2010). *Teaching and learning pragmatics: Where language and culture meet*. Longman.

Ismail, K. A., & Abdul Wahid, N. (2020). A review on technology readiness concept to explain consumer's online purchase intention. *International Journal of Information Management, 6*, 49–57. DOI: 10.15282/ijim.6.0.2020.5629

Jarrar, Y., Awobamise, A. O., & Sellos, P. S. (2020). Technological Readiness Index (TRI) and the intention to use smartphone apps for tourism: A focus on inDubai mobile tourism app. *International Journal of Data and Network Science*, 297–304. DOI: 10.5267/j.ijdns.2020.6.003

Jegede, O. O.Olusegun Oladele Jegede. (2024). Pragmatic implicature and the articulation of protest in Femi Osofisan's plays. *Creative Saplings, 3*(9), 21–40. DOI: 10.56062/gtrs.2024.3.9.712

Jenkins, H. (2006). *Convergence Culture: Where Old and New Media Collide*. New York University Press.

Jewitt, C. (2008). Multimodality and literacy in school classrooms. *Review of Research in Education, 32*(1), 241–267. DOI: 10.3102/0091732X07310586

Jewitt, C. (Ed.). (2009). *The Routledge Handbook of Multimodal Analysis*. Routledge.

Jewitt, C., & Oyama, R. (2001). Visual meaning: A social semiotic approach. In van Leeuwen, T., & Jewitt, C. (Eds.), *Handbook of visual analysis* (pp. 134–156). SAGE Publications.

Johnson, C., & Williams, A. (2018). The digital divide in co-operative movements: Challenges and solutions. *Global Co-operative Review, 7*(4), 120–134.

Jones, R. H., & Hafner, C. A. (2012). *Understanding Digital Literacies: A Practical Introduction*. Routledge. DOI: 10.4324/9780203095317

Joyce, M. (Ed.). (2010). *Digital activism decoded: The new mechanics of change*. International Debate Education Association.

Karatzogianni, A. (2015). *Firebrand waves of digital activism 1994–2014: The rise and spread of hacktivism and cyberconflict*. Palgrave Macmillan. DOI: 10.1057/9781137317933

Karatzogianni, A., Miazhevich, G., & Denisova, A. (2017). A comparative cyberconflict analysis of digital activism across post-Soviet countries. *Comparative Sociology*, *16*(1), 102–126. DOI: 10.1163/15691330-12341415

Kaun, A., & Uldam, J. (2018). Digital activism: After the hype. *New Media & Society*, *20*(6), 2099–2106. DOI: 10.1177/1461444817731924

Kaun, A., & Uldam, J. (2018). The digital divide and its impact on activism in the 21st century. *Journal of Social Media and Society*, *6*(2), 47–65.

Knobel, M., & Lankshear, C. (2007). Online Memes, Affinities, and Cultural Production. In Knobel, M., & Lankshear, C. (Eds.), *A New Literacies Sampler*. Peter Lang.

Kondo, S. (2010). Apologies: Raising learners' cross-cultural awareness. In Martinez-Flor, A., & Usó-Juan, E. (Eds.), *Speech act performance: Theoretical, empirical and methodological issues* (pp. 145–162). John Benjamins. DOI: 10.1075/lllt.26.09kon

Kress, G. (1993). Against arbitrariness: The social production of the sign as a foundational issue in critical discourse analysis. *Discourse & Society*, *4*(2), 169–193. DOI: 10.1177/0957926593004002003

Kress, G. (2010). *Multimodality. A Social Semiotic Approach to Contemporary Communication*. Routledge.

Kress, G. (2010). *Multimodality: A social semiotic approach to contemporary communication*. Routledge.

Kress, G. (2010). *Multimodality: A Social Semiotic Approach to Contemporary Communication*. Routledge.

Kress, G., & van Leeuwen, T. (1996). *Reading Images: The Grammar of Visual Design*. Routledge.

Kress, G., & van Leeuwen, T. (2001). *Multimodal discourse: The modes and media of contemporary communication*. Arnold.

Kress, G., & van Leeuwen, T. (2001). *Multimodal Discourse: The Modes and Media of Contemporary Communication*. Arnold.

Kress, G., & van Leeuwen, T. (2020). *Reading images. The grammar of visual design* (3rd ed.). Routledge. DOI: 10.4324/9781003099857

Kress, G., & van Leeuwen, T. (2021). *Reading images: The grammar of visual design* (3rd ed.). Routledge.

Lam, S. Y., Chiang, J., & Parasuraman, A. (2008). The effects of the dimensions of technology readiness on technology acceptance: An empirical analysis. *Journal of Interactive Marketing*, *22*(4), 19–39. DOI: 10.1002/dir.20119

Letamendia, A. (2017). Towards the aestheticisation of the resistances in the Digital Age? A critical approach. *Precarity within the Digital Age: Media change and social insecurity*, 135-149.

Letamendia, A. (2017). Towards the aestheticisation of the resistances in the digital age? A critical approach. In Heidkamp, B., & Kergel, D. (Eds.), *Precarity within the Digital Age. Prekarisierung und soziale Entkopplung – transdisziplinäre Studien*. Springer VS., DOI: 10.1007/978-3-658-17678-5_9

Lu, J., Mao, Z., Wang, M., & Hu, L. (2015). Goodbye maps, hello apps? Exploring the influential determinants of travel app adoption. *Current Issues in Tourism*, *18*(11), 1059–1079. DOI: 10.1080/13683500.2015.1043248

Machin, D. (2007). *Introduction to Multimodal Analysis*. Hodder Arnold.

Machin, D., & Mayr, A. (2012). *How to do critical discourse analysis: A multimodal introduction*. SAGE Publications.

Makhortykh, M., & González Aguilar, J. M. (2020). Memory, politics and emotions: Internet memes and protests in Venezuela and Ukraine. *Continuum (Perth)*, *34*(3), 342–362. DOI: 10.1080/10304312.2020.1764782

Martínez-Flor, A. (2019). Speech acts in online discourse. *Journal of Pragmatics*, *143*, 92–104.

Mathew, P., & Krishnan, R. (2020). Impact of problematic internet use on the self-esteem of adolescents in the selected school, Kerala, India. *Archives of Psychiatric Nursing*, *34*(3), 122–128. DOI: 10.1016/j.apnu.2020.02.008 PMID: 32513461

McKie, R. (2017, December 10). *Scientists trace 2002 SARS virus to colony of cave-dwelling bats in China*. The Guardian, https://www.theguardian.com/world/2017/dec/10/sars-virus-bats-china-severe-acute-respiratory-syndrome

Menon, V. A., Prasad, A., Puthur, L. A., K K, S., & Joseph, L. (2023). Social media dependency and Facebook usage among the older adults of Kerala. *Studies in Media and Communication*, *11*(4), 202. DOI: 10.11114/smc.v11i4.6060

Moerdisuroso, I. (2014). Social semiotics and visual grammar: A contemporary approach to visual text research. *International Journal of Creative and Arts Studies*, *1*(1), 80–91. DOI: 10.24821/ijcas.v1i1.1574

Mohammed, W. F. (2019). Online activism: Centering marginalized voices in activist work. *Ada: A Journal of Gender. New Media, and Technology, 15*, 1–11.

Mohan, N., Zakkariya, & Bobby, R. R. (. (2023). Technology readiness motivators and Online Behavioural Advertising: A perceived benefits-risk assessment using Privacy Calculus Theory. *International Journal of Professional Business Review, 8*(6), e02297. DOI: 10.26668/businessreview/2023.v8i6.2297

Monogbe, B. O. (2019). ASUU strike and Nigerian educational system: An empirical investigation of the Nigerian tertiary institution. *American Journal of Social Sciences and Humanities, 4*(1), 56–67. DOI: 10.20448/801.41.56.67

Moussa, M. B., Benmessaoud, S., & Douai, A. (2020). Internet memes as "tactical" social action: A multimodal critical discourse analysis approach. *International Journal of Communication, 14*, 5920–5940.

Muhideen, S., Jianxun, C., Akintunde, T. Y., Olayemi, R. H., Koroma, J., Amosum, T. T., & Shahani, R. (2021). Nexus between students' attitude towards self-learning, tencent app usability, mobile-learning, and innovative performance. SSRN *Electronic Journal*. DOI: 10.2139/ssrn.3926083

Munandar, J. M., & Munthe, R. C. F. (2019). How technology affects behavioral intention (case study of online transportation in Indonesia and Thailand). *The South East Asian Journal of Management, 13*(2), 222–236. DOI: 10.21002/seam.v13i2.11343

Munoz, P., & Navas, L. (2020). Social media and grassroots mobilisation: The case of co-operatives. *Social Media Studies, 18*(2), 75–88.

Murphy, J., Denyer, D., & Pettigrew, A. (2021). The Role of Framing Mechanisms in Explaining System-Wide Change: The Case of the Northern Ireland Conflict and Peace Process. *British Journal of Management, 32*(2), 322–341. DOI: 10.1111/1467-8551.12393

Nassef, M., Eba, B., Islam, K., Djohy, G., & Flintan, F. (2023). *Causes of farmer-herder conflicts in Africa: A systematic scoping review*. SPARC.

Naugle, D. A., Smith, J. P., & Lee, R. T. (2024). Fear, efficacy, and stigma: Behavioral responses during the COVID-19 pandemic. *Health Psychology Review, 18*(1), 112–130.

Ndzinisa, N., & Govender, E. (2024). Cultural interpretations and government policies: Impact on individuals' positionality towards COVID-19 vaccines in Eswatini. *Journal of Health Communication, 29*(3), 245–260.

Neate, R. (2020, July 21). *Jeff Bezos, the world's richest man, added £10bn to his fortune in just one day*. The Guardian, https://www.theguardian.com/technology/2020/jul/21/jeff-bezos-the-worlds-richest-man-added-10bn-to-his-fortune-in-just-one-day

Norrick, N. R., & Ilie, C. (Eds.). (2018). *Pragmatics and its interfaces*. John Benjamins.

Norris, S. (2004). *Analyzing Multimodal Interaction: A Methodological Framework*. Routledge. DOI: 10.4324/9780203379493

Nwabunwene, D., & Waive-Aghante, R. (2024). A pragmatic analysis of the slang expressions, no gree & oya in Nigerian English. *PREORC Journal of Arts and Humanities*, *9*, 115–141.

Nwankwo, C. F. (2021). Discursive construction of the farmer-pastoralist conflict in Nigeria. *Open Political Science*, *4*(1), 136–146. DOI: 10.1515/openps-2021-0014

Nwankwo, C. F. (2024). Constructing farmer-pastoralist conflict as Islamization: Transformation and adaptation of resource competition discourse in the Nigerian Benue Valley. *Geoforum*, *148*, 1–9.

Nwankwo, C. F., Ayadiuno, R. U., Ali, A. N., & Madu, I. A. (2020). Farmer-herder conflict: The politics of media discourse in Nigeria. *International Journal of Scientific Research*, *76*(1), 191–221. DOI: 10.21506/j.ponte.2020.1.13

Nwoke, C. (2022). Representations of the Nigerian Police and Policing in Stand-up Comedy: Tracking Embedded Meanings and Implications. *Nokoko 10.*

O'Halloran, K. (2011). 'Multimodal Discourse Analysis'. In K. Hyland and B. Paltridge (eds.) Companion to Discourse (London: Continuum): 120–137. O'Halloran, K. and Smith, B.A. (2011). 'Multimodal Studies'. In K. O'Halloran and B.A. Smith (eds.)

O'Halloran, K. L. (2008). Systemic functional-multimodal discourse analysis (SF-MDA): Constructing ideational meaning using language and visual imagery. *Visual Communication*, *7*(4), 443–475. DOI: 10.1177/1470357208096210

Obadare, E. (2009). *Humor, Silence, and Civil Society in Nigeria*. Cambridge University Press.

Oghuvbu, E. A., & Oghuvbu, O. B. (2020). Farmers-herdsmen conflict in Africa: The case of Nigeria. *Vestnik RUDN.International Relations*, *20*(4), 698–706. DOI: 10.22363/2313-0660-2020-20-4-698-706

Ogunyemi, B. (2022). Digital activism and civic engagement in Nigeria: A study of the #RevolutionNow and #EndSARS movements. *African Journalism Studies*, *43*(2), 37–55. DOI: 10.1080/23743670.2022.2035692

Ohaja, E. U., & Momoh, T. N. (2023). Multimodal analysis of the aesthetic appeals of cartoons in selected Nigerian dailies. *GVU Journal of Management and Social Sciences*, *8*(2), 119–130.

Oh, J. C., Yoon, S. J., & Chung, N. (2014). The role of technology readiness in consumers' adoption of mobile internet services between South Korea and China. *International Journal of Mobile Communications*, *12*(3), 229. DOI: 10.1504/IJMC.2014.061460

Ojebode, A., Adedayo, A., & Adedeji, W. (2021). Social media activism and police accountability in Nigeria: The #EndSARS movement. *African Journal of Criminology and Justice Studies*, *14*(1), 1–19.

Okesola, S., & Oyebode, O. (2023). "The soro-soke [speak up] generation": Multimodality and appraisal choices in selected #EndSars civil protest-related memes in Nigeria. *Language and Semiotic Studies*, *9*(2), 290–312. DOI: 10.1515/lass-2022-0016

Okunade, S. K., & Aduloju, A. A. (2023). Hashtag activism and youth political engagement in Nigeria: A study of the #EndSARS protest. *Journal of African Media Studies*, *15*(1), 45–62. DOI: 10.1386/jams_00059_1

Olaniyan, A., & Yahaya, A. (2016). Cows, bandits, and violent conflicts: Understanding cattle rustling in northern Nigeria. *Africa Spectrum*, *51*(3), 93–105. DOI: 10.1177/000203971605100305

Oli, N. P., Ibekwe, C. C., & Nwankwo, I. U. (2018). Prevalence of herdsmen and farmers conflict in Nigeria. *International Journal of Innovative Studies in Sociology and Humanities*, *3*(1), 30–39.

Olomojobi, O., & Ajilore, K. (2018). Press coverage of herders-farmers conflict in selected Nigerian newspaper. *Journal of Communication and Media Research*, *10*(1), 38–51.

Olowojolu, O. (2022). Positive media portrayal of the Nigerian Police: A discourse analysis of institutional rebranding strategies. *Medicine and Society*, *10*(1), 78–92.

Oluremi, T. A., & Olaniyan, O. R. (2023). Nigeria Policemen's Abuse of Power Memes as Reformative Indices. Anaphora. *Journal of Language, Literary, and Cultural Studies*, *06*(02). Advance online publication. DOI: 10.30996/anaphora.v6i2.9651

Omolabi, I., & Adebayo, K. T. (2024). A pragmatic analysis of selected ASUU strike memes motivated humour on social media. *Integrity Journal of Arts and Humanities*, *5*(2), 61–72. DOI: 10.31248/IJAH2024.130

Online, S. A. L. T. (2020a). *Resmi internet sitesi (Official web page).*http://www.saltonline.org

Online, S. A. L. T. (2020b). *Çevrimiçi gösterim: The Wolfpack (Online screening: The Wolfpack).* https://saltonline.org/tr/2232/cevrimici-gosterim-the-wolfpack?tag=11

Online, S. A. L. T. (2020c). *Salon: Modern denemeler 4.* https://saltonline.org/tr/277/modern-denemeler-4?q=salon

Online, S. A. L. T. (2020d). *Çevrimiçi sunum: 1932'den 1973'e Gazi Eğitim Enstitüsü (Online presentation: The history of Gazi Eğitim Enstitüsü from 1932 to 1973).* https://saltonline.org/tr/2244/cevrimici-sunum-1932den-1973e-gazi-resim-is?q=google

Online, S. A. L. T. (2020e). *Ev-kesit (Home-segment).* https://saltonline.org/projects/evkesit/

Online, S. A. L. T. (2020f). *Osmanlı İstanbul'unda kadın bani yapıları.* https://saltonline.org/projects/kadinbaniyapilari/

Opeibi, T. (2020). Multimodal discourse in digital protest communication: An analysis of #EndSARS online activism in Nigeria. *Discourse & Society, 31*(6), 680–698. DOI: 10.1177/0957926520939674

Oscarsson, M., Carlbring, P., Andersson, G., & Rozental, A. (2020). A large-scale experiment on New Year's resolutions: Approach-oriented goals are more successful than avoidance-oriented goals. *PLoS One, 15*(12), e0234097. DOI: 10.1371/journal.pone.0234097 PMID: 33296385

Osisanwo, A. (2024). Gunmen, bandits and ransom demanders: A corpus-assisted critical discourse study of the construction of abduction in the Nigerian press. *Corpus-based Studies across. Humanities (Washington), 2*(1), 1–22. DOI: 10.1515/csh-2024-0003

Osisanwo, A., & Alugbin, M. (2024). Metaphorical constructs and semiotic expressions in the BBC Yoruba Internet memes of English Premier League match results. *Language and Semiotic Studies, 10*(3), 415–436. DOI: 10.1515/lass-2024-0032

Osisanwo, A., & Atoloye, L. (2024). "Silence is the best answer for a bully": An exploration of humour techniques in selected Nigerian newspaper political cartoons. *Language and Semiotic Studies, 10*(3), 367–396. DOI: 10.1515/lass-2024-0009

Osisanwo, A., & Falade, T. (2024). Directives and references in selected coronavirus-motivated internet memes. *Language and Semiotic Studies, 10*(2), 245–266. DOI: 10.1515/lass-2024-0008

Panchanathan, S., & Raj, K. (2022). A study on impact of social media among students of adolescent age group on individual performance. *International Journal of Professional Business Review, 7*(3), e0505. DOI: 10.26668/businessreview/2022.v7i3.0505

Papacharissi, Z. (2020). *Affective publics: Sentiment, technology, and politics.* Oxford University Press.

Parasuraman, A., & Colby, C. L. (2015). An updated and streamlined Technology Readiness Index: TRI 2.0. *Journal of Service Research, 18*(1), 59–74. DOI: 10.1177/1094670514539730

Pavlović, L. M. (2016). Internet memes as a field of discursive construction of identity and space of resistance. *AM Časopis za studije umetnosti i medija*, (10), 97-106.

Porter, M. E. (2008). On competition (Updated and expanded edition). *Harvard Business Review.*

Poulsen, S. V. (2015). "Multimodality." In Key Terms in Multimodality: Definitions, Issues, Discussions, edited by Nina Nørgaard. https://multimodalkeyterms.wordpress.com/

Pradhan, M. K., Oh, J., & Lee, H. (2018). Understanding travelers' behavior for sustainable smart tourism: A technology readiness perspective. *Sustainability (Basel), 10*(11), 4259. DOI: 10.3390/su10114259

Ranaeiy, S., Taghavi, M. R., & Goodarzi, M. A. (2015). The effect of Loneliness on Social Networking Sites use and its related behaviors. *Global Journal of Health Science, 8*(8), 162. DOI: 10.5539/gjhs.v8n8p162 PMID: 27045407

Reynolds, M., & Weiss, S. (2020, May 27). *How coronavirus started and what happens next, explained.* Wired, https://www.wired.co.uk/article/china-coronavirus

Rintel, S. (2013). Crisis memes: The importance of templatability to internet culture and freedom of expression. *Australasian Journal of Popular Culture, 2*(2), 253–271. DOI: 10.1386/ajpc.2.2.253_1

Rivas-Carmona, M. (2014). Cartooning for gender equality: A multimodal expression of 'humour' and 'vindication'. *Research on Humanities and Social Sciences, 4*(24), 8–19.

Roberts, D., & Taylor, P. (2020). Sociocultural barriers to digital activism in cooperatives. *Journal of Social Media and Activism, 8*(3), 33–48.

Rosen, L. D., Whaling, K., Carrier, L. M., Cheever, N. A., & Rokkum, J. (2013). The Media and Technology Usage and Attitudes Scale: An empirical investigation. *Computers in Human Behavior, 29*(6), 2501–2511. DOI: 10.1016/j.chb.2013.06.006 PMID: 25722534

Rowat, R. (2020, March, 13). *The Berlin Philharmonic made its digital concert hall free for everyone*. CBC, https://www.cbc.ca/music/the-berlin-philharmonic-has-made-its-digital-concert-hall-free-for-everyone-1.5497260

Saji, T. G., & Paul, D. (2018). Behavioural intention to the use of mobile banking in Kerala: An application of extended classical technology acceptance model. *Metamorphosis, 17*(2), 111–119. DOI: 10.1177/0972622518792802

Saka, E. (2022). Researching political trolls as instruments of political conservatism in Turkey: A historical framework and methodological reflections on a discourse community. In Costa, E., Lange, P. G., Haynes, N., & Sinanan, J. (Eds.), *The Routledge Companion to Media Anthropology*. Routledge. DOI: 10.4324/9781003175605-44

Schneider, C. J. (2016). *Policing and Social Media: Social Control in an Era of New Media*. Lexington Books. DOI: 10.5040/9781978725768

Scholz, T. (2010). *Digital labor: The internet as playground and factory*. Routledge.

Seo, J.-Y., Kim, S.-I., & Jeong, C. (2018). Effects of technology readiness on usage intention of smart-phone tourism applications: An application of the technology readiness and acceptance model. *The Tourism Sciences Society of Korea, 42*(8), 109–127. DOI: 10.17086/JTS.2018.42.8.109.127

Shareef, M. A., Kapoor, K. K., Mukerji, B., Dwivedi, R., & Dwivedi, Y. K. (2020). Group behavior in social media: Antecedents of initial trust formation. *Computers in Human Behavior, 105*(106225), 106225. DOI: 10.1016/j.chb.2019.106225

Shifman, L. (2013). Memes in a digital world: Reconciling with a conceptual troublemaker. *Journal of Computer-Mediated Communication, 18*(3), 362–377. DOI: 10.1111/jcc4.12013

Shifman, L. (2013). *Memes in digital culture*. The MIT Press. DOI: 10.7551/mitpress/9429.001.0001

Shukla, S., & Sharma, P. (2018). Emotions and media multitasking behaviour among Indian college students. *Journal of Creative Communications, 13*(3), 197–211. DOI: 10.1177/0973258618790794

Smith, G., & Jansson, A. (2019). Transnational advocacy through digital tools: Case studies of co-operative movements. *International Journal of Digital Activism, 15*(1), 12–27.

Snow, D. A., Vliegenthart, R., & Ketelaars, P. (2019). The framing perspective on social movements: Its conceptual roots and architecture. In Snow, D. A., Soule, S. A., Kriesi, H., & McCammon, H. J. (Eds.), *The Wiley Blackwell Companion to Social Movements* (2nd ed., pp. 392–410). Wiley Blackwell., DOI: 10.1002/9781119168577.ch22

Sorce, G., & Dumitrica, D. (2022). Transnational dimensions in digital activism and protest. *The Review of Communication, 22*(3), 157–174. DOI: 10.1080/15358593.2022.2107877

Sorce, S., & Dumitrica, D. (2022). Emojis and memes as tools of digital activism. *New Media & Society, 24*(6), 825–843.

Stake, R. E. (1995). *The art of case study research.* Sage Publications.

Steyn, B. (2003). From strategy to corporate communication strategy: A conceptualization. *Journal of Communication Management (London), 8*(2), 168–183. DOI: 10.1108/13632540410807637

Steyn, B., & Puth, G. (2000). *Corporate communication strategy.* Heinemann.

Stock, R., & Gross, M. (2016). How does knowledge workers' social technology readiness affect their innovative work behavior? *2016 49th Hawaii International Conference on System Sciences (HICSS).*

Stornaiuolo, A., & Thomas, E. E. (2017). Disrupting educational inequalities through youth digital activism. *Review of Research in Education, 41*(1), 337–357. DOI: 10.3102/0091732X16687973

Sultana, A. (2021). Impact of online advertising and the use of cosmetic products: A study on the influence of online advertisements and change in the purchasing behaviour of women in Kerala. *International Journal of Communication and Society, 3*(2), 112–119. DOI: 10.31763/ijcs.v3i2.214

Tagg, C. (2015). *Exploring Digital Communication: Language in Action.* Routledge. DOI: 10.4324/9781315727165

Tahir, H. (2013, August 28). ASUU strike and faltering university education. *Vanguard.* https://www.vanguardngr.com/2013/08/asuu-strike-and-faltering-university-education/

Tatsuki, D. H., & Houck, N. R. (Eds.). (2010). *Pragmatics: Teaching speech acts.* TESOL.

Tella, A. (2018). Humour generation and multimodal framing of political actor in the 2015 Nigerian presidential election campaign memes. *The European Journal of Humour Research, 6*(4), 95–117. DOI: 10.7592/EJHR2018.6.4.tella

The Guardian. (2024, January 15). 'No gree for anybody' slang could be message of rebellion, Nigerian police claim. https://www.theguardian.com/world/2024/jan/15/no-gree-for-anybody-slang-message-rebellion-nigerian-police-claim

Thomas, L. P., Chaudhary, R., Thomas, J., & Menon, V. A. (2023). Assessing Instagram addiction and social media dependency among young adults in Karnataka. *Studies in Media and Communication, 11*(6), 72. DOI: 10.11114/smc.v11i6.6102

Thomas, L. P., Menon, V. A., Thomas, J., Ali, K. A. A., Soman, K. K., & Kumar, T. K. S. (2024). Towards a model: Exploring fatigue factors in ZOOM online classes. *2024 International Conference on Current Trends in Advanced Computing (ICCTAC).* DOI: 10.1109/ICCTAC61556.2024.10581300

Tiwa, D. F. (2024). Institutional distrust trap: An analysis of the effect of public distrust in the Nigeria Police Force. *Policing and Society, 34*(8), 846–860. DOI: 10.1080/10439463.2024.2341121

TrendMind. (2025). *How social media is transforming protest culture.* TrendMind Report.

Treré, E. (2019). *Hybrid media activism: Ecologies, imaginaries, algorithms.* Routledge.

Treré, E., Jeppesen, S., & Mattoni, A. (2017). Comparing digital protest media imaginaries: Anti-austerity movements in Greece, Italy & Spain. *TripleC, 15*(2), 405–424. DOI: 10.31269/triplec.v15i2.772

Treré, E., & Mattoni, A. (2015). Media ecologies and protest movements: Main perspectives and key lessons. *Information Communication and Society, 19*(2), 290–306.

Treré, E., & Mattoni, A. (2021). De-westernising digital activism. *Global Media and Communication, 17*(1), 79–98.

Trillò, T., Hallinan, B., & Shifman, L. (2022). A typology of social media rituals. *Journal of Computer-Mediated Communication, 27*(4), zmac011. DOI: 10.1093/jcmc/zmac011

Tufekci, Z. (2017). *Twitter and tear gas: The power and fragility of networked protest.* Yale University Press.

Uche, L. U., & Ngwu, C. C. (2023). Media activism and digital resistance in Nigeria: A study of youths' engagement during the #EndSARS protest. *Communication and the Public*, *8*(1), 23–39. DOI: 10.1177/20570473221141891

Udoudom, U., Obong, U. A., Etifit, S., & Idiong, E. (2024). Social media activism and sloganeering in Nigeria: Examining the socio-political contexts in the "no gree for anybody" mantra. *International Journal of Diverse Discourses*, *1*(2), 12–27.

Ugwuona, C. (2016). 2013 ASUU strike discourses in Nigeria: A critical discourse analysis. *Mediterranean Journal of Social Sciences*, *7*(2), 435–444. DOI: 10.5901/mjss.2016.v7n2p435

Ulmer, R. R., Sellnow, T. L., & Seeger, M. W. (2017). *Effective crisis communication: Moving from crisis to opportunity*. Sage Publications.

UNDP. (2020). *Four in every five SMEs substantially impacted by COVID-19 crisis*. https://www.tr.undp.org/content/turkey/en/home/presscenter/pressreleases/2020/04/B4G-anket.html

Unuabonah, F. O., & Oyebode, O. O. (2021). 'Nigeria is fighting Covid-419': A multimodal critical discourse analysis of political protest in Nigerian coronavirus-related internet memes. *Discourse & Communication*, *15*(2), 200–219. DOI: 10.1177/1750481320982090

Unuabonah, F. O., & Oyebode, O. O. (2021). "Nigeria is fighting Covid-419": A multimodal critical discourse analysis of political protest in Nigerian coronavirus-related Internet memes. *Discourse & Communication*, *15*(2), 200–219.

Usman, S. O., & Nuhu, M. T. (2016). Satire as Tool of Political Cartoons in the Nigerian National Dailies: A Critical Discourse Analysis. *European Scientific Journal*, *12*(29), 124–138. DOI: 10.19044/esj.2016.v12n29p124

Vahdat, A., Alizadeh, A., Quach, S., & Hamelin, N. (2021). Would you like to shop via mobile app technology? The technology acceptance model, social factors and purchase intention. [AMJ]. *Australasian Marketing Journal*, *29*(2), 187–197. DOI: 10.1016/j.ausmj.2020.01.002

Van De Velde, C. (2024). The power of slogans: Using protest writings in social movement research. *Social Movement Studies*, *23*(5), 569–588. DOI: 10.1080/14742837.2022.2084065

van Dijk, T. (2001). Critical discourse analysis. In D. Tannen, D. Schiffrin, & H. Hamilton (Eds.), *Handbook of discourse analysis* (pp. 352–371). Blackwell.

van Dijk, T. A. (2000). Ideology and Discourse: A Multidisciplinary Introduction. https://www.discourses.org/download/books

Van Dijk, J. (2005). *The Deepening Divide: Inequality in the Information Society*. Sage Publications.

van Dijk, T. A. (1993). Principles of critical discourse analysis. *Discourse & Society*, *4*(2), 249–283. DOI: 10.1177/0957926593004002006

van Dijk, T. A. (2006). Discourse and manipulation. *Discourse & Society*, *17*(3), 359–383. DOI: 10.1177/0957926506060250

van Leeuwen, T. (2005). *Introducing Social Semiotics*. Routledge.

van Leeuwen, T. (2008). *Discourse and Practice: New Tools for Critical Discourse Analysis*. Oxford University Press. DOI: 10.1093/acprof:oso/9780195323306.001.0001

Vásquez, C., & Aslan, E. (2021). "Cats be outside, how about meow": Multimodal humor and creativity in an internet meme. *Journal of Pragmatics*, *171*, 101–117. DOI: 10.1016/j.pragma.2020.10.006

Veg, S. (2016). Creating a textual public space: Slogans and texts from Hong Kong's Umbrella movement. *The Journal of Asian Studies*, *75*(3), 673–702. DOI: 10.1017/S0021911816000565

Vlachaki, C. (2021). Humour in digital discourse: Memes, multimodality and relevance (M.A. thesis). National and Kapodistrian University of Athens, Greece.

Vlavo, A. (2017). Visual semiotics in digital activism: Memes, GIFs, and emojis. *Media Culture & Society*, *39*(5), 789–804.

Vlavo, F. A. (2017). *Performing digital activism: New aesthetics and discourses of resistance* (1st ed.). Routledge. DOI: 10.4324/9781315692869

Waheed, A., Zhang, Q., Farrukh, M., & Khan, S. Z. (2021). Effect of mobile social apps on consumer's purchase attitude: Role of trust and technological factors in developing nations. *SAGE Open*, *11*(2), 215824402110067. DOI: 10.1177/21582440211006714

Waugh, E. (2014). Teaching pragmatics and intercultural communication online. *TESL Canada Journal*, *30*(7), 98–107. DOI: 10.18806/tesl.v30i7.1154

WHO. (2015). *Ebola situation report*. https://apps.who.int/ebola/current-situation/ebola-situation-report-22-july-2015

Wilson, J., & Ogden, J. (2008). *Strategic communication planning*. Kendal Hunt.

Wodak, R. (1996). *Disorders of discourse*. Longman.

Wolfson, T. (2014). *Digital rebellion: The birth of the cyber left.* University of Illinois Press. DOI: 10.5406/illinois/9780252038846.001.0001

Word Gate. (2025). *Understanding pragmatics in online communication.* Word Gate Linguistics Blog.

World Bank. (2020). *Proposed sustainability checklist for economic recovery interventions.* http://pubdocs.worldbank.org/en/223671586803837686/Sustainability-Checklist-for-Assessing-Economic-Recovery-Investments-April-2020.pdf

World-o-Meter. (2020). [*Coronavirus pandemic.* https://www.worldometers.info/coronavirus/]. *COVID, 19,* •••.

Wu, A. W., Connors, C., & Everly, G. S.Jr. (2020). COVID-19: Peer support and crisis communication strategies to promote institutional resilience. *Annals of Internal Medicine, 172*(12), 822–823. Advance online publication. DOI: 10.7326/M20-1236 PMID: 32251512

Wu, Y., & Wall, M. (2021). COVID-19 and viral anti-Asian racism: A multimodal critical discourse analysis of memes and the racialization of the COVID-19 pandemic. *Journal of Contemporary Chinese Art, 8*(2–3), 107–127. DOI: 10.1386/jcca_00040_1

Xian, C., Wang, Z., & Wang, L. (2021). Multitasking habits of Chinese smartphone users: Under the influence of social media apps. *2021 International Conference on Information Science, Parallel and Distributed Systems (ISPDS).* DOI: 10.1109/ISPDS54097.2021.00054

Xie, C., & Yus, F. (2018). Digital pragmatics: New theoretical frameworks. *Journal of Language and Digital Communication, 5*(1), 1–20.

Xie, C., & Yus, F. (2018). Introducing internet pragmatics. *Internet Pragmatics, 1*(1), 1–12. DOI: 10.1075/ip.00001.xie

Yang, G. (2016). Activism. In Peters, B. (Ed.), *Digital keywords: A vocabulary of information society and culture* (pp. 1–17). Princeton University Press.

Yang, G. (2016). *The Red Guard generation and political activism in China.* Columbia University Press.

Yi, G., Zainuddin, N. M. M., & Bakar, N. A. B. A. (2021). Conceptual model on Internet Banking acceptance in China with social network influence. *JOIV: International Journal on Informatics Visualization, 5*(2), 177–186. DOI: 10.30630/joiv.5.2.403

Yin, R. K. (2014). *Case study research: Design and methods* (5th ed.). SAGE Publications.

Yus, F. (2018). Multimodality in memes: A cyberpragmatic approach. In Storbeck, J. E. R., & Jedlowski, A. (Eds.), *Analyzing digital discourse: New insights and future directions* (pp. 105–131). Springer International Publishing., DOI: 10.1007/978-3-319-92663-6_4

Yus, F. (2019). An outline of some future research issues for internet pragmatics. *Internet Pragmatics*, *2*(1), 1–33. DOI: 10.1075/ip.00018.yus

Zappavigna, M. (2012). *Discourse of Twitter and Social Media: How We Use Language to Create Affiliation on the Web.* Bloomsbury Academic. DOI: 10.5040/9781472541642

Zerfass, A., & Huck, S. (2007). Innovation, communication, and leadership: New developments in strategic communication. *International Journal of Strategic Communication, 1*(2), 107–122. DOI: 10.1080/15531180701298908

Zorlu, F. (2020, March 11). *Turkey confirms first case of coronavirus.* Anadolu Agency, https://www.aa.com.tr/en/latest-on-coronavirus-outbreak/turkey-confirms-first-case-of-coronavirus/1761522

Zorlu. (2020). *Kurumsal.* https://www.zorlupsm.com/tr/kurumsal/basin-bultenleri/psmyle-kal-online-konserler

# About the Contributors

**Rotimi Taiwo** is a Professor of English and New Media Studies in the Department of English Obafemi Awolowo University, Ile-Ife. He holds Ph.D. from Obafemi Awolowo University, Ile-Ife (2003). He joined the University in January, 1997 as an Assistant Lecturer and rose through the ranks to become a professor in October, 2011. Between June 2008 and August 2009, he was an Alexander von Humboldt Post-doctoral Fellow at the Department of English, University of Freiburg, Germany. He was also a Visiting Professor at the University of Munster, Germany (2014); Covenant University (2017-2018) and Olabisi Onabanjo University (2022-2023). In Obafemi Awolowo University, Ile-Ife, he has served as the Coordinator, Use of English (2006-2008), Head of the Department English, (2018 - 2020), Editor-in-Chief, Ife Studies in English and Linguistics (2018-2020) He also served as the Editor of the Journal of English Scholars' Association of Nigeria (2018-2020). He is currently member of editorial boards of Linguistik Online (Berne, Germany), International Journal of Language, Society and Culture (Tasmania, Australia), Covenant Journal of Language Studies (Ota, Nigeria) and CLAREP Journal of English and Linguistics, among others. He has equally served as member of the Board of Regents (Council), Landmark University, Omu Aran (2019-2022). Over 100 of his papers, which are mainly in the areas of lexical studies, media, political, and religious discourse analysis, as well as pragmatics of online discourse, have appeared in reputable and high impact journals in his discipline. For almost two decades, Professor Taiwo has been working on computer-mediated discourse analysis and he has published extensively on this area of research. Some of his most outstanding works in this area of research are: Handbook of Research on Discourse Behavior and Digital Communication: Language Structures and Social Interaction Volumes I & II (IGI Global, New York, 2010); Computer Mediated Discourse in Africa (Nova, New York, 2012), Language and Mobile Telecommunication in Nigeria: SMS as a Digital Age Lingual-cultural Expression (OAU Press, 2012); The Discourse of Digital Civic Engagement: Perspectives from the Developing World

(New York: Nova Science, 2016) His current research is discursive marketisation in higher institutions' online spaces in which he is editing a book titled: Transformation of Higher Education Through Institutional Online Spaces slated to be released by IGI Global, Hershey, Pennsylvania, USA in the last quarter of 2023. Prof Taiwo has successfully supervised 30 M.A, 5 MPhil 8 PhD candidates. Outside the university setting, Professor Taiwo is currently the President Gideons International, Central West State Association, and Coordinator, Pastoral Support Group, All Souls' Chapel (Interdenominational), OAU, Ile-Ife.

***

**Vishnu Achutha Menon** is an independent journalist, writer, researcher, and an Indian percussionist. He is a recipient of the Junior Scholarship the Ministry of Culture awarded. His research interests are film studies, verbal & nonverbal communication, south Asian performances, Natyasastra, media studies, media analysis techniques, Laban Movement Analysis, and Ethnomusicology.

**Matthew Alugbin**, PhD, lectures in the Department of English, Edo State University, Uzairue, Nigeria. His research agenda broadly includes critical/multimodal discourse analysis, migration discourse, conflict studies in (new) media, socio-political African discourse, and social movement studies.

**Moses O. Ayoola** was born in Omuo-Ekiti, Ekiti State Nigeria. He attended University of Ado-Ekiti, Ekiti State, Nigeria for his bachelor of Arts degree in English and Literary studies and University of Ilorin, Nigeria for both master of Arts and PhD in English language. He has taught English Language at various levels of education. He currently teaches at Department of English and Literary studies, Bamidele Olumilua University of Education Science and Technology (BOUESTI) Ikere-Ekiti, Nigeria. His areas interest are Syntax, applied linguistics, political discourse and Systemic functional Linguistics and he has many publications to his credit in these areas, in reputable international Journals. Dr. Ayoola is a member of English Scholars' Association of Nigeria (ESAN) and many other academic / professional bodies.

**Sahika Dogan** is an associate professor at Faculty of Communication, Istanbul Bilgi University, where she also serves as the Director of the Public Relations and Corporate Communication MA Program. Her recent research interests include the emerging business models in digital media and social inclusion patterns in human resources practices.

**Deborah Abiola Fifelola** obtained her Master's degree in English from the Department of English, Redeemer's University, Ede, Nigeria. Her areas of research include (multimodal) discourse analysis, and (corpus) pragmatics. She has published papers in international journals such as Visual Communication and Discourse & Communication.

**Omolade Ilesanmi** is a doctoral student at the Department of English, University of Ibadan, Ibadan, Nigeria. She works as a lecturer in the Department of English and Literary Studies, McPherson University, Nigeria. Her research interests include Critical and Multimodal Discourse Analysis, Pragmatics, Protest Studies, Queer Discourse, Parenting Discourse, Media Discourse and Humour.

**Olusegun Oladele Jegede** is a lecturer in the Department of Languages and Literature, Lead City University, Ibadan, Nigeria. He is a distinguished researcher with a prolific publication record in language and His scholarly articles span diverse topics including rhetorical strategies, politeness dynamics, and pragmatic functions in political speeches. His research also encompasses inclusive education, digital language teaching, mobile-assisted language learning, syntactic analysis, and code-switching in Nigerian education, reflecting his broad expertise and dedication to advancing linguistic studies. He has published extensively in learned journals and contributed to books in these areas.

**Foluke O. Unuabonah** received her PhD from University of Ibadan, Nigeria and is currently a Professor in English Department, Redeemer's University, Nigeria. Her areas of research include (corpus) pragmatics and discourse analysis. She has published articles in Communication and the Public, Visual Communication, Journal of Pragmatics, Discourse & Society, Discourse & Communication, Pragmatics, Pragmatics & Society, Intercultural Pragmatics and Text & Talk. She compiled the Historical Corpus of English in Nigeria with other colleagues in Redeemer's University.

# Index

## A



## C



## D



## E



## F



## H



## I



## K



## M

www.ingramcontent.com/pod-product-compliance
Lightning Source LLC
LaVergne TN
LVHW062118200926
848484LV00007B/1709